Play Therapy Interventions with Children's Problems

Play Therapy Interventions with Children's Problems

Case Studies with DSM-IV-TR Diagnoses

Second Edition

Garry L. Landreth, Daniel S. Sweeney, Dee C. Ray,
Linda E. Homeyer, Geraldine J. Glover

JASON ARONSON
Lanham • Boulder • New York • Toronto • Plymouth, UK

Published in the United States of America
by Jason Aronson
An imprint of Rowman & Littlefield Publishers, Inc.

A wholly owned subsidiary of
The Rowman & Littlefield Publishing Group, Inc.
4501 Forbes Boulevard, Suite 200, Lanham, Maryland 20706
www.rowmanlittlefield.com

Estover Road
Plymouth PL6 7PY
United Kingdon

British Library Cataloguing in Publication Information Available

The hardback edition of this book was previously cataloged by the Library of Congress as follows:

Library of Congress Cataloging-in-Publication Data

Play therapy interventions with children's problems : case studies with DSM-IV-TR diagnoses / Garry L. Landreth ... [et al.].— 2nd ed.
   p. cm.
   Includes bibliographical references and index.
   1. Play therapy—Abstracts. 2. Play therapy—Case studies—Abstracts I. Landreth, Garry L.
RJ505.P6T488 2005
618.92'891653—dc22   2004026255

ISBN 978-0-7657-0381-1 (cloth : alk. paper)
ISBN 978-0-7657-0801-4 (pbk : alk. paper)
ISBN 978-0-7657-0807-6 (electronic)

Printed in the United States of America

♾™ The paper used in this publication meets the minimum requirements of American National Standard for Information Sciences—Permanence of Paper for Printed Library Materials, ANSI/NISO Z39.48-1992.

Contents

Introduction

Play therapy is not an approach based on guess, trial and error, or the whims of the play therapist at the moment. Play therapy is a well-thought-out, philosophically conceived, developmentally based, and research-supported approach to helping children cope with and overcome the problems they experience in the process of living their lives. This book is unique in play therapy literature in that for the first time the existing findings of play therapy research studies and case reports have been brought together in one volume. As the reader will note, the popular myth that play therapy requires a long-term commitment of many months is dispelled by the findings of many of the studies reported in this book.

The focus of this book is on interventions and methodologies that have been helpful in alleviating problems of children who have been referred for play therapy. Concise digests of play therapy procedures based on case studies and research reported in the literature highlight the results achieved. These digests provide the reader with a concise reference text to the most difficult, as well as the most common, problems encountered by play therapists in their work with children. In addition, this book contains play therapy approaches based on a variety of theoretical positions for dealing with a broad range of specific problems experienced by children. This practical reference book provides quick access to documented studies that demonstrate the effectiveness of different theoretical models of play therapy and a wide variety of play therapy approaches, such as individual play therapy, group play therapy, sibling group play therapy, sand play, puppet play, structured and nonstructured procedures, "Theraplay," and activity play therapy, in a variety of settings including private practice, agencies, hospitals, elementary schools, prisons, and homes.

Unlike in the first edition, filial therapy research studies are not included in this second edition in order to keep the focus exclusively on play therapy. There are enough research studies in filial therapy to constitute a volume devoted to that topic alone. Thirteen of the studies included in the first edition were removed because they did not report conclusive results or lacked a specified research design. This second edition contains the addition of nineteen research studies in the literature that report specific and identifiable results supporting the effectiveness of play therapy.

The research studies and case reports included in this volume are the result of an exhaustive literature search and comprehensive holdings of the Center for Play Therapy Library at the University of North Texas, which included more than four thousand journal articles related to the field of play therapy. In addition, extensive use was made of the references in *The World of Play Therapy Literature: A Definitive Guide to Authors and Subjects in the Field* by Garry Landreth, Brandy Schumann, Sue Bratton, Amy Kale, and Kim Hilpl (2003), published by the Center for Play Therapy. The diligent library research by Gena Minnix for the second edition is gratefully acknowledged.

The purpose of this book is to make available to mental-health professionals and students in the play therapy field research-based play therapy procedures that have been demonstrated to be effective with a myriad of specific children's problems. In fact, this book contains every research study and case report with definitive results that we could locate in the literature.

Our experience in training and supervising play therapists has shown that they often begin to doubt themselves and the effectiveness of play therapy when they are not familiar with substantiated results. This book aims to rectify that problem by providing research to encourage and nurture confidence. When practitioners know that what they are doing is based on research, they are more likely to be consistent in their approach and thus more effective.

In this day of accountability demanded by lawyers in courtroom experiences and by managed care providers, play therapists must increasingly be able to document the effectiveness of play therapy procedures. This book should prove to be a significant asset to those who are required to justify their recommendations for play therapy services.

The reader will note that at the end of each study or case report there is a listing of possible DSM-IV-TR diagnoses. In many instances the case report or research study did not provide the detailed criteria necessary for actual diagnosis. Therefore, the suggested diagnosis is provided only to assist the play therapist in exploring possible options.

CHAPTER 1

Abuse and Neglect

The typical approach to child abuse is to remove the child from the home, but in such cases the inner dynamics of the child's reaction to the abuse still exist. The emotional dynamics resulting from abuse must be matched by an equally dynamic therapeutic process, such as that found in the play therapy relationship. Children who have been abused cannot be expected to verbally describe their experience and their reaction because they lack the cognitive-verbal ability to do so. Abused children come from inconsistent environments. The play therapy relationship provides them with an absolutely consistent environment, for without such, the child cannot feel safe; it is this dimension of predictable safety that allows children to express, explore, and resolve through play deep-seated emotional pain. Abuse and neglect cause serious inner conflicts and relationship problems for children, and play therapy provides the modality necessary for children to develop adaptive and coping mechanisms on their own terms and at their own emotional pace.

Processing Physical and Emotional Abuse through Puppet Play

Charles A. Burch

FOCUS

Puppet play is used as a technique in play therapy to assist a thirteen-year-old boy in dealing with physical and emotional abuse.

INTRODUCTION

Abused children often have very high levels of anxiety. The use of puppet play to distance the self from the content of the play, and thus the anxiety, is used with Carl. Therapeutic issues for Carl involve his ethnicity; abuse, neglect, and abandonment by his birth parents; the death of his adoptive father; and rejection by his adoptive mother, who wanted to "unadopt" him.

CASE STUDY

Carl was born to an unmarried teenage mother. At the age of four months, he was placed with a foster family. Although the investigating social worker found evidence of frequent, severe, and abusive physical punishment by the foster parents, Carl was allowed to be adopted. Four years later, after the family had moved twice, the adoptive father died. The adoptive mother indicated that her husband's last wish was that Carl be "unadopted." While seeking a placement for Carl, the adoptive mother indicated that Carl was stupid, mean, jealous, stubborn, and had "bad blood." Carl was then placed in a foster home but continued to have regular contact with his adoptive mother and sister.

INTERVENTION

Increasing social and school problems resulted in Carl's initial involvement in therapy. He worked with a female therapist for a year. When the female therapist left the clinic, Carl was referred to the author because of the recommendation that a male therapist would be appropriate, given Carl's entry into adolescence.

Carl was seen in a play therapy setting. During the early stages, Carl revealed conflicts regarding his African American identity and his rage about being abandoned. He wanted to discover what was wrong with him and get the right medicine to be cured. A strong therapeutic alliance was developed during this initial stage.

During his seventh session, Carl selected two hand puppets: an aggressive-looking parrot and a woodpeckerlike red bird, which he used to ask the therapist questions after a verbal patient-therapist interchange resulted in a high level of anxiety. He asked the therapist to have these puppets available for subsequent sessions.

In the next session Carl immediately sought out the puppets and asked that the play be recorded. After the puppet play was finished, the tape was played, and Carl and the therapist discussed various points in the play.

There was significant puppet play during the next four sessions, each followed by a time for listening to the audiotape. The first puppet play revolved around a baby bird (Carl) who hatched after the mother bird left. The baby bird had no one to feed it and even had no name or understanding of what kind of bird it might be. A neighbor bird came and took the baby bird to its home.

The second puppet play continued to reveal Carl's need to understand why he was abandoned, even though the reason was demeaning to his view of himself. The play also indicated his fantasy that he had his father's name.

The third play focused on a meeting between the red bird (Carl) and his biological mother (the parrot). Although excited about meeting his mother, when she expressed the desire to take him home, he stated that she was "too late" and that he wanted to stay with the birds who had taken care of him. The play continued to reveal that Carl still desired to be with his adoptive mother, although he was rejected by her and abandoned, through his death, by his adoptive father.

The final drama revealed Carl's view of the inevitability of abuse from parental figures. During this puppet play, his current foster parents mistreated, threatened, and abused him. The play ended when his biological mother came to the rescue and took him away to live in a pleasurable setting. Carl still hoped to have his birth mother be the perfect parent he had never had.

According to the author, the puppet play revealed how severely Carl had suffered and how he viewed himself as bad, rather than viewing his birth, adoptive, or foster mothers as not meeting his needs. The author indicated that he worked with Carl to develop insight within the metaphor of the puppet play. This allowed Carl the opportunity to work through his view of himself and his feelings toward parental figures.

COMMENTARY

Carl reportedly was very spontaneous regarding development of the puppet play; this activity clearly offered insight into his past and his hopes for the future. The play provided the means through which he was able to replay and master his childhood traumas. By requesting that the puppet play be audiotaped and then played, Carl allowed the therapist to participate in the process at a deeper, more active level.

SOURCE

Burch, C. A. 1980. Puppet play in a thirteen-year-old boy: remembering, repeating, and working through. *Clinical Social Work Journal* 8 (2): 79–89.

POSSIBLE DSM-IV-TR DIAGNOSES

300.02	Generalized Anxiety Disorder
309.21	Separation Anxiety Disorder
995.5	Physical Abuse of Child
V61.20	Parent-Child Relational Problem

Overcoming the Effects of Severe Deprivation, Dehydration, and Coma through Play Therapy

David Friedman

FOCUS

A severely neglected child participated in play therapy after hospitalization and placement in a foster home.

INTRODUCTION

Six-year-old Sean had been deprived of all fluid by his mother during a heat wave in an attempt to "cure" his enuresis. His two-year-old sister died from the same deprivation. Sean was comatose when hospitalized for severe dehydration. After his release, he was referred for therapy. Sean was hypervigilant to his environment. He did not speak during intake sessions but responded by shaking his head.

CASE STUDY

From a self-psychology perspective, Sean was conceptualized as a child who had learned to serve as his own hypervigilant self-object, risking disintegration if he did not meet his mother's needs. Repression of his own developmentally appropriate narcissistic needs resulted in a lack of pleasure, of activities, and of initiative. Self-psychology believes that reflecting, or mirroring, the child's needs not only validates these needs but also facilitates the developmental process of integration for the child.

INTERVENTION

When Sean began play therapy, he displayed no affect, appeared almost mechanical, was nonverbal, and did not play. Play was initiated by the author through the use of stimulating toys and food. To help relieve Sean's anxiety about being close, the author played by himself until eventually Sean, who responded only to the most indirect invitation to play, was able to join in.

After four months of weekly sessions, Sean finally was able to ask for a toy or food. Continued reflecting was needed to maintain contact with him. The author indicated that the slightest response that was not in touch with Sean's subjective world disrupted the fragile therapeutic alliance: Sean would look bewildered and immediately withdraw.

After seven months an important change occurred. Sean's flat and monotonous play became animated and filled with affect. Sean's play with a mother and baby doll revealed a baby who was able to smash the "bad mommy" doll into the wall. This play continued for fifteen minutes. Subsequent play included the now-labeled "baby man," who built prisons where the "bad mommy" could be kept without escaping.

Sean's play was now spontaneous and filled with strong emotion. However, the author indicated that the reflections, or mirroring, still had to be focused on the baby. If direct questions were asked, Sean retreated to the previous behavior of bewilderment and withdrawal.

Change was seen outside of therapy as well. Sean was able to be assertive, even to the point of saying "no" to authority figures. The play therapist also assisted Sean's foster parents in facilitating Sean's developmental needs and his emerging self.

COMMENTARY

Long-term, severe deprivation results in the need for long-term therapeutic intervention. Deprivation, or child neglect, often results in children who are unable to play. Many experts agree that the first step to remediation is to help the child learn to play. Once this key developmental task is accomplished, the child is able to use play in an expressive, healing manner.

SOURCE

Friedman, D. 1983. A self-psychology perspective. *Association for Play Therapy Newsletter* 2 (3): 6–8.

POSSIBLE DSM-IV-TR DIAGNOSES

313.89   Reactive Attachment Disorder of Infancy or Early Childhood
995.5   Neglect of Child

Play Therapy and Disclosure of Abuse

Patricia R. Klem

FOCUS

A case study describes how a child used a dollhouse in a play therapy session to disclose physical and sexual abuse and produce healing solutions.

INTRODUCTION

The case study presented is that of James, a six-year-old boy referred for counseling due to substantial emotional and behavioral disturbance. Play therapy offered James the freedom to overcome his developmental delays and fear so he could disclose sexual abuse by a sibling. The reenactment of physical abuse in the play eventually forced James's mother to admit to physical abuse by the father.

CASE STUDY

James, a developmentally delayed boy who lived with his mother, father, and four siblings, was described by school personnel as disruptive and destructive. He was also preoccupied with death. When he was discovered exposing himself and attempting to touch other boys at school, James told police officers, "my brother does it to me." The family was referred for family therapy and marital counseling, and James was referred for play therapy.

INTERVENTION

In the first play therapy session, James appeared very interested in the dollhouse but would not initiate playing with it. When the play therapist indicated that the dollhouse could be played with and suggested that it could be moved to the middle of the room, James began to explore it with great interest. As he re-arranged the dollhouse, he described his own house in detail and selected just the right number of dollhouse figures, labeling them with the names of his family. He quickly went on to describe and act out the nighttime physical and sexual abuse by his older brother. He laid the James doll down on the bottom bunk bed and said, "I'm sleeping now." Then, the brother doll came in the bedroom, hit the James doll, and touched it in the crotch. Before the brother doll left the room, it said, "If you tell, I'll kill you." This same sequence of interaction was repeated three times before the mother doll called the children dolls to wake up and get ready for school. James then described a typical day's routine and repeated the nighttime abuse. The entire scenario was played out three times in the first session. James did not want to leave the playroom when the time was up. He left only after reassurance that he could play with the dollhouse during the next session.

In the second and third sessions, James continued to act out the abuse with the dollhouse figures. He also introduced an unnamed male who would hit the James doll, throw him against the wall, and pull him by the hair. When the play therapist asked James to identify the new male doll, James answered, "I can't tell you, and you can't make it stop."

The father was away on business and did not attend the family therapy sessions. When the therapist told the family about James's abuse and asked who might have abused him, no one in the family would reveal any information.

During the fourth play therapy session, James placed the James doll on the top bunk of his bed and announced, "I feel safe on the top now that you know the secret." James told the play therapist that the night invasions had stopped, but the brother still threw him against the walls and yelled at him during the day.

Only after the father physically abused James in public did the mother, fearing Child Protective Services might remove James from the home, act to protect him. She revealed the long-term physical abuse of James by his father and stated that the older brother had also been physically and verbally abused by him. The mother took the children and left the home.

COMMENTARY

James was able to use the safety of the play therapy sessions and the availability of concrete play (especially necessary, given James's developmental delay) with the dollhouse to act out his abuse. Manipulating the doll figures to repeatedly reenact his abuse gave James the ability to communicate the threats made against him and his fear of being attacked with no internal or external sources to protect him. Through continued play, James was quickly able to develop a sense of control and place himself in a position of safety.

SOURCE

Klem, P. R. 1992. The use of the dollhouse as an effective disclosure technique. *International Journal of Play Therapy* 1:69–73.

POSSIBLE DSM-IV-TR DIAGNOSES

995.5   Physical and Sexual Abuse of Child
V61.8   Sibling Relational Problem

The Impact of Play Therapy on Self-Concept and Self-Mastery in Sexually Abused Children

Charles Lee Perez

FOCUS

Individual and group play therapy in the treatment of sexually abused children are studied. Mediating variables of gender, age, type of abuse, and living arrangements were examined.

INTRODUCTION

As the need to provide treatment for sexually abused children increases, questions regarding the most effective treatment model also increase. In this study, individual play therapy and group play therapy were used to determine the most effective treatment modality for sexually abused children. Age of the child, gender, type of abuse, and living arrangements (whether at home or in foster care) were examined as possible factors affecting the child's response to therapy.

Sexual abuse forces children to experience behavior for which they are not developmentally or emotionally prepared. This disruption of the typical developmental process often directly affects a child's self-concept and self-mastery. With this in mind, this study measured the change of self-concept and self-mastery over the course of treatment.

RESEARCH METHODS AND DESIGN

Fifty-five children who had been verified by social services, police, or both as having been sexually abused took part in this research. The children ranged in age from four to nine years. They were carefully screened to ensure that there had been no previous therapy and that no more than six months had elapsed since the disclosure of the sexual abuse.

Severity of abuse, degree of exposure, type of sexual activity, length of time exposed to abuse, number of incidents, other physical abuse, and emotional response of the child after disclosure varied with each child. The sexual abuse was both incestual and extrafamilial (babysitters, teachers, day care providers, strangers). The abusers were primarily males.

The Primary Self-Concept Inventory and the Locus of Control Scale were used to measure self-concept and self-esteem both before and after treatment. Analysis of variance, analysis of covariance, and multiple regression analysis were used to analyze the resulting data.

INTERVENTION

The children were divided into three groups. The first received individual play therapy and the second received group play therapy in once-a-week, sixty-minute sessions for twelve weeks. The third group, the control group, received no therapeutic intervention.

Both individual and group play therapy followed the relationship model developed by Clark Moustakas[1] and used Ray Bixler's[2] limit setting. In addition, structured techniques, such as art projects, role-playing, mutual storytelling, literature, and snack time, were included. Each group comprised three to five children of the same gender who ranged from four to six or seven to nine years in age. One purpose of the group play therapy was to facilitate the development of a pseudofamily in which the children could unconsciously relate to the therapist as a parent and other group members as siblings.

---

1. Clark Moustakas, *Children in Play Therapy* (Northvale, N.J.: Jason Aronson, Inc., 1973).
2. Ray Bixler, Limits Are Therapy, *Journal of Consulting Psychology* 13: 1–11.

The play therapists were four social workers who were part of a local sexual-abuse treatment team. They received twelve weekly sessions of training and supervision regarding the principles and methodology of play therapy.

RESULTS

The results indicated that play therapy benefits sexually abused children regardless of gender, age, type of abuse experienced, or current living arrangements. The results of both individual and group play therapy were statistically significant ($p > .05$) when compared to the control group. There were no significant differences in the effects of treatment between individual and group play therapy.

Play therapy gave the children the opportunity to reorganize the negative events of sexual abuse, gain self-control over these events, and begin developing a positive self-concept. The measured self-concepts of the children receiving play therapy increased ($p < .05$), while the children in the control group actually scored lower at the post-test.

Self-mastery is a key therapeutic issue for sexually abused children. The violation of physical and emotional boundaries results in the belief that they are not entitled to privacy and exist merely to be used by a more powerful person. These children thus come to believe they have no control, or mastery, over their environment. The self-mastery scores of the children in play therapy rose significantly ($p < .05$), while those of the children in the control group dropped, and their sense of helplessness increased.

COMMENTARY

Although there was no significant difference in outcome between individual and group play therapy, the author identified advantages of group play therapy. The group allows the children to identify with other sexually abused children, thus reducing their feeling of isolation. The group also acts as a pseudofamily and allows the child to experience parental and sibling relationships in which sexual abuse does not occur.

The relationship of the child to the abuser did appear to have some effect on the results of treatment. Victims of incest had higher average group scores than victims of extrafamilial abuse on both the self-concept and self-mastery instruments. While these increases did not reach a statistically significant level, the results do seem to imply that children involved in incest improve more in the areas of self-concept and self-mastery when compared to the victims of extrafamilial abuse.

SOURCE

Perez, C. 1987. A comparison of group play therapy and individual play therapy for sexually abused children. Ph.D. diss., University of Northern Colorado. *Dissertation Abstracts International* 48(12A).

POSSIBLE DSM-IV-TR DIAGNOSIS

995.5 Sexual Abuse of Child

Play Therapy with a Severely Neglected, Emotionally Abused Child

Janet West

FOCUS

Play therapy is used to allow a child the freedom to regress and then emotionally mature.

INTRODUCTION

Severe neglect and emotional abuse often result in acting-out behavior and impaired academic achievement. Child-centered play therapy provides a child with the opportunity to deal with her multiple therapeutic issues in the order of her preference.

CASE STUDY

Rosy, an underweight, six-year-old girl, had recently been placed in a children's home. She was manipulative, sought attention, and wanted to run her life by her rules. She spent a great deal of time wandering around aimlessly and showed very little academic achievement. Although long-term foster care appeared inevitable, it was decided that she needed therapeutic intervention before a foster home would be appropriate.

Rosy was the fifth child of a mother in her late twenties. Two children were placed with grandparents, and the other two suffered permanent developmental damage from severe neglect. Rosy's family moved several times as her father was frequently unemployed. Her mother was a prostitute. Her parents offered her some love, although it was expressed in inappropriate ways.

Several events immediately preceded Rosy's placement in the children's home. Her mother had killed a male client in their home, and Rosy assisted in cleaning up the blood. The mother was jailed, and Rosy moved in with a neighbor. Rosy's father was later hospitalized after she discovered him attempting suicide; she was then admitted into foster care. Three months after her placement, Rosy began play therapy.

INTERVENTION

The author identified her approach as child-centered play therapy and conceptualized the process of treatment with the use of Moustakas's[3] stages of play therapy. Because of Rosy's severe deprivation, food was added to the play therapy setting. The primary goal of each session was to provide a safe, therapeutic environment. Rosy was allowed to work at her own pace and to express whatever she desired (within appropriate limits). Thus, material surfaced in the sessions as Rosy's needs dictated, not in a logical, adult-directed sequence.

Rosy was actively involved in play from the beginning of her first session. She easily picked up being in charge of the play and gave directions to her play therapist. A primary theme in Rosy's play was mother-baby relationships. In the first four sessions, Rosy was an angry, bossy, unloving mother and directed the therapist to be the abused baby. Rosy, as the mother, threatened the baby with abandonment. So specific and detailed were many of the interchanges that the play therapist believed they were reenactments of actual incidents.

The fifth session proved pivotal in the parenting play. Rosy continued to insist on playing the mother but chose to interact in a much more positive manner with a doll as the baby. Rosy soon decided she wanted to be the baby and demanded to be held, rocked, and fed by the play therapist. She snuggled into the arms of the therapist, fully trusting the care and nurturing of the therapist-mother.

From this point on, Rosy continued to increase the developmental level of her play. She initiated play in which she was the little girl and the therapist was the mother. As trust in her therapist-mother continued to develop, she occasionally played the part of the baby again, as if to reassure herself that she was valued and accepted as a baby. Rosy used the play of the baby to reintegrate what it meant for her to be reparented. After she was able to enjoy being a baby, she had less need to take control in her everyday environment.

---

3. Clark Moustakas, *Children in Play Therapy* (Northvale, NJ: Jason Aronson, Inc., 1973).

The therapist believed that the provision of food assisted in the strong relationship between her and this very deprived child. Not only did the real food meet the real need of a hungry child, but play food and play surrounding the issue of food continued to meet her emotional cravings as well. Rosy often pretended to feed herself and the therapist using mixtures of water, sand, and clay. The symbolism of her being the provider of the food also gave insight into her need to care for herself after her perceived abandonment by both parents.

Jigsaw puzzles were also available for Rosy's use. The author indicated that Rosy selected increasingly more developmentally mature puzzles throughout the course of her treatment. The author believed that Rosy used the puzzles symbolically as a way to express her need to puzzle something out and integrate herself. These times of reintegration were additionally identified by her need to play the baby role again.

Other play themes included negative mother symbols of Dracula and a witch. A ghost contained many childhood illusions and fears. An old man, played by the therapist at Rosy's instruction, seemed to be the embodiment of her mother's clients.

COMMENTARY

During fifteen months of play therapy, Rosy was able to use the freedom of the self-directed, child-centered play therapy to deal with her needs in her own way. It is exciting to see that a severely neglected and emotionally abused child is able to know what it is best to deal with first, and even repeat dealing with, in order to get to a healthy place in life. In the presence of the play therapist, who knew how to facilitate therapy appropriately from the pseudomother role, Rosy used play therapy effectively.

SOURCE

West, J. 1983. Play therapy with Rosy. *British Journal of Social Work* 13:645–61.

POSSIBLE DSM-IV-TR DIAGNOSES

995.5   Neglect of Child
V61.20 Parent-Child Relational Problem

CHAPTER 2

Aggression and Acting Out

Unlike the typical response to aggression and acting-out behavior by teachers, parents, and adults in authority positions, the objective in play therapy is not to stop the behavior but rather to understand the child and provide an acceptable avenue for the child to express unfulfilled feelings, wants, and needs. Many play therapists find it difficult to respond appropriately to acts of aggression because such acts in the playroom are often directed toward themselves. In such cases, the therapist may react emotionally as though the act were a personal attack, thus shifting the focus to an issue of transference that must be worked through. As shown in the studies in this section, parents and therapists can successfully use play to help children effectively release aggressive feelings and in the process significantly improve their attitudes and behavior outside the playroom. Once the feelings and needs behind aggressive acts have been accepted and children are allowed to express them, they are able to go on to explore more positive behaviors.

Play Therapy with an Aggressive Child

John Allan and Keith Brown

FOCUS

Jungian play therapy is used as an approach to treat an aggressive third-grade boy.

INTRODUCTION

Allan and Brown describe the framework for Jungian play therapy and the evolution of themes through three major stages: chaos, struggle, and resolution. Emphasis is placed on the importance of the human psyche as a self-regulating structure capable of self-healing. The Jungian therapist provides a safe and protected setting in which painful unconscious struggles and negative feelings can be externalized and projected onto the toys. The chaos of the first stage is transformed into themes of struggle between good and evil, with evil generally winning. As therapy approaches the resolution stage, good tends to take control, and themes of construction and healing become common. Essential to Jungian play therapy are materials that allow the psyche to communicate through creative processes and symbolism. Consequently, the play therapy room should contain wet and dry sand tables, a sink for water play, a large dollhouse, and art materials.

CASE STUDY

Darren, an eight-year-old third grader, was referred to counseling because of his disruptive behavior in the classroom and aggression on the playground. Darren's father and mother had separated just prior to Darren's starting school. Darren's mother defended his behavior by protesting that he was being unfairly treated. After two assessment sessions, the school counselor saw Darren every day in play therapy the first week because of his severe problems both in and outside the classroom.

INTERVENTION

During the first three sessions, the therapist reflected Darren's actions and identified feelings evident in the play. Darren was apparently upset by such affective statements and would stop any comments he had been making for a period of time. Also during this time, Darren displayed aggression and destruction and tested limits, to which the therapist responded with redirection and limit setting.

In the fourth session Darren was asked to draw a picture and tell a story about the picture. A depiction of "good guys" versus "bad guys" was portrayed, and the therapist took this opportunity to provide some interpretation. During the same session, Darren created a sand tray scene, and again the therapist provided an interpretation, this time drawing a connection between the feelings depicted in the sand tray scene and feelings Darren might possibly be experiencing in school. The struggles between the good guys and the bad guys continued to session thirteen, with interpretations generally kept within the context of Darren's play.

By the thirteenth session Darren was able to resolve the conflict between good and evil in a socially acceptable way by having good marginally defeat evil in a hockey game. During this session, Darren expressed some of his angry, confused, and hurt feelings related to his father's abandonment. In the final two sessions he chose to work in the sand tray. The theme of aggression was considerably neutralized, and on the whole, good feelings predominated over bad.

RESULTS

At the beginning of treatment, Darren was considered the number one priority for counseling service in the school he attended. A year later, he was coping and behaving in more positive ways at home and at school. His mother's only visits to school were for teacher interviews to discuss routine academic matters.

COMMENTARY

Allan and Brown found that a good relationship with a child, one that allows the child to release hurt and aggressive feelings through play, can positively improve behavior outside the play therapy room. In Jungian play therapy, interpretive language serves as a catalyst that translates the unconscious material for the conscious ego. When a healthy connection is established between the child's conscious and unconscious, the child's psyche is able to grow and move toward self-actualization and a more fulfilling and socially acceptable way of being in the world. An interesting note in this study is the use of play therapy every day during the initial work of therapy as dictated by the severity of problem.

SOURCE

Allan, J., and Brown, K. 1993. Jungian play therapy in elementary schools. *Elementary School Guidance and Counseling* 28 (1): 30–41.

POSSIBLE DSM-IV-TR DIAGNOSES

V71.02 Child or Adolescent Antisocial Behavior
312.9   Disruptive Behavior Disorder NOS
313.81   Oppositional Defiant Disorder

Play Therapy and Video Feedback of Play Sessions with Oppositional Disordered Children

Patricia Beers

FOCUS

The effect of individual play therapy in conjunction with parent counseling and focused, videotaped feedback of parent-child play sessions on parent-child interactions is studied.

INTRODUCTION

A research study was conducted to determine the effectiveness of two differing interventions for children exhibiting oppositional and disruptive behaviors. The treatment approaches selected included individual play therapy accompanied by parent counseling and focused, videotaped feedback in which the parent(s) participated in videotaped play sessions with the child, followed by a feedback session between the parents and therapist. Statistically significant results were reported.

RESEARCH METHODS AND DESIGN

Twenty intact families with a one- to nine-year-old child diagnosed with oppositional disorder of childhood (according to the DSM-III) were selected from a variety of area mental-health agencies and clinics. The families were randomly placed into three groups: (1) traditional play therapy for the child and counseling with parents, (2) focused, videotaped feedback, and (3) control group.

The treatment goals were to improve parent-child interaction, described as increasing positive affect, decreasing both controlling and submissive behaviors, decreasing negative affect, changing physical and verbal interactions, and improving parental perception of the child. Also, the treatment sought to change the parental perceptions of their child's problems.

The Eyberg Child Behavior Inventory and the Interpersonal Behavior Constructs Scale were used to collect information about changes in behavior. Data were collected before treatment, in the middle of treatment (after eight weeks), at the end of treatment (after sixteen weeks), and at follow-up (four weeks after treatment ended, or at twenty weeks).

INTERVENTION

One group consisted of traditional play therapy for the child and individual counseling with each of the parents; each session lasted fifty minutes. The parent's sessions initially focused on the child and then seemed to focus on the intrapersonal issues of the parent.

The focused, videotaped feedback treatments consisted of one two-hour session weekly. The session began with three seven-minute sessions in the playroom, which were videotaped: first, the mother and child; next, the father and child; and finally, both parents and the child. The child then went to the waiting room and was watched by the receptionist. For the remainder of the session, the parents had a conjoint session with the therapist that focused on a review of the videotaped activities in a therapeutic setting with attention directed to salient verbal and nonverbal behaviors in parent-child interactions. The control group received no treatment.

RESULTS

Generally speaking, after eight weeks significant improvement was seen in the children participating in play therapy with the parents participating in counseling, while the videotaped-feedback groups showed no significant improvement until follow-up.

Nonacceptance behavior in parent-child interactions decreased significantly for the children in the play therapy group after eight weeks of treatment ($p <$ .05). However, when nonacceptance was measured again at the follow-up, some of this positive change had been lost (score of 2.17 at eight weeks, 1.43 at twenty weeks). The videotaped-feedback group actually had a statistically significant increase in nonacceptance behavior at both midtreatment and at follow-up (score of 1.95 at pretreatment, 3.58 at eight weeks, and 2.16 at follow-up). Thus, the play therapy group had less nonacceptance behavior at follow-up than the videotaped group, even with the slight loss of their previous improvement.

The play therapy group increased at statistically significant levels in the amount of time a parent and child worked together (score of 1.8 to 5.1). There was little change in the videotaped feedback group (score of 3.7 to 4.2).

In the area of shared conversations, the videotaped feedback group showed a significant increase. The play therapy group actually showed a slight decrease in the number of shared conversations between child and parent.

Each of the groups—play therapy, video feedback, and control— demonstrated a decrease in perceived problems and intensity of problems. The author hypothesized that the increased attention the parents were giving the children, in order to log their behavior, may have had a positive effect on both the parents and the children. Also, the contact between the parents and the researcher, who called regularly to get the weekly behavioral log information, may have become therapeutic in nature and thereby influenced all three groups.

COMMENTARY

This study revealed interesting information: the children who received play therapy showed the most dramatic positive changes after eight weeks. This may indicate that children with oppositional defiant disorder respond well to the individual therapeutic contact. While these findings cannot be generalized to the entire population of children in play therapy, it may indicate that this possibility does exist. It appears unclear why the children in the videotaped treatment group did not show significant positive changes until follow-up. One conclusion may be that having only the parents working directly with the child may have caused the positive changes to occur more slowly. The combination of individual therapeutic intervention for both the child and the parent results in quicker relief for problematic child-parent interactions.

SOURCE

Beers, P. 1985. Focused videotape feedback psychotherapy as compared with traditional play therapy in treatment of the oppositional disorder of childhood. Ph.D. diss., University of Illinois, Urbana-Champaign. *Dissertation Abstracts International* 46 (04): B1330.

POSSIBLE DSM-IV-TR DIAGNOSIS

313.81 Oppositional Defiant Disorder

Play Therapy as an Intervention for Acting-Out Children

Viola A. Brody

FOCUS

Developmental play therapy uses the dialog of touch to impact behavior change in acting-out children.

INTRODUCTION

The core of developmental play therapy is touch. Brody asserts that a child who experiences touch from a capable toucher will grow toward healthy maturity and will heal from earlier trauma and neglect. A disturbed child who experiences caring touch feels truly seen, validated, and acknowledged by another person, often for the first time.

CASE STUDY #1

Alan was one of eight four-year-old boys in a developmental play group referred for severe acting out and unmanageable behavior. He was paired with a therapist who played with him each week through the medium of physical touch. The treatment period spanned twenty weeks. In the initial sessions, Alan resisted the cradling. He displayed hyperactive and unfocused behavior, running about the room disturbing other pairs, unable to keep to his designated mat. The therapist set the limits of the session, explaining to Alan that he would be held for short periods of time each week. Alan was held loosely in an upright position so that he had room to push against the therapist, which he did in the beginning. Within a few sessions, Alan had stopped running around and wanted to be with the therapist. He came to enjoy the touching contact with the therapist and was also aware that he was experiencing this as pleasing. He could communicate his awareness to the therapist and was able to provide much of the structure in their touching dialog, directing the therapist and inventing games.

RESULTS

The goal of developmental play therapy is not to solve problems or to change the child's behavior but rather to build a relationship. Alan's behavior showed that he had accepted a core self and that he could relate to others. One year later, the therapist accidentally ran into Alan during a visit to his classroom. The therapist was impressed by the quiet, comfortable, and confident way in which Alan was able to interact with him.

CASE STUDY #2

Mira was a normal four-year-old child whose mother wanted her to participate in the developmental play training program. Mira was described as being very difficult as a baby and now constantly fought with her older sister. The therapist observed that she was a very controlling child who constantly called attention to herself. During the initial sessions, Mira resisted everything the therapist did, screamed, threw her shoes, and disturbed others in the room. At the third session, the therapist used redirection to provide Mira with an acceptable way of touching after she had spit at and bit the therapist. By the end of the third session, Mira had invented a special game in which her leg would work only if the therapist kissed it ten times. By the sixth session, Mira could not get enough touching, was very babyish, and enjoyed being sung to by the therapist. During the twelfth session, Mira shifted out of this attachment phase into the separation phase and began to treat the therapist less like a parent and more like a friend, asking the therapist how to do things and competing with her. Mira's treatment period ended with session sixteen.

RESULTS

When the therapist felt seen, heard, and acknowledged by Mira, she knew that Mira had shifted out of the attachment phase into the separation phase and was becoming more independent. Near the end of the treatment period, Mira was able to compose a special poem that expressed her affection for and connection to the therapist.

COMMENTARY

Touch, if done sensitively and appropriately, enables the child to experience the therapist's physical presence, as well as the child's own presence. A special dialog develops between the therapist and child through touch, taking the child back to an earlier stage of development. The child is given the opportunity to regress to that earliest of touching experiences, being cradled and held like a baby. The child is then able to pick up and bring forward what is needed for healing.

SOURCE

Brody, V. A. 1992. The dialogue of touch: developmental play therapy. *International Journal of Play Therapy* 1:21–30.

POSSIBLE DSM-IV-TR DIAGNOSES

Case #1
314.01   Attention-Deficit/Hyperactivity Disorder, Predominantly Hyperactive-
         Impulsive Type
314.9   Attention-Deficit/Hyperactivity Disorder NOS

Case #2
313.89   Reactive Attachment Disorder of Infancy or Early Childhood

Both
V71.02   Child or Adolescent Antisocial Behavior
312.9   Disruptive Behavior Disorder NOS
313.81   Oppositional Defiant Disorder

A Group Play Technique for Rewarding Social Responsibility

Albert S. Carlin and Hubert E. Armstrong

FOCUS

Social-learning theory is utilized in a playgroup to reduce hostility in four severely disturbed boys.

INTRODUCTION

Carlin and Armstrong drew on social-learning theory and operant techniques to
devise a group treatment program with two main characteristics: (1) the encouragement of social responsibility, that is, teaching children that the behavior of
other group members is partially their own responsibility; and (2) the token reinforcement of social participation in a natural setting.

CASE STUDY

Physical fighting and teasing among four boys in a children's day care unit had
become sufficiently intense that it was interfering with treatment, not only of
the boys concerned but also of the rest of the children on the unit. Tony, age

seven, was a minimally brain-damaged child who engaged in hyperactive, but not antisocial or destructive, behavior. John, age nine, was a schizophrenic child who engaged in ritualistic play and became enraged if other children did not carry out his directions. Paul, age twelve, was a schizophrenic and minimally brain-damaged child who generally seemed completely puzzled by the world around him. He engaged in erratic aggressive behavior, impulsively lashing out at anyone within reach. Tom, age seven and a half, was explosive, hostile, and destructive. All four boys had difficulty interacting with peers and adults.

INTERVENTION

Four days a week, for five weeks, the boys were brought together in a group for a ninety-minute period of cooperative play. Carlin and Armstrong, together with the two nurses regularly assigned to the boys at this time, acted as therapists. The planned procedure was for the children to be involved in a situation structured so that cooperative play would be encouraged. For sequences of appropriate interaction involving at least three of the boys, token rewards would be placed in a common pool. Sequences of socially inappropriate behavior, such as spitting, hitting, kicking, or destroying a project, would result in a fine, and tokens would be taken from the pool. Effort on the part of one or more children to solve group problems or to be extra helpful to the group would be rewarded by bonus tokens added to the pool. Fines or payments would be preceded by verbal evaluation of the behavior and announcement of rewarding or fining action. At the end of the session, the tokens in the pool would be evenly divided among the children, and they could cash them in for toys and sweets.

After several days of observation during which the boys typically interacted by teasing and physically attacking one another, the plan was presented. It was mentioned that since the boys seemed to have difficulty getting along, the staff had decided to pay them to get along. The rest of the intervention was then outlined for the boys, and they were reminded about the specifics each day before they began their group session.

The boys seemed enthusiastic about the plan, and the first day produced a remarkable change in their behavior. Rather than provoking each other as usual, they worked together in harmony to build a spaceship out of blocks. When tokens were paid to the boys during the session, the amount and reason for payment were disclosed at the same time. When a fine was levied near the end of the session because of Tom's misbehavior, the group members were told it was their responsibility to stop Tom from throwing things at the adults. With the help of adult suggestions, the group was able to engage Tom in a constructive activity, which meant that the remainder of the earnings was preserved.

After several sessions, it became obvious that the system of fines was not sufficient to halt all the disruptive behaviors. The group was just not able to cope with some members. Thus, a "penalty box" was initiated, that is, an out-of-control child was physically placed in a penalty box by the adults. During this period, the child could not receive rewards earned by the rest of the group; nor could his behavior in the box penalize the rest of the group.

Tony was discharged from the unit at this time, resulting in a group of three children. By this time, John and Tom had become friendlier and begun to work together more, although Tom often had difficulty relinquishing control. They seemed to derive more satisfaction from their positive relationship than from the reward of including Paul in their play. At this point, the fining procedure was eliminated, and the boys were rewarded just on the basis of appropriate behaviors. All misbehavior was simply ignored. During the remaining sessions, a genuine warmth seemed to be developing among the three group members. There was also far less acting-out behavior during the sessions. The program was terminated on the discharge of a second group member.

COMMENTARY

Carlin and Armstrong stated that although their purpose was not to provide a sound methodological analysis of the principles attempted, these children, who were presumed to be "uncontrollable" as a result of brain damage and childhood schizophrenia, were found to be quite capable of inhibiting their aggressive acting-out behavior and working together in reasonable harmony. Although dramatic changes in aggressive behavior occurred almost immediately, a general reduction in aggression toward the rest of the ward was also reported by the staff. During the play sessions, the children helped one another behave properly by the use of such techniques as distraction, avoidance, and reminders. Through the flexible use of operant and group techniques, Carlin and Armstrong were able to instill a sense of social responsibility. Disturbed children do not seem to lack the capacity to enjoy interpersonal relationships. Rather, they are more likely to lack the ability to experience interpersonal relationships that can supply a satisfying result. The token system provided an opportunity for these boys to experience positive social interaction.

SOURCE

Carlin, A. S., and Armstrong, H. E. 1968. Rewarding social responsibility in disturbed children: a group play technique. *Psychotherapy: Theory, Research and Practice* 5:169–74.

POSSIBLE DSM-IV-TR DIAGNOSES

295.90 Schizophrenia, Undifferentiated Type
314.01 Attention Deficit/Hyperactivity Disorder, Predominantly Hyperactive-
        Impulsive Type
312.34 Intermittent Explosive Disorder
V71.02 Child or Adolescent Antisocial Behavior
312.9   Disruptive Behavior Disorder NOS
313.81 Oppositional Defiant Disorder
312.8   Conduct Disorder

Play Group Counseling as an Effective Intervention for Children with Behavior Problems

Gary Lloyd Gaulden

FOCUS

Developmental play group counseling is explored as a potential intervention for reducing classroom-disturbance behavior of second-grade students.

INTRODUCTION

Developmental play group counseling was hypothesized to facilitate positive change in disadvantaged second-grade students who were exhibiting behavior problems in the classroom. The study was designed to measure change in self-concept, attitudes toward school, and classroom-disturbance behavior of identified students who participated in developmental play group counseling, play group counseling, and a control group.

INTERVENTION

Subjects for the study were selected from a pool of fifty-six second graders from a Title I program who were rated by their teachers to be one or more standard deviations above the mean on the "classroom-disturbance" factor of the Devereux Elementary School Behavior Rating Scale. Participation in the Title I program required that the students be economically and educationally deprived and functioning one to two years below grade level in reading and/or math. Students were randomly assigned in groups of four to developmental play group counseling and play group counseling. The remaining fifteen students were assigned to the control group. Students in the two experimental groups received treatment in two forty-five minute sessions per week for seven weeks for a total of fourteen sessions.

Developmental play group counseling combines the techniques of developmental group counseling and play group counseling. Developmental group counseling is a structured verbal approach in which the child can learn to verbally express and explore feelings by participating in a discussion triad as talker, listener, or observer. The discussion triad took place within the first fifteen to twenty minutes of a forty-five minute session and was followed by thirty to thirty-five minutes of play group counseling.

Play group counseling is an unstructured approach that uses play media to help the child experience self. The children are permitted to use the session as they wish. The therapist's primary emphasis is on relating to the here and now, interacting with each child by observing, listening, and reflecting content and feelings.

RESULTS

Children in the play group counseling approach made significant changes of one or more standard deviations in the reduction of "classroom-disturbance" behavior and maintained that level of improvement eight weeks after the end of the study. There were no significant changes in measured self-concept or attitude toward school. The developmental play group counseling subjects and the control group did not achieve any significant change on measurement instruments.

COMMENTARY

Although the author had expected the combined approach of developmental play group counseling to be superior, the findings suggest that play group counseling alone was the more effective approach in dealing with classroom-disturbance behavior of deprived second-grade students. In play group counseling, children are free to use play materials as their natural language of expression. The author suggested that the discussion phase of the developmental play group counseling approach may have been facilitated by limiting to three the number of children in the group; however, all of the counselors involved in the research project concluded that the children in developmental play group counseling were much too young and immature to benefit from this approach.

SOURCE

Gaulden, G. L. 1975. Developmental-play group counseling with early primary-grade students exhibiting behavioral problems. Ph.D. diss., North Texas State University. *Dissertation Abstracts International* 36 (05): A2628.

POSSIBLE DSM-IV-TR DIAGNOSIS

Insufficient information provided in the study.

Brief Play Therapy for a Preschooler with Severe Temper Tantrums

David M. Levy

FOCUS

A form of brief play therapy is used with a two-year-old girl who had severe temper tantrums.

INTRODUCTION

Jane had reportedly been an "easy baby" until a nanny had begun toilet training her at twelve months. Jane did not take to toilet training easily, battling the nanny every time she was placed on the potty-training chair. After a few months, however, bowel training was achieved, followed by bladder control at twenty-five months. It was believed that the temper tantrums and other behavioral problems were directly tied to the strict regime of toilet training by a highly disciplinarian nanny. The tantrums would last approximately two hours (if allowed to run their course) and consisted typically of Jane lying on the floor, kicking and screaming. Jane also showed little affection toward her parents or four-year-old brother and displayed a generally negative and sulky attitude.

INTERVENTION

Jane was seen for a total of ten sessions. In her first sess'
into the room without her mother. In fact, she clung
would not release it. The play therapist put several t<
would not play with them. The therapist then took a play gun a..~
clay figures. When Jane was asked whom else the therapist should shoot, sne
pointed at her mother and then at the play therapist. After the therapist shot
both, Jane began to play, but when the therapist attempted to approach her, she
hid under a chair. The therapist attempted to give toys to her, but Jane shoved
them aside. After several such attempts, Jane again went to her mother and
clung to her skirt. The therapist believed that the reluctance to play was due to
Jane's negative attitude, not because of her fear of a stranger. He attempted to
model destructive behavior in order to give Jane permission to release her own
feelings.

The second session began much like the first. After several minutes, however, Jane's mother slipped out of the playroom, and Jane accepted some clay
from the therapist and began to form babies. Later, she was able to initiate spontaneous play with other toys.

In the third session, she again needed her mother present at the beginning
of the session. Once her mother had slipped out, Jane again played with the clay,
making babies, and frequently wanted her hands cleaned. The session ended
with Jane playing easily and occasionally laughing. After this session, Jane's parents reported she began to display "sudden and unusual affection." Additionally,
there was a reduction of the negative attitude, more positive compliance with
parental requests, and freer play with other children.

In the next several sessions, Jane made her clay babies sit on the potty-chair.
Some clay babies stood near the potty-chair. Jane explained she had attempted
to urinate at home like her older brother.

During the fifth play therapy session, Jane placed bits of clay in a bowl.
When the therapist reflected that the clay represented bowel movements, Jane
looked at the play therapist and smiled. After this session, Jane began soiling at
home, several times a day. Initially, the therapist advised the mother to ignore the
behavior. During the eighth session, Jane displayed a marked increase in destructive play. This included pulling her clay babies apart, throwing the clay all
over the room, tearing paper off the crayons, and so on. The next day, Jane
smeared herself with feces. At this point, the therapist allowed the mother to intervene, and Jane stopped soiling that same day. In the ninth session, one week
after the cessation of soiling, Jane smeared clay and pretended to eat it. With her
presenting behaviors successfully resolved, the tenth and final session was used
for closure and termination.

he decision to select this form of brief therapy, general release play therapy, was based on the belief that the symptomatic behavior was the result of excessive demands or prohibitions made at too early a developmental age. In this approach, the child is able to release anxieties through the use of therapeutic self-regression. Released from constricting emotions, the child is free to express self through the various play materials. This approach to play therapy would be applicable to many other children who have various maladaptive responses to general stressors during early childhood. It should also be noted that the author stressed that release play therapy should be used only with children whose problematic behavior is not related to other family problems.

SOURCE

Levy, D. 1939. Release therapy in young children. *Child Study* 16 (1): 141–43.

POSSIBLE DSM-IV-TR DIAGNOSES

312.9   Disruptive Behavior Disorder NOS
300.00 Anxiety Disorder NOS
309.4   Adjustment Disorder with Mixed Disturbance of Emotions and Conduct

Play Therapy for the Institutionalized Child

Helen E. Miller

FOCUS

A mentally and physically normal six-year-old girl who was displaying behavioral problems related to abandonment and institutionalization was successfully treated with nondirective play therapy.

INTRODUCTION

Deprived of their original family group, children in institutions feel rejection and have less opportunity to develop positive relationships. Play therapy provides an opportunity for a relationship with an understanding, accepting adult. This case study exemplifies the particular difficulties that face the institutionalized child and the positive impact of play therapy intervention.

CASE STUDY

Lucy was four years old when her father was killed in a mine accident, and she came to live at Mooseheart Institution with her mother and three older brothers. After two years, Lucy's mother remarried and left Mooseheart without the children. Two months later, Lucy, who was now six years old, was referred for play therapy following uncontrollable outbursts after visits from her mother. She attended play therapy once a week for four months, then every day for a short period, for a total of twenty-two contacts. Lucy had one therapist for the first five sessions and a different therapist for the remaining seventeen sessions.

During the sessions, Lucy was allowed to direct the play. She did not interact directly with the first therapist but primarily engaged in nurturing behavior with dolls. When abruptly changed to a new therapist at the sixth session, Lucy reacted by limiting her play to rolling a peg around on the floor. She resumed active play during the eighth session, shifting back and forth from nurturing to aggressive behavior. She remained nonverbal until the eighteenth session, when two unique procedural changes occurred. Given the opportunity, Lucy chose to attend play therapy every day. In this same session, another child whom Lucy knew happened to join the session. In this session, Lucy began to talk to the therapist and affectionately hugged and kissed her, both firsts.

RESULTS

During the final four sessions, Lucy was verbally expressive and displayed affection for the therapist. She was able to use toys and materials that were of special significance to her. Lucy worked through her difficulties in accepting her new stepfather and his children. She was able to verbally request affection from her therapist. Lucy decided when it was time for her final session and announced that she might return when all the snow was off the ground. Reports from Lucy's teachers indicated that she was no longer uncontrollable after visits from her mother and was getting along better in school.

COMMENTARY

Although the author found it difficult to imagine that these play sessions held any significance for Lucy because of what was described as a "dearth of interplay between the therapist and child," the significance of the relationship was clearly demonstrated by the drastic behavior change when Lucy lost her first therapist. Lucy's second therapist often did not accurately reflect Lucy's actions and feelings during the play sessions. In fact, Lucy's first advances toward the therapist occurred only when she was in the presence of another child. However, if the therapist's recognition of what the child was trying to express was inadequate at times, the therapist's willingness to fulfill the role assigned by the child minimized these deficits. Play therapy provided an opportunity for the therapist to function as a therapeutic agent in the life of an institutionalized child by demonstrating that she could and would be able to meet the child's basic needs.

SOURCE

Miller, H. E. 1948. Play therapy for the institutionalized child. *Nervous Child* 7:311–17.

POSSIBLE DSM-IV-TR DIAGNOSES

309.3 Adjustment Disorder with Disturbance of Conduct
312.9 Disruptive Behavior Disorder NOS

Play Therapy for Behavior Problems Centered around Issues of Anger, Fear, and Control

Mary Ann Par

FOCUS

Sand and water play were used by a child in play therapy to deal with numerous behavior problems that included aggressive tendencies, phobias about the dark and animals, noncompliance with authority figures, poor peer relations, and poor dietary habits.

INTRODUCTION

Four-year-old James, the oldest of four siblings, came from an environment that did not facilitate the expression of emotions. His father was often unavailable to the family. His mother was considered overly strict and showed some compulsive tendencies. Both parents expected James to show far more control in his behavior than is generally expected from a child of comparable age. Expression of his feelings often involved noncompliant and controlling behaviors. His problems extended to the school setting, where he had problems relating to authorities and peers. Play therapy was used to allow James to face his issues of anger, fear, and control and to free him to express his emotions in more acceptable ways.

INTERVENTION

Play therapy for James followed a child-centered approach in a playroom with typical toys and objects. James selected sand and water play as his primary play while in the playroom. During the beginning sessions, he was apprehensive about entering the room and protested verbally and physically. Once inside, his play was serious, purposeful, and guarded. He initiated little contact with the therapist and played cautiously with the sand and water, careful not to mix the two. If the sand stuck to his body, he would compulsively wash every grain away before returning to play. The water used to wash with had to be warm because the use of cold water greatly disturbed him. His play centered primarily around the careful preparation of food. Such play was intentional and serious. Before leaving each session, he was careful to clean up all of the sand, even though he was not asked to do so.

The author specified two turning points during the course of therapy. The first involved James's expression of his repressed feelings about a new sibling in the family. Expressing these feelings allowed him in turn to exhibit the more nurturing qualities of a big brother. After building sand houses for two animal figures, James found a motorcycle man figure. The animals were terrorized by the figure until he buried the figure in the sand. After a short period of more play, James unburied the now happy motorcycle man. The animals and the motorcycle man played together in the following session. James expressed and laid to rest his aggressive feelings toward his new brother. He could then accept the new role as a caring older brother.

The second experience occurred when James was facing some obvious anxiety and fear due to a number of incidents occurring between his family and an aggressive neighbor. James entered the playroom, although he made it clear that he did not wish to do so. After violently throwing all the water and sand onto the floor, he assumed the role of a courteous bus driver as he carefully drove a busload of children through the sand-water obstacles to the safety of their homes. After dealing with his out-of-control emotions, James found he could provide a safe and nurturing environment for those he cared about. At the end of the session, James seemed content with the mess he had made on the floor and made no attempt to clean it up. He seemed proud of the mark he had made on the room.

RESULTS

Toward the end of therapy, James was less fearful of cold water and experimented with different temperatures of water by combining hot and cold. His play centered around less emotionally charged issues and more around typical childhood themes. The therapist remembered fondly James's use of sand to represent snow as he sang "Jingle Bells" in preparation for Christmas. The therapeutic experience was positive for James, and he was reported to be better adjusted in dealing with his emotions and with those around him. He was more liked by himself and his peers.

COMMENTARY

Anticipating the possible reaction to the liberal use of sand and water play as demonstrated in this case, the author pointed out that the behaviors in the playroom with these mediums never "spilled over" into the classroom. James played with sand and water in acceptable and appropriate ways while in the school setting. The author also points out that if, with another child, such uses of sand and water threatened the structure and guidelines of the play setting, clearly defined limits about the use of the medium should be set.

SOURCE

Par, M. A. 1990. Sand and water play: a case study. *Association for Play Therapy Newsletter* 9 (1): 4–6.

POSSIBLE DSM-IV-TR DIAGNOSES

309.4   Adjustment Disorder with Mixed Disturbance of Emotions and Conduct
V71.02 Child or Adolescent Antisocial Behavior
312.9   Disruptive Behavior Disorder NOS

Psychoanalytic Play Therapy with an Acting-Out Child

Anneliese Ude-Pestel

FOCUS

Psychoanalytic play therapy uses expressive art with a child demonstrating serious acting-out and self-injuring behavior.

INTRODUCTION

Six-year-old Betty's parents requested therapy due to her severe acting-out behaviors. These behaviors included screaming, temper tantrums, beating her head against the floor, pulling out her hair, running around the house naked, and aggression toward her sibling. Psychoanalytic play therapy was employed, with Betty taking the lead in the play activities and Ude-Pestel interpreting the play and art expressions.

CASE STUDY

Betty lived with her parents, a two-year-old brother, and a live-in babysitter. Following Betty's birth, the death of a relative caused severe depression in the mother, who reportedly sought comfort from Betty instead of providing her with appropriate nurturing. Severe constipation and persistent thumb sucking were reported in Betty's early development. A neurological examination revealed no abnormal conditions.

In addition to the behavioral history noted, Betty expressed her emotional pain in art creations in the home. Her parents brought approximately fifteen hundred pictures and paintings to the initial parent consultation. According to Ude-Pestel, Betty had a particular penchant for ghosts and skulls, which, Ude-Pestel hypothesized, Betty "had to paint, driven by her unconscious, in order to survive, lest she be flooded with these frightening pictures which are the mirror images of her inner fears."

INTERVENTION

Ude-Pestel provided a detailed description of the treatment process with Betty, including thirty-nine chapters and twenty-six color or black-and-white pictures of the artwork Betty drew during the process. The course of her treatment is exemplified in the first and last pictures displayed in the case study, "Crucified" and "Dancing Girl," respectively.

The play materials provided for Betty included a wide variety of toys in addition to art materials. Betty's established preference for expressing herself in art continued within the therapeutic process. In describing the play materials to Betty's parents, Ude-Pestel noted that children "aren't expected to do anything. Everything you see in this room is simply an invitation. If a child wants to, he can play with these things, but he is not forced or influenced in any way."

During the initial phase of treatment, Betty engaged in nurturing activities with Ude-Pestel, including making milk and swinging together. These were accompanied by Betty's artwork involving ghosts, monsters, skeletons, and crocodiles. Child- and therapist-initiated storytelling was also a part of the initial stages of therapy, with fairy tales as the focus. The drawings and stories were interpreted as Betty's illustrating and processing her unconscious fears. As the therapeutic alliance was established, Betty was able to express her emotions more openly and to become verbally and behaviorally aggressive. She ordered the therapist around and, during one session, threw numerous toys at Ude-Pestel, requiring her to shield her face with a pillow. Betty grabbed the pillow, shoved it into the therapist's face, and threw her whole body weight onto Ude-Pestel. This was followed by a calm, trancelike state.

Concurrent with the play therapy, Ude-Pestel also worked with Betty's parents and her teachers, both to obtain further background information and to provide therapeutic direction. As the treatment progressed, Betty's artwork reflected changes in her life: the drawings of ghosts and monsters were replaced by pictures of friends, animals, and ice-skating. The progress of treatment is described by Ude-Pestel in terms of a particular play item that had been used throughout the therapy process. A cardboard box had initially been a cradle for Betty (interpreted as the womb). It later became a pirate ship with a death banner. As the therapy approached termination, it became a playhouse with an open door. The behaviors for which Betty had been referred had ameliorated, and Ude-Pestel reported that a follow-up several years later revealed that Betty continued to function well.

COMMENTARY

Before Betty entered treatment for her difficulties, she was already expressing her emotional pain through expressive art and play, as well as the acting-out behaviors for which she was referred.

In the play and art therapy process, Betty was allowed to continue expressing herself in her own way, rather than being compelled to pursue an adult therapeutic agenda. Although Ude-Pestel's interpretations may be open for discussion, Betty's emotional and behavioral history and the healing change brought about in the play process cannot be disputed. Allowing Betty to express herself and to heal on her terms through the play therapy process changed her life.

SOURCE

Ude-Pestel, A. 1977. *Betty: History and Art of a Child in Therapy.* Palo Alto, CA: Science and Behavior Books, Inc.

POSSIBLE DSM-IV-TR DIAGNOSES

312.8   Conduct Disorder
313.81   Oppositional Defiant Disorder
300.02   Generalized Anxiety Disorder

Play Therapy with Conduct-Disordered Children

Archana Dogra and V. Veeraraghavan

FOCUS

Individual play therapy is combined with parental counseling as an intervention for children diagnosed with conduct disorder.

INTRODUCTION

The purpose of this study was to determine the effect of play therapy along with parental counseling on the behaviors of children diagnosed with conduct disorder. The researchers specifically measured the severity of typical conduct disorder symptoms, such as excessive levels of fighting and bullying; cruelty to animals or other people; severe destructiveness to property; repeated lying; persistent, severe disobedience; and defiant provocative behavior.

RESEARCH METHODS AND DESIGN

Twenty participants who were referred to a child guidance clinic located in India for manifesting aggressive conduct disorder were chosen to participate in the study. Once chosen for the study, they were diagnosed by two psychiatrists and one psychologist with conduct disorder. The sample consisted of children mainly from a lower socioeconomic range between the ages of eight and twelve. Gender was not reported. Each child's behavior was measured according to a pretest/post-test design by the Picture-Frustration Test and the Child Behavior Rating Scale. The twenty children were randomly and evenly split into an experimental group and a control group. The Wilcoxon Signed Ranks Test was used for the analysis of results.

INTERVENTION

For the experimental group, each child participated in individual play therapy according to a nondirective approach. The children received two sessions per week for a period of two months, totaling sixteen sessions per child. The parents participated in parental counseling to help them better understand their child and to change their own attitudes and behavior toward the child. The control group did not receive intervention.

RESULTS

According to the Picture-Frustration Test results, the experimental group showed significantly lesser extrapunitive (tendency to blame some person or circumstance for their frustration) responses and significantly higher impunitive and need-persistence responses as compared to the control group. The Child Behavior Rating Scale showed a significant change in the posttreatment scores of the experimental group after the intervention on the six dimensions of adjustment to self, home, school and social, physical, and personality total adjustment. The child's aggressive conduct disorder also changed significantly, including less fighting and bullying, less violence against adults, more obedience, less frequent and severe temper tantrums, decrease in the parents' use of corporal punishment, decrease in parental neglect, and decrease in the child's strong dislike for school.

COMMENTARY

Individual play therapy along with parental counseling appeared to be an effective treatment for children diagnosed with conduct disorder. The experimental group demonstrated significantly less severity in conduct disorder behaviors. Researchers commented that play therapy offered a cathartic effect that helped the child express his or her hidden, repressed needs through a constructive and creative outlet. They also noted that play therapy was helpful to these children because of their ability to communicate pleasant and unpleasant feelings without the fear of consequences.

SOURCE

Dogra, A., and Veeraraghavan, V. 1994. A study of psychological intervention of children with aggressive conduct disorder. *Ind. Journal of Clinical Psychology* 21:28–32.

POSSIBLE DSM-IV-TR DIAGNOSIS

312.8 Conduct Disorder

Effect of Play Therapy on Withdrawn and Aggressive Behavior

Julius Seeman, Edyth Barry, and Charlotte Ellinwood

FOCUS

Play therapy is used with children demonstrating withdrawn behavior and high aggression.

INTRODUCTION

The authors conducted this study early in the research on play therapy. They attempted to provide substantial research that would address previous research flaws, such as controlling for motivation of clients, measuring personality organization, and providing research on child therapy. Through the use of a standardized measure to determine participation in the study and the matching of experimental and control groups, the authors were able to present the field of play therapy with a solid research study to support its use.

RESEARCH METHODS AND DESIGN

In a predominantly upper-middle-class school, the researchers administered the Tuddenham Reputation Test to 150 children in the second and third grades. The teachers also completed a teacher rating scale for each child. Based on these measures, children were classified into three groups: high adjustment, aggression, and withdrawal. The sixteen children rated lowest in adjustment on these scales were chosen for the study. Eight children were randomly assigned to the experimental group and eight children were randomly assigned to the control group. There was equal representation in the groups among boys and girls and among aggressive and withdrawn children. The teacher rating scale and reputation tests were administered on three occasions: once before therapy, once at the end of the school year, and one year after the second testing. The interval from first to last testing was nineteen months. A priori directional hypotheses specified that score changes for the experimental group would exceed significantly those of the control group.

INTERVENTION

Each child in the experimental group was brought to a clinical facility once a week for individual play therapy. Length of therapy was determined by the therapist's judgment of need in conjunction with the children's attitudes toward continuing, without reference to test data. Median length of therapy for the group was thirty-seven sessions. No differential contact was made with the parents of either group. The control group received no intervention.

RESULTS

On the teacher rating scale, the experimental group showed marginally significant improvement as compared to the control group on the post-test versus follow-up. The reputation test results also favored the experimental group. It is noted that at pretest, all of the participating children were more aggressive than the class average. By follow-up time, all children in the experimental group had lower aggression scores than the average child in the class, while all control children still had higher than average aggression scores.

COMMENTARY

The authors concluded that children who are involved in a therapy experience are perceived by others as significantly less maladjusted after therapy. The findings also indicate that a striking reduction in aggressiveness may result from a permissive therapeutic climate. Finally, behavior appeared to change without working with parents. This may demonstrate that young children may change even in the absence of systematic environmental alteration.

SOURCE

Seeman, J., Barry, E., and Ellinwood, C. 1964. Interpersonal assessment of play therapy outcome. *Psychotherapy: Theory, Research, and Practice* 1:64–6.

POSSIBLE DSM-IV-TR DIAGNOSIS:

312.9   Disruptive Behavior Disorder NOS
V62.81 Relational Problem NOS
V62.3   Academic Problem

Effectiveness of Individual and Group Play Therapy for Kindergartners with Adjustment Problems

Robyn Rennie

FOCUS

The effect is studied of group and individual child-centered play therapy on kindergarten children with adjustment problems.

INTRODUCTION

Children with adjustment difficulties need early intervention in their school setting. Play therapy provides children the opportunity to resolve adjustment problems that hinder emotional and social development and assists them in gaining the maximum benefit from learning experiences, thus increasing their academic success. The purpose of this study was to determine the effectiveness of individual child-centered play therapy offered in the school setting on kindergartners with adjustment problems, specifically on self-concept, externalized behavioral problems, internalized behavior problems, and self-control. A secondary objective was to compare the participants involved in individual child-centered play therapy with participants in a previous study who were involved in child-centered group play therapy.

RESEARCH METHODS AND DESIGN

For the purpose of this study, adjustment difficulties included children who were exhibiting shy, withdrawn, anxious, depressed, or inattentive behaviors or who were experiencing life changes such as divorce, moving, or a new sibling. Children were identified and referred by their teachers. The experimental group, consisting of fourteen kindergarten children experiencing adjustment difficulties, received ten to twelve thirty-minute individual play therapy session in a twelve-week period in their elementary school. The comparison group, utilized from a previous study, consisted of fifteen children with adjustment problems who received twelve to fourteen forty-five minute group play therapy sessions in fourteen weeks in their elementary school. The control group, consisting of thirteen children experiencing adjustment problems, received no play therapy intervention over a twelve-week period. Prior to and following treatment, parents completed the Child Behavior Checklist, Filial Problem Checklist, and the Self-Control Rating Scale. Teachers completed the Early Childhood Behavior Scale and the Self-Control Rating Scale, and children were administered the Joseph Pre-School and Primary School Self-Concept Screening Test. Scores obtained from the instruments administered to the experimental group were analyzed and compared to scores obtained from the previous group play therapy study, as well as to scores from the control group. An analysis of covariance was computed to test the significance of the differences between the experimental group, comparison group, and control group.

INTERVENTION

The children who participated in individual play therapy received child-centered play therapy in the school. The children who participated in group play therapy received child-centered group play therapy in the school. The children in the control group received no intervention. The play therapists were doctoral students trained in play therapy.

RESULTS

Children with adjustment problems in the experimental group exhibited a significant reduction in total behavior problems and a significant reduction in externalizing behavior problems as measured by the Child Behavior Checklist—Parent Form. Additionally, individual play therapy was significantly more effective than group play therapy in helping children maintain an acceptable level of classroom behavior as perceived by teachers on the Early Childhood Behavior Scale.

COMMENTARY

This study demonstrated promising results for play therapy with kindergarten children experiencing adjustment difficulties. Notably, this study reveals that play therapy can serve as a positive intervention for children at risk for problem behavior, problems with self-control, and negative self-concept. In addition, the prospect of decreasing external behavior problems may lead to the creation of new patterns of interacting with peers, teachers, and family members.

SOURCE

Rennie, R. 2000. A comparison study of the effectiveness of individual and group play therapy in treating kindergarten children with adjustment problems. Unpublished Ph.D. diss., Denton: University of North Texas.

POSSIBLE DSM-IV-TR DIAGNOSES

296.xx   Major Depressive Disorder
300.02   Generalized Anxiety Disorder
309.xx   Adjustment Disorder
V62.3   Academic Problem

CHAPTER 3

Attachment Difficulties

Attachment can be defined as a bond of affection that endures difficulties and is imperative for children's healthy development and adjustment. Emotionally needy children, especially those who have experienced severe neglect, often experience strong needs for affiliation, attachment, and acceptance. Children who experience poor mother-child attachment often become "hard-to-reach" children. The acting out of these needs in the playroom can cause the play therapist considerable difficulty because these children may have such a powerful need to be special to the play therapist. Maintaining a sense of objectivity and compassionate understanding is crucial at such times, particularly when limits may need to be set. The play therapist must be careful not to become overly responsive when the child insists on knowing that he or she is the most important person in the whole world to the therapist. Children who do not have a secure attachment bond have great difficulty accepting themselves and other people. The play therapist's acceptance of the child enables the child to accept self.

Child-Centered Play Therapy for Problems Associated with Attachment

Lucy Colbert

FOCUS

Long-term child-centered play therapy is used with an angry, defiant, destructive child who had experienced constant rejection from her parents.

INTRODUCTION

Child-centered play therapy provides a situation in which the child can grow by playing out feelings of tension, frustration, insecurity, aggression, fear, bewilderment, and confusion in the presence of a warm and accepting person who displays genuine interest in and liking for the child as an individual. As described by Virginia Axline,[1] this play setting allows the child the opportunity to bring feelings out into the open, face them, and learn to control them or abandon them.

CASE STUDY

Debra, a nine-year-old girl from an unstable and inconsistent home situation, had experienced constant rejection from her parents, who apparently favored her three younger siblings. She was described by her parents as impulsive, aggressive, destructive, quick-tempered, and cruel to animals and other children. Her teachers said she was restless, inattentive, quarrelsome, defiant, sullen, and often involved in stealing and lying. From the age of four on, Debra had exhibited behavior problems that culminated in a juvenile court hearing, at which time she was made a ward of the court. After two years of foster care, Debra was eventually hospitalized for psychiatric care because of fighting, stubbornness, impulsiveness, setting fires, and sexual misbehavior with animals.

INTERVENTION

Debra's therapy took place in a playroom equipped with sand, running water, art materials, three games, and a variety of nurturing, aggressive, and constructive toys. Debra's treatment plan, as determined by her psychiatric team, included fifty-five-minute play therapy sessions twice a week. This schedule was rigidly maintained for seven months of treatment. Any need to reschedule was explained to Debra, and she was reassured of the next meeting time.

Structuring limitations were decided upon before the play therapy began. However, no limits were presented to Debra until the need arose. If Debra refused to go to the playroom, the therapist stayed with her long enough to reassure her that the choice was hers and that the next session would be held as usual. Sessions were always held in the playroom, and Debra was not allowed to stay longer than the time allotted. The session was terminated if Debra became bored

---

1. Virginia Axline, *Play Therapy* (New York: Ballantine Books, 1969).

and uninterested and left the room. The therapist straightened the room before and after each session. Debra was not allowed to remove any toys from the playroom but could take drawings she had made. She was not allowed to attack the therapist, and if she became unduly destructive in any way, this behavior was redirected using a four-step limit-setting sequence. The therapist (1) recognized Debra's feelings or wishes, (2) clearly stated the limit, (3) provided alternatives through which the feeling or wish could be expressed, and (4) helped Debra bring out feelings of resentment that arose when the restriction was invoked.

During her seven months of therapy, Debra progressed through the four stages of the therapeutic process as identified by Clark Moustakas[2]: (1) undifferentiated hostility and anxiety, (2) directed anger and hostility, (3) ambivalence, and (4) positive and negative feelings separate from and consistent with reality. Debra's progress was observable in her changing behavior with the knockdown clown "Bozo," in her appearance, and in the way she played. In the beginning, Debra beat Bozo up, threw him around the room, and shouted obscenities. This was followed by gluing curls to Bozo and calling him a "girl." In subsequent sessions, Debra alternated between beating and hugging Bozo. During the last sessions, Debra hugged Bozo and apologized when she bumped his nose. Debra came to the first ten sessions with her hair covering her face. By session fourteen, she had combed her hair out of her eyes and was able to look directly at the therapist. During early sessions, Debra would stop before completing a project, game, or activity. For a period beginning around the ninth session, Debra found it necessary to win at everything, often cheating and changing the rules in order to do so. She was unwilling to chance playing a game to its conclusion according to the rules until session forty-three.

At session twenty, Debra was told of her parents' plan to have her return home. During the following twenty sessions, Debra spent most of her time working out feelings of ambivalence toward her mother and also toward the therapist. She was able to accept both her parents and the therapist only after the therapist clarified for Debra that she (the therapist) would be happy for Debra if she wanted to go home and that she wanted to spend time with Debra but would do so only as long as Debra was in the hospital. After two successful home visits, Debra was permanently reunited with her family.

COMMENTARY

Debra had entered play therapy as a negative, angry, defiant, and destructive little girl who had felt completely rejected. The accepting, safe environment of the

<hr/>

2. Clark Moustakas, *Children in Play Therapy: A Key to Understanding Normal and Disturbed Emotions* (New York: McGraw-Hill, 1953).

play therapy relationship is freeing to children, enabling them to risk exploring more positive behaviors. With long-term and consistent intervention by Colbert through the medium of child-centered play therapy, Debra learned that it was all right to be angry, that it was safe to relate to another person, that she was liked for herself regardless of her actions, and that someone understood her pain.

SOURCE

Colbert, L. 1971. Debra finds herself. *Nursing Outlook* 19 (1): 50–3.

POSSIBLE DSM-IV-TR DIAGNOSES

313.89   Reactive Attachment Disorder of Infancy or Early Childhood
V71.02   Child or Adolescent Antisocial Behavior
312.9   Disruptive Behavior Disorder NOS
313.81   Oppositional Defiant Disorder
312.8   Conduct Disorder

Cognitive, Reflective, and Psychodynamic Play Therapy Techniques for Promoting the Attachment Process in an Adopted Boy

Ann Milston

FOCUS

Structured, behaviorally based play therapy within the framework of Kleinian theory is used with an emotionally disturbed seven-year-old boy who was experiencing attachment difficulties with his adoptive mother.

INTRODUCTION

Milston utilized an eclectic series of techniques, beginning with free reflective play, while also focusing on transference and countertransference issues. Within the context of specific, identifiable themes, Milston introduced affirmation, writing, and meditation to assist in changing unconscious negative thoughts into positive self-statements. In addition, the child's mother, as primary caretaker, was brought into the play sessions for a period to help her learn to relate to her child in new and more positive ways through imaginative play. This case study illustrates the use of a combination of cognitive-type therapy, reflection, and psychodynamic techniques within the context of play therapy.

CASE STUDY

Adam was born to a seventeen-year-old girl who was hospitalized for depression shortly after Adam's birth. Adam had been in and out of foster care due to his mother's neglect and possible physical abuse and was adopted at age two. His adoptive family included a mother who was described as bright, but rather tense and strict; a father who was described as easygoing; and an eleven-year-old sister. At age seven, Adam was referred for outpatient treatment for being overly aggressive, lying, and stealing. His teachers described him as a bright, but very unhappy, child with no friends. He showed no signs of emotion or remorse and took little pleasure in life.

INTERVENTION

Treatment consisted of one-hour play therapy sessions each week for two years and then every other week for six months. In the initial phase of therapy, Adam was living at home. He was then placed in a residential treatment center for children. During the last six months of therapy, he was again living at home. In the initial phase of therapy, Adam's behavior in the playroom was aggressive, lacking imagination, helpless, and rude. Early play included throwing things at and trying to frighten the therapist from the safety of a playhouse. Milston interpreted this as a reenactment of the birth mother's seemingly hostile rejection of Adam as an infant and Adam's need to test this new relationship with the therapist.

After a few weeks of free reflective play, Milston altered the play sessions. During the first fifteen minutes, Milston was "the boss" and directed Adam in affirmation writing and meditation to help him change his unconscious negative life thoughts into positive statements about himself. During the rest of the session, Adam was allowed self-direction. After six weeks, Adam's mother joined some of the sessions. In one particularly memorable session, Adam was inside a sleeping bag and instructed his mother and Milston to hide. Holding a toy zebra, Adam then wriggled over to where they were hidden and told his mother to first find the zebra and then she would find him. Adam's mother was able to become involved in this play and, at the therapist's suggestion, was overjoyed to find a baby boy inside the sleeping bag. The symbolic rebirth from out of the sleeping bag into his mother's arms was reported to be a turning point for both mother and son.

RESULTS

Although Adam suffered several setbacks during therapy and was not able to control his aggressiveness consistently and sufficiently, upon termination with this therapist, Adam was able to show remorse for inappropriate behavior and to show affection, enjoyed life, and had greater flexibility in relationships. His adoptive parents reported that Adam came out of his tantrums much more quickly and was more willing to accept responsibility for his actions.

COMMENTARY

Although the number of sessions in which this mother participated with her son was not clear, the inclusion of the mother as an integral part of the therapy seemed to be most beneficial for this child. At the end of their therapeutic relationship, Milston related that not all issues had been properly worked through, but hopefully the emotional bond that had developed between mother and son would provide the foundation for further healing. The process of recovery for some very disturbed and damaged children may necessarily be long-term.

SOURCE

Milston, A. 1989. Establishing bonding: a case of rebirth? *British Journal of Occupational Therapy* 52 (11): 437–39.

POSSIBLE DSM-IV-TR DIAGNOSES

313.89   Reactive Attachment Disorder of Infancy or Early Childhood
V71.02   Child or Adolescent Antisocial Behavior
312.8   Conduct Disorder
300.4   Dysthymic Disorder

CHAPTER 4

Autism

The little-understood condition of autism seems to defy explanation of cause, and counseling procedures with autistic children have seldom been written about in counseling, psychology, or social work journals. Even fewer references can be found in the play therapy literature. Psychoanalytically oriented therapists have produced the only two case reports that were found on the application of play therapy procedures to autistic children. Both studies offer dramatic possibilities for making emotional contact with some autistic children. Lessons evident in these studies are that autistic children need to be in control of their play and their relationship with the therapist, and they feel safer in interacting with the therapist through toys, such as puppets. The technique described in this chapter of having a puppet verbalize for the therapist offers positive possibilities for the play therapist who experiences a wide variety of reluctant or withdrawn children.

Psychodynamic Play Therapy with a High-Functioning Autistic Child

Richard Bromfield

FOCUS

The relevance of traditional psychodynamic play therapy to the milder variants of the autistic syndrome is reaffirmed.

51

INTRODUCTION

Autistic children are often viewed as too limited in language and symbolic thought to benefit from therapy. However, higher-functioning autistic children seem capable of benefiting from traditional play therapy. These children appear autistic, yet display greater intellect and social interest than is typical of pervasive autism. This case history was presented to encourage the use of traditional play therapy with children who may seem suited solely for more highly structured and educative experiences.

CASE STUDY

Tim was born of an uncomplicated pregnancy and experienced no significant medical problems as an infant. Tim's mother described him as an unaffectionate infant, neither seeking nor appearing to enjoy her attention. Although early developmental milestones were met in a timely fashion, a general lack of responsiveness to others continued to increase. By age three, other signs of autism had become evident, such as gross language deficits, inordinate need for sameness, aberrant eye contact, and delayed motor skills.

At age six, Tim was referred to Bromfield for therapy at the point of transition from a therapeutic day program to a self-contained special education classroom in a public school. He had been treated by two previous therapists for approximately six months each. Both therapists described him as too autistic and unreachable to benefit from therapy. Tim's mother was described as well intentioned and overly involved with her only child. She had only recently begun to acknowledge the serious nature of her son's developmental delays. Tim's father was described as caring but strange, often sharing Tim's idiosyncratic view of the world.

INTERVENTION

Bromfield met with Tim in twice-weekly play therapy sessions during the first year of treatment. The first few sessions lasted only about fifteen minutes each, as Tim became unduly anxious. Early sessions involved solitary play with a race-track game board, joylessly pursuing laps around the track, stopping only to spit occasionally or to smell the game materials. Although Tim rejected Bromfield's rare overtures to join in his activity, he would watch the therapist closely whenever Bromfield turned away.

The first instance of verbal interaction involved Bromfield's use of a puppet. Bromfield had commented that Tim was smelling the game. Direct verbal interaction proved to be too invasive. However, when the puppet copied Tim's frequent action of smelling the racetrack, Tim responded to the puppet by saying, "You smell stuff," and the puppet verbally agreed. Several weeks later, Tim recalled this play with the puppet, which provided an opportunity for Bromfield to explain how the puppet smelled in order to learn more about the world. Tim confessed that he also "smells the things that happen to him." He was able to use the puppet during a later session to direct anger at Bromfield, indicating that he was capable of processing and integrating the therapeutic experience, however slowly.

Tim's use of the play therapy sessions progressed as he moved from reclusive play in the corner of the office to the use of mailboxes and telephones to receive letters and calls. By doing so, he provided himself modes of communication allowing for varied degrees of intimacy. Throughout play therapy, puppets also served as vehicles for Tim's communication. Different puppets were attributed specific characteristics, such as the angry wolf, the hungry pig, and the baby cow. The therapist was also assigned a puppet through which Bromfield was expected to communicate. A predominant theme during the play therapy sessions was Tim's wish to be liked by the therapist. Tim would work hard to obtain gifts and extra time, and the therapist's failure to provide gratification resulted in tremendous frustration, anger, and intensification of autistic behaviors.

After a year of play therapy, Tim showed increased comfort and more direct communication with Bromfield. Tim's parents and teachers observed positive growth outside of therapy. He also showed enhanced capacity to express himself, to tolerate frustration and anxiety, and to manage closeness with peers and school staff. An extensive neurodevelopmental assessment conducted at age seven showed considerable positive change in Tim's intellectual functioning as compared with an assessment done two years earlier.

COMMENTARY

Play therapy permitted Tim to experience play in which he could securely be in control. The therapist's responsiveness to Tim's need to control the relationship helped Tim feel less vulnerable and thereby more willing to risk greater investment in the therapist. Through nonverbal and spoken validations of his autistic life experience by way of the puppets, Tim experienced himself and the therapist more directly.

This case history tends to reaffirm the use of traditional forms of play therapy as being helpful in treating milder forms of childhood autism. Therapy that addresses the child's inner world and relationships can complement broader educational and behavioral programs. Bromfield admits that play therapy with a high-functioning autistic child can be a labored experience, but rewarding for both the child and the therapist. Nonintrusively seeking meaning in the child's behaviors and unusual verbalizations conveys an interest in the child's communication. Bromfield warns that preconceived notions of what constitutes valuable fantasy or play will blind the therapist to what is there and workable.

SOURCE

Bromfield, R. 1989. Psychodynamic play therapy with a high-functioning autistic child. *Psychoanalytic Psychology* 4:439–53.

POSSIBLE DSM-IV-TR DIAGNOSES

299.00   Autistic Disorder
300.00   Anxiety Disorder NOS

Treating Autism with Psychoanalytic Play Therapy

Monica Lanyado

FOCUS

Psychoanalytic play therapy with a child with autism involves the therapist's patience in the process of waiting for the child's cues.

INTRODUCTION

Lanyado describes a child's new experience of awareness of separateness and subsequent positive development through the formation of symbols.

CASE STUDY

Five-year-old Enid was described as an autistic child hovering between fleeting awareness of people and events around her and total withdrawal. A psychologist had found her to be untestable and possibly mentally subnormal. Enid's parents experienced severe marital problems during the mother's pregnancy and the first year of Enid's life and divorced when she was two years old. The mother then literally lost herself in her child. Mother and child retreated into their own private world until the mother experienced some recovery from the trauma of the divorce and realized the need for help for Enid and herself.

INTERVENTION

For a variety of reasons, Enid was seen only once a month. During the same interval, Enid's mother was seen by another psychoanalyst. For the first four sessions, Enid was absorbed in obsessional sand play. At the fifth session, a dramatic change occurred. Enid arrived for therapy carrying a doll. She stood directly in front of the therapist and stared into her eyes as if to say, "Here I am." Enid initiated communication by showing the therapist that the doll's batteries were missing. She then began to stare at the sand tray but seemed unable to move away from the therapist. The therapist responded to this dilemma, verbally recognizing that Enid wanted the therapist to go with her to the sand tray. As in previous sessions, Enid absorbed herself in the sand play, occasionally asking about her mother. Only at this point was the therapist able to interpret the symbolic meaning in Enid's attempts at communication. For Enid, being separated from her mother was like having a piece of her body missing, just like the doll whose battery was missing. Enid responded to this interpretation with a nod and a grin; she had experienced a need to communicate, and she had been heard. Over time, Enid became more able to tolerate her separateness from her mother. She first used primitive sign language and then more complex verbal and playful communication with others. She continued toward normal development at a steady, although much delayed, pace.

COMMENTARY

The disturbed attachment between Enid and her mother interrupted normal development and did not allow Enid to see herself as separate from her mother. This attachment manifested itself in autistic behaviors. Through play therapy, Enid was able to express her separation anxiety symbolically and to be understood. Psychoanalytic play therapy's emphasis on symbolism and interpretation supported Enid in developing a symbolic language and the ability to communicate with others.

SOURCE

Lanyado, M. 1987. Asymbolic and symbolic play: developmental perspectives in the treatment of disturbed children. *Journal of Child Psychotherapy* 13 (2): 33–44.

POSSIBLE DSM-IV-TR DIAGNOSES

299.00   Autistic Disorder
315.31   Expressive Language Disorder
313.89   Reactive Attachment Disorder of Infancy or Early Childhood
V61.20   Parent-Child Relational Problem
309.21   Separation Anxiety Disorder

CHAPTER 5

Burn Victims

Pediatric burn patients present a multifaceted challenge to child-care personnel who must help them cope with emotional issues of trauma, separation, loss of control, isolation, disfigurement, and chronic pain. Prolonged hospitalization is accompanied by an array of emotional reactions: anxiety, fear, anger, depression, aggression, disorientation, and withdrawal. These reactions can be exacerbated by the never-ending process of changing the victim's dressing, which can be an especially anxiety-provoking time for child burn victims.

Modifications in play materials may be necessary for children who require a sterile environment. If a sand tray is being used, glass beads or paper punch holes can be substituted for the sand as these can be sterilized. It is important that child burn victims be provided an opportunity to develop a feeling of control. The manipulation of toys and the creation of play scenarios serve this purpose. It is not necessary for these children to experience actual control of their environment; the important dimension is that they feel they are in control, which will then enable them to begin the process of dealing with the trauma of their experience.

Multimodal Treatment of a Burned Child

Lilly Schubert Walker and Mark Healy

FOCUS

Multimodal treatment is studied of an eight-year-old girl with severe burns, using medication, relaxation exercises, and behavior therapy for the treatment of trauma and pain, and play therapy and storytelling for emotional adjustment.

INTRODUCTION

The case study presented is that of eight-year-old Amy, who was hospitalized with second- and third-degree burns covering 80 percent of her body. In addition to the medical treatment for pain, relaxation, imagery, and behavior therapy were designed to help Amy adjust to the hospitalization. Play therapy and storytelling were used to assist Amy in gaining "understanding of herself, her emotions, and her motivations."

CASE STUDY

Walker and Healy described Amy as a "controlled" child who did not readily express emotions. Her parents described her as normal, active, and self-confident. She was additionally reported to be very sensitive to others' disapproval and nonacceptance and felt very guilty following any misbehavior. The burn injuries were a result of an accident in which her nightgown caught fire from a gas heater. Following her hospitalization, Amy was delirious and her chances of survival uncertain. Her hospital behavior was "whiny, easily irritated, and ingratiating." As the burn treatment continued, Amy developed fears of the medical procedures, resisted the hospital staff with combative behavior, and refused to eat or to participate in physical therapy.

INTERVENTION

The first intervention focused on Amy's difficulty with the medical procedures, primarily the dressing changes. The chosen intervention was relaxation training, emotive imagery, and a behavior therapy program. The reward for cooperative behavior was "time spent in play" (see below).

The refusal to eat, a common issue for pediatric burn victims, was also dealt with by a behavioral intervention. Amy was able to maintain an adequate daily caloric intake, but the results of the psychotherapeutic intervention were inconsistent.

Storytelling, using Gardner's[1] mutual storytelling technique, was also employed to help Amy in her adjustment. The specific treatment goal was to assist her with self-concept and body-image issues. The storytelling intervention con-

---

1. Richard Gardner, *Storytelling in Psychotherapy with Children* (Northvale, NJ: Jason Aronson, Inc., 1993).

sisted of Amy reading stories to the playroom director, with a therapist later reviewing them, and Amy occasionally composing her own stories with similar themes.

The play therapy interventions included artwork, games, and so on. The authors suggested that some of the play materials promoted catharsis (e.g., play dough and artwork), some were mediums to deal with control issues (e.g., board games), and some facilitated the goals of physical therapy (e.g., coloring and embroidery).

Parent counseling was also included in Amy's treatment. This included both training in behavior management and designed play activities involving Amy's mother.

COMMENTARY

Walker and Healy suggested that psychotherapy needs to be indirect and nonthreatening for pediatric burn patients. The primary interventions that meet those criteria in this case are the modalities of storytelling and play therapy. The authors noted that "play therapy provided a useful mode to help this child discuss some of her concerns." This certainly appeared to be the case. It is interesting to note the relationship between the behavioral interventions and play therapy. The "reward" for Amy's cooperative behavior was time to play, often in the hospital playroom. It might be assumed that Amy cooperated with the medical procedures in order to have the opportunity to process her emotions surrounding the situation in the play experience. Although various therapeutic interventions were employed with Amy, it appears that the play therapy interventions were crucial elements in her adjustment to the challenging medical circumstance.

SOURCE

Walker, L. S., and Healy, M. 1980. Psychological treatment of a burned child. *Journal of Pediatric Psychology* 5 (4): 395–404.

POSSIBLE DSM-IV-TR DIAGNOSES

293.89   Anxiety Disorder Due to a General Medical Condition
309.81   Posttraumatic Stress Disorder

Development of a Preoperative Play Program for Burned Children

Debra L. Walls

FOCUS

The development of a play therapy program using preoperative techniques for burned children based on a survey of pediatric play programs in the United States.

INTRODUCTION

A review of the literature did not reveal the existence of a standard preoperative play program for burned children. A survey was conducted to research the existence and development of such programs for children hospitalized for burn treatment. The focus was on programs that included preoperative play for their patients and on determining the procedures, materials, and staff involved in the programs. The author's objective was to develop a model program.

RESEARCH METHODS AND DESIGN

The development of the program consisted of five phases: (1) a literature search of the topic, (2) compiling and analyzing data obtained from a questionnaire and follow-up telephone interviews, (3) development of a preoperative play program for burned children, (4) evaluation of a developed program by a panel of experts, and (5) field testing of the program with five burned children.

INTERVENTION

A nineteen-item questionnaire was distributed to 239 pediatric play therapy programs in the United States to determine the number of programs that used preoperative play, procedures and materials used, and the medical events for which pediatric patients are prepared. Follow-up telephone interviews were conducted with those agencies that included preoperative play for burned children. Using the information gathered from the questionnaire and telephone interviews, a program was developed to teach these children about their burn care and treatment, including tanking, debridement, donor sites, and skin grafts.

The program was then sent to a panel of experts for review, including people in the fields of medicine, burn care and treatment, therapeutic recreation, and special education.

RESULTS

Of the 239 questionnaires sent out, 145 (62%) were returned, with 58 (40%) indicating the existence of a preoperative play program for burned children. A follow-up telephone interview was conducted with these fifty-eight, of which eighteen (31%) responded. Based on the findings and a review of the literature, a curriculum was developed. The program was evaluated by a panel of four experts and accordingly revised and field-tested with five children admitted to the North Carolina Jaycees Burn Center in Chapel Hill, North Carolina. A qualitative evaluation following each preoperative preparation session was completed with positive results.

COMMENTARY

Walls concluded that the programs surveyed in the study were inconsistent and disorganized and that the developed program for burned children was a relevant and potentially valuable teaching tool. Although there are common issues for children experiencing hospitalization (see chapter 13), burned children face unique challenges that make a program tailored to their needs essential. Walls concluded her research with recommendations that the program be expanded to adolescents and that development of further tactile and visual play materials would be beneficial to accommodate children with other disabilities or from varied cultural backgrounds.

SOURCE

Walls, D. L. 1981. The development of a pre-operative play program for burned children. Unpublished Ph.D. diss., Virginia Polytechnic Institute and State University.

POSSIBLE DSM-IV-TR DIAGNOSES

293.89   Anxiety Disorder Due to a General Medical Condition
309.81   Posttraumatic Stress Disorder

CHAPTER 6

Chronic Illness

Chronically ill children often experience high levels of pain, stress, and anxiety that can prevent their natural coping behaviors from being utilized. Episodes of severe asthma attacks, for example, may be so frightening and stressful as to debilitate the child. The natural calming effect of play can help the child to relax and experience natural recovery. Chronically ill children often feel helpless and, in play therapy, can experience being in control of their play and in charge of the outcome, thus returning to a state of feeling in control. Play reduces the world of reality to a child's dimension in which the child is the master and the person who determines direction. Adaptations in play materials or expectations of play may be necessary when working with the chronically ill child who may be immobilized or whose physical activity has been significantly restricted due to the illness. These children may not be able to fully act out the range of their emotions in typical kinds of play activities, for example, being physically aggressive to express anger.

Play Therapy with an Asthmatic Child

Joanne Bentley

FOCUS

Play therapy was used to treat a boy with severe asthma and eczema, with the aim of reducing the number and severity of asthma attacks while he was in a residential treatment program.

INTRODUCTION

Bentley presented the case of John, a nine-year-old boy who had been placed in a residential treatment center for severe, persistent asthma and eczema. John was referred for psychotherapeutic treatment after being in the treatment center for five months. His skin condition had worsened, and he was wheezing almost daily. Unlike the other children at the center, John had to remain on corticosteroid medication. The staff was also concerned about his social relations as John constantly complained about the other children's treatment of him. They discovered, however, that John was provoking attacks upon himself and was a primary scapegoat at the center. Therapy was conducted for a period of fourteen months.

CASE STUDY

Before being placed in the center, John had been hospitalized several times for severe asthma attacks. During the most recent episode, a tracheotomy had been performed, which assisted respiration for two days. John was reported to have had a skin rash since the age of one month and daily sneezing from eight months. At age two, he was diagnosed with severe asthma and eczema. By the time of admission to the residential program, John was having severe attacks almost every week.

There was no information about John's biological parents or the conditions under which he lived prior to his adoption at eight months other than that John had lived in at least two foster homes. Bentley reported that the parents had a genuine affection for John and there was no evidence of pathology in either parent.

INTERVENTION

Before treatment began, John met with the therapist for an initial diagnostic impression. Bentley remarked on this because John was initially on guard when the therapy began, viewing the therapist as a person who asked many questions. During the first stage of treatment, John set up scenarios with toy soldiers in which both sides were destroyed. He also played competitive games with the therapist in which he would become belligerent when losing and depressed when winning, often stopping the game or trying to lose. Bentley interpreted this as anger related to wanting things and feeling guilt about wanting. She believed that a major therapeutic task was to help John accept and find appropriate ways to gratify his wishes.

As the treatment progressed, the therapist took a more active role, responding to John's destruction with the modeling of healing and nurturing. John would create clay dinosaurs and destroy them; the therapist would repair the dinosaurs and feed them. John initially resented the therapist as interfering, but eventually began to identify with her role. Interestingly, if the therapist had to change the appointment time or if John felt cheated out of another activity by coming to therapy, he reverted to smashing animals and preventing their repair.

In the final phase of therapy, John became more focused on the theme of food. He moved from making dinosaurs to making food with the clay and began to be less depressed about winning games. He also "fed" himself and the therapist. Bentley posited that John was beginning to communicate in a new way at this point and that he was processing the issue of having needs and wants and the appropriateness of having those met. John began to accept both real food and play food from the therapist. An important incident that occurred outside of therapy, which pointed to John's progress, was his initiation of a fight with one of his tormentors at the treatment center; this was "the first time he [the residential counselor] had seen John stick up for himself."

John's parents removed him from the treatment facility before therapy was completed. Although Bentley believed that the termination was premature, she reported that John had no serious asthma attacks after returning home.

COMMENTARY

The effects of play therapy in the processing of intrapsychic issues have a corresponding benefit for the physiological condition of chronically ill children. The frequency and severity of John's asthma attacks was substantially ameliorated through the play therapy process. Bentley suggested that John was able to process some of his internalized anger related to his infant deprivation through the play therapy. His aggressive and passive-aggressive behaviors, related to the fear of having needs and wanting them to be met, emerged in the play, were accepted by the therapist, and were resolved to some degree. The experimentation that John was allowed to act out in the latter stages of treatment led to his learning new behaviors that translated outside of the playroom.

SOURCE

Bentley, J. 1975. Psychotherapeutic treatment of a boy with eczema and asthma. *The Journal of Asthma Research* 12 (4): 207–14.

POSSIBLE DSM-IV-TR DIAGNOSES

313.81   Oppositional Defiant Disorder
V61.9   Relational Problem Related to a Mental Disorder or General Medical
         Condition

Individual Play Therapy for Children with Insulin-Dependent Diabetes Mellitus

Elizabeth M. Jones

FOCUS

Effectiveness is studied of play therapy on depression, anxiety, and overall health adjustment for children diagnosed with insulin-dependent diabetes mellitus (IDDM).

INTRODUCTION

IDDM is a disease of childhood that requires the child and the family to manage a host of factors influencing the child's physical health on a daily basis. Poor diabetes management has been linked to increased anxiety, low self-concept, depression, lack of family support, poor coping skills, and overall poor psychological adjustment. The purpose of this study was to determine the effectiveness of play therapy for children diagnosed with IDDM. Specifically, the researcher examined the effects of the intervention on depression symptoms, anxiety symptoms, behavioral difficulties, healthy adjustment, and adherence to a diabetes regime.

RESEARCH METHODS AND DESIGN

Subjects were selected from a summer camp for children with diabetes. The children attending the camp were from varying ethnic and socioeconomic backgrounds and all were diagnosed with IDDM. Thirty volunteer children between the ages of seven to eleven years were selected to participate in the study. Children were equally assigned to the experimental or control group. Each parent completed the Filial Problems Checklist and the Diabetes Adaptation Scale. Each child was administered the Children's Depression Inventory, the Revised Children's Manifest Anxiety Scale, and the Diabetes Adaptation Scale—Child Form. Data from all instruments were collected prior to intervention, postintervention, and three months following intervention for all participants. Analysis of covariance was computed to test the significance of the difference between the experimental group and the control group on the post-test means and follow-up means.

INTERVENTION

The children in the experimental group received twelve child-centered play therapy sessions during the three-week camp term. Each session lasted thirty minutes, provided as each child's camping schedule allowed. The play sessions were held in a small room in the hospital building on the campgrounds. Sessions were facilitated by three graduate students trained in play therapy. The control group received no play therapy but participated in the therapeutic summer camp.

RESULTS

Analysis of covariance revealed that the children in the experimental group significantly improved their adaptation to their diabetes following intensive play therapy as reflected by the Diabetes Adaptation Scale. Statistical trends noted increased improvement in the experimental group in the areas of behavior difficulties and adherence behavior.

COMMENTARY

The author concluded that providing play therapy in an intensive format in the summer camp setting was both practical and effective, as therapeutic changes seemed to occur more rapidly and the therapeutic relationship formed quickly and easily. Also, parents were eager for their children to receive play therapy, indicating the lack of preventative therapeutic services available to them and their awareness of a need for such services. By including play therapy as a part of a multidisciplinary approach to diabetes treatment for young children, there is the potential to address problems before they present difficulties for children and families.

SOURCE

Jones, E. M. 2000. The efficacy of intensive individual play therapy for children diagnosed with insulin-dependent diabetes mellitus. Unpublished Ph.D. diss., Denton: University of North Texas.

POSSIBLE DSM-IV-TR DIAGNOSES

293.83 Mood Disorder Due to Insulin-Dependent Diabetes Mellitus
293.84 Anxiety Disorder Due to Insulin-Dependent Diabetes Mellitus
V15.81 Noncompliance with Treatment

CHAPTER 7

Deaf and Physically Challenged Children

Children who are physically challenged are often reacted to in terms of what is physically observable, with the resulting effect that they may feel incomplete, unworthy, or unacceptable. The problems and challenges these children face are of only secondary concern to the play therapist. What is important is that these children are people in their own right, and as such, they experience the same feelings and reactions as all other children. Their condition does not make them any less of a person, just as a child who experiences reading difficulties, speech difficulties, academic problems, poor peer relationships, overwhelming anxiety, or some other difficulty is not thought to be less of a person. All children need understanding, acceptance, feelings of adequacy, and a sense of personal worth. A child's physical condition does not change these needs. It is understandable that these children may be slow to trust the play therapist because of the rejection they may have experienced from other significant adults in their lives.

The play therapist will need to be sensitive to the fact that some challenges these children have faced may have resulted in their approaching the world differently, as in the case of deaf children. Studies show that during the preoperational stage, ages two to seven, these children display less mature play patterns, exhibit very little make-believe play, and engage in less symbolic solitary play. Such information is essential for the play therapist to adequately understand the play of these children. Likewise, the play therapist may need to make significant adjustments to accommodate the physically challenged child; for example, they may have to tape a paintbrush to the hand of a cerebral-palsied child.

Sand Play with Hyperkinetic, Epileptic Children

Itsuo Kawai, Hayao Kawai, and Hiroshi Naniwa

FOCUS

The effect is studied of sand play therapy on the restless behavior of epileptic children.

INTRODUCTION

The authors explored the use of sand play therapy with psychomotor epileptic children with hyperkinetic or restless behavior disorders in which medication had little to no effect.

CASE STUDY

Eleven children ages five to fourteen were seen for sand play therapy once a week for a total of 30 to 150 sessions. Anticonvulsant and psychotropic medicines did not seem to affect the behavior disorders in eight of the cases. Although the three other children developed seizures during the sand tray sessions, the restless behavior did not decrease with the introduction of medication.

INTERVENTION

The authors report the use of Kalff's[1] style of sand play. Over the course of the sessions, three primary characteristic features of children with epilepsy were noted: irrelevant or irrational content, a stormy or rigidly ordered world, and persistent battles. An example of irrelevant or irrational content would be the child having a witch and a monster jump out of a volcano or baseball bats and airplanes laid out together in a line. Another child displayed stormy and rigidly ordered worlds, violent throwing of sand, and splashing of water "floods," which contrasted with ordered lines of miniatures such as animals, cavalry, and vehicles. The authors note that battles are often displayed by neu-

---

1. Dora Kalff, *Sandplay*, 2nd ed. (Santa Monica, CA: Sigo, 1980).

rotic children and that epileptic children never tire of repeating them. One therapist indicated that catharsis had occurred upon seeing a town reappear where there had been destruction after a fierce battle, only to have the destruction begin again.

RESULTS

The behavior of five of the eleven children improved remarkably. At a five-year follow-up, these five had no recurrence of restless behavior. Four other children became less restless, their school adjustment was above average, and they displayed only occasional violence with their families. The final two children showed no improvement during their sand play therapy, and participation in this study was terminated.

Six children experienced seizures during sand play therapy. Three of these children improved psychologically, two showed less restless activity, and one remained unaffected by the sessions and continued to have seizures.

COMMENTARY

The results of this study serve as encouragement for further psychotherapy with children who are epileptic. Although little information is given by the authors on the sand play sessions, the three major characteristics identified in the sand play could reveal some of the inner thoughts of the child with epilepsy and behavior disorders, such as the ongoing struggle of living a life that can be out of control and chaotic and certainly, for a child, filled with irrational content.

SOURCE

Kawai, I., Kawai, H., and Naniwa, H. 1980. Effects of play therapy on hyperkinetic children with psychomotor epilepsy. *Folia Psychiatrica et Neurologica Japonica* 34 (3): 400–401.

POSSIBLE DSM-IV-TR DIAGNOSES

312.9   Disruptive Behavior Disorder NOS
293.9   Mental Disorder NOS Due to a General Medical Condition

Play Therapy with Preschool Deaf Children

Viola Jackson Oualline

FOCUS

Short-term child-centered play therapy is used with preschool deaf children having behavioral disturbance.

INTRODUCTION

Since deaf children rely on nonverbal means of communication, play therapy as a nonverbal intervention should be expected to yield positive results. The investigation involved the effects of short-term child-centered play therapy with preschool deaf children exhibiting some level of behavioral difficulty.

RESEARCH METHODS AND DESIGN

The children who participated in this investigation had impaired hearing and had been referred for therapy to classes for the deaf. The children selected for the study were those (1) whose hearing impairment had existed prior to language acquisition; (2) who had a hearing loss of seventy decibels or more; (3) who had an IQ of 80 or above; (4) who were between four and six years of age; and (5) who were described by a hearing therapist as having behavioral problems. Twenty-four children met the selection criteria and were paired according to age and gender. They were then assigned randomly to a treatment or control group.

Pre- and post-tests administered included the Vineland Social Maturity Scale, the Child Behavior Rating Scale, and the Behavior Problem Checklist. Parents and hearing therapists completed questionnaires concerning the children before and after the intervention.

INTERVENTION

Children assigned to the treatment group received fifty minutes of individual play therapy per week for ten weeks with a trained play therapist. The therapeutic approach was described as nondirective, following Virginia Axline's[2] eight basic principles. The play materials used were standardized and included toys recommended by Virginia Axline and Haim Ginott.[3] Children assigned to the control group were given thirty minutes of free individual play with an untrained volunteer.

RESULTS

Statistical analysis of the scores on the Vineland indicated a significant increase in mature behavior patterns for the children who had experienced the play therapy intervention. The scores on the other instruments did not show significance, although Oualline suggested that the instruments may not be adequate measures for children with severe hearing impairment. On the qualitative level, data from questionnaires revealed that all the parents and teachers of seven of the children in the treatment group reported positive behavioral change in the children at the completion of the play therapy intervention.

COMMENTARY

Oualline noted that the true "language" of the deaf child is nonverbal communication. This fact would appear to indicate that play therapy would be a very appropriate and beneficial intervention for the deaf child requiring counseling. The child born deaf does not have the ability to inquire orally about the curious world in which he or she lives, which may result in frustration and anger or withdrawal and apathy. Oualline asserted that all children's need to experience self-acceptance is unfulfilled for the deaf child because of these dynamics. Play therapy can be a means to reach these children and to provide them with an opportunity to "communicate" in a way that was previously impossible.

SOURCE

Oualline, V. J. 1975. Behavioral outcomes of short-term nondirective play therapy with preschool deaf children. Unpublished Ph.D. diss., North Texas State University, Denton.

---

2. Virginia Axline, *Play Therapy* (New York: Ballantine Books, 1969).
3. Haim Ginott, *Group Psychotherapy with Children: The Theory and Practice of Play Therapy* (New York: McGraw-Hill, 1961).

POSSIBLE DSM-IV-TR DIAGNOSES

309.3   Adjustment Disorder with Disturbance of Conduct
309.4   Adjustment Disorder with Mixed Disturbance of Emotions and Conduct
313.81 Oppositional Defiant Disorder

CHAPTER 8

Dissociation and Schizophrenia

According to Gil, "Dissociation is understood as a process of separating, segregating, and isolating chunks of information, perceptions, memories, motivations, and affects. Dissociation serves as a defense against severe stress, allowing the individual to protect against the original trauma but leaving a predisposition to react to subsequent stress or familiar stimuli as if they were a reoccurrence of the trauma."[1] Dissociative identity disorder is the most severe of the dissociative disorders, and it is important to note that although the age of onset is almost invariably childhood, it does not typically come to attention until much later. Reports in the literature support the conclusion that there is a significant correlation between ongoing or severe childhood sexual or physical abuse and dissociated states. Due to the secretive nature of posttraumatic play, direct observation by therapists of posttraumatic play is most likely to occur only in a play therapy experience and then only after therapeutic conditions of acceptance and great safety are felt by the child. Play therapy seems to offer the most promise for effecting change and trauma resolution for traumatized children. There have also been promising reports in the literature describing the use of play therapy with child alters (personality states) of adults with multiple personality disorder.

---

1. E. Gil. *The Healing Power of Play: Working with Abused Children* (New York: Guilford, 1991), 22.

Jungian Play Therapy with a Schizophrenic Boy

John Allan and Sarah Lawton-Speert

FOCUS

Jungian play therapy is used with a profoundly sexually abused boy diagnosed as schizophrenic.

INTRODUCTION

The case study presented is that of a boy named Kim, referred for treatment by his adoptive parents. Kim's history included severe neglect and sexual abuse; it was noted that he had been diagnosed with schizophrenic disorder, disorganized type. Jungian play therapy was utilized, and the play therapy was conducted by a graduate student under the supervision of John Allan.

CASE STUDY

Kim was four-and-a-half years old at the start of treatment and had been diagnosed as schizophrenic. His behavior at the time of referral was characterized by incoherent and disorganized speech, a wide range of affect, loose associations, and bizarre and illogical language. Kim thought that toy snakes were real and would bite him. Much of his play was sexual in nature, including frequent masturbation, indiscriminate urination, touching adults' genitals, and attempted sex acts with other children. He also suffered from sleep disturbances, including night terrors.

Kim and his older brother were initially raised by their mother, who exhibited several abusive parenting patterns: severe neglect, abandonment for up to three days, physical abuse of the older boy, and sexual abuse of Kim. Kim was removed from his mother's care at the age of four months (for a four month period), and then permanently at the age of ten months. He remained in foster-care settings until twenty-three months of age, when he went to live with his adoptive parents. Kim was adopted together with his older brother.

INTERVENTION

The eighteen-month treatment process consisted of three stages: initial, middle, and termination. The initial stage of therapy was marked by terror and rage. Kim refused to enter the playroom and would kick, scream, and run away. After being carried into the playroom, he would spit, swear, throw toys and water, and attempt to hurt the therapist. Kim would occasionally have to be restrained. By the seventh session, his anger having gradually diminished, he would respond to limits and engage in some nurturing play.

Seductive and erotic play emerged following the seventh-session and continued for the next three months. Kim took off his clothes and attempted to engage the therapist in sexual activity. When the therapist set a limit on this, Kim became angry and began to stimulate himself with the play materials. He also frequently washed himself with sand, soap, and water during this stage and urinated in a tub. After sixteen sessions, Kim moved to some intense infantile play, including sucking on a bottle and being fed and diapered by the therapist. This evolved into Kim's providing these nurturing behaviors for himself. Following this, Kim moved to tender play toward the therapist, with occasional conflicted moves into aggressive and sexualized play. He processed emerging feelings of attachment with the therapist and the conflict he felt, in comparison, toward his adoptive mother.

After a year of play therapy, much of the play activity centered around themes of domestic animals, cars, and houses. Kim included the therapist less frequently in his play. Toy animals that had been attacking became pets. Sexual themes disappeared. Doll play involved typical family scenes.

Toward the end of the treatment (eighteen months), Kim's behavior was no longer characterized by unpredictable outbursts. His behavior improved significantly at school, he did not act out sexually inappropriately, and he was a play leader with other children. His parents reported that he was responsive and affectionate, and he was integrated into a regular kindergarten class.

COMMENTARY

This case study demonstrates the Jungian position that the psyche knows how to heal itself and that children will go where they need to go. It should be pointed out that careful supervision and consultation were an integral part of the effectiveness of the play therapy intervention in this case. The profound nature of Kim's situation and diagnosis was certainly not outside the effective sphere of the play therapy intervention. The integration and development that occur for the severely abused and fragmented child in play therapy is testimony to the resilience of children and the effectiveness of play therapy.

SOURCE

Allan, J., and Lawton-Speert, S. 1993. Play psychotherapy of a profoundly incest abused boy: a Jungian approach. *International Journal of Play Therapy* 2 (1): 33–48.

POSSIBLE DSM-IV-TR DIAGNOSES

295.10 Schizophrenia, Disorganized Type
V61.21 Sexual Abuse of Child
312.8   Conduct Disorder
313.81 Oppositional Defiant Disorder

Play Therapy with a Dissociative Child

Jane Gorman

FOCUS

Child-centered play therapy is used with a dissociative ten-year-old boy.

INTRODUCTION

Steve was referred for psychotherapeutic intervention by his school. He exhibited bizarre and problematic behavior in the classroom and dissociative behavior in the playroom. A child-centered play therapy approach was utilized.

CASE STUDY

Steve was ten years old and in the fourth grade when referred for psychotherapeutic services. Although he spoke in complete sentences and had a large vocabulary, he was difficult to understand. Steve's teacher reported that he was not able to write but was able to read. In the classroom, he was easily distracted, sought attention, disrupted the class, continued talking, and wandered out into the halls.

Evaluations indicated that Steve had average intelligence, speech difficulties, impulsive behavior, impaired attention and concentration, fine motor difficulties, perceptual problems, poor peer relationships, and severe emotional problems. Speech therapy and special academic placement were recommended in addition to mental-health services.

INTERVENTION

The treatment process included twenty weeks of twice-weekly play therapy sessions. Initially, Steve used the play times to talk fast and throughout the session. He began to play for brief periods and, by the fifth session, was engaged in play for the entire session. Despite the wide variety of play materials available, Steve seldom used the toys, preferring instead to use empty boxes, water, window shades, and other miscellaneous objects.

In the play therapy sessions, Steve immediately began referring to "Thomas," to whom Steve attributed much of his activity. There were sessions in which Steve would use "Thomas," "Thomas and me," or "I" interchangeably. This changed markedly in the fifteenth session, in which Steve locked the punching bag in the closet and began increasingly to use "I"; in the next ten sessions he no longer attributed his actions to Thomas. Although in the last four sessions prior to termination Steve referred to "John," he was able to claim many parts of his own behavior.

Steve's behavior in the playroom was characterized by his constant separation of affect from various situations, particularly by the use of loose associations. Gorman notes that loose associations served to allow expression of emotional content without clearly connecting it to a specific or appropriate context. Steve would use Thomas to accomplish this, to tell sadistic fantasies or explain playroom behavior that was aggressive, destructive, regressive, or messy. He would also use Thomas to extend his solitary activity into shared experiences in fantasy, thus addressing his feelings of aloneness and poor peer relationships.

The play therapy intervention was based on three goals: reduction of anxiety through the release of repressed impulses, opportunities for ego development, and enhancement of self-esteem. Steve's expression of impulses was described in his selection and use of play materials, many of which could be destroyed or used aggressively. Ego development occurred for Steve as he mastered the environment of the playroom. Gorman suggested that as Steve developed his mastery over objects, he was able to imagine that he was the master of his life predicament as well. As Steve experienced the acceptance and regard of the therapist in the play process, his self-esteem grew.

Steve exhibited positive progress in the play therapy process. He moved from verbally expressing aggressive fantasies to acting them out in the play. Increased mastery of particular motor skills was evident, as well as an improved ability to communicate effectively. Steve's verbal behavior became more related to the content of his play. Articulation improved, and he was able to seek and acknowledge feedback on his communication. Steve progressed from "Thomas tells me what I can do and what I can't do" to claiming his own behavior. Although Gorman recommended continued therapeutic intervention, Steve's progress at the point of termination was clearly evident.

COMMENTARY

Steve's dissociative behavior in the play served the purpose of giving expression to the deficits in his emotional integration. This process was facilitated by the environment and process of play therapy. The freedom to express himself in an accepting and caring environment, combined with the structure of the playroom and the relationship, enabled Steve to address anxiety-producing and frightening issues. The safety of the play therapy process allows the child with dissociative behaviors to get past the hypervigilance of protecting self in order to explore self.

SOURCE

Gorman, J. N. 1972. Dissociation and play therapy: a case study. *JPN and Mental Health Services* 10 (2): 23–6.

POSSIBLE DSM-IV-TR DIAGNOSES

300.14   Dissociative Identity Disorder
295.10   Schizophrenia, Disorganized Type
314.01   Attention Deficit/Hyperactivity Disorder, Combined Type
313.81   Oppositional Defiant Disorder
315.2   Disorder of Written Expression
315.39   Phonological Disorder

Play Therapy with a Regressed Schizophrenic Adolescent Girl

Bernadine Irwin

FOCUS

Play therapy is used with a schizophrenic girl hospitalized for decompensation and regressive behavior.

INTRODUCTION

Jane (name given by reviewer) was a sixteen-year-old female who had been hospitalized with the diagnosis of schizophrenic disorder, chronic undifferentiated type. The author's experience as a nurse in various psychiatric facilities led her to conclude that regressed patients were often ignored because of their inability to respond to traditional treatment methods. A brief play therapy program was developed with specific treatment objectives, using a child-centered approach.

CASE STUDY

The adolescent female presented in this case had been hospitalized following eight months of progressive decompensation. A social worker assigned to Jane's case described her home situation as "intolerable." She was unable to attend school, where she had been making high grades, and regressed to the point of necessitating hospitalization.

Jane was unable to control urine and feces and was mute except for frequent repetitions of the word "yellow," particularly when anxious. She remained in bed throughout the day, except when taken to meals. There was no indication of affect, and she would stare without any expression. The social worker noted that during her two weeks in the hospital prior to the play therapy intervention, there was no eye contact given to any person.

INTERVENTION

Six sessions of child-centered play therapy were included in the treatment process. Prior to the beginning of treatment, seven behavioral objectives were established in order to assess progress: making occasional eye contact with others, leaving bed voluntarily and interacting, controlling urine and feces, occasionally making a facial expression, taking voluntary showers, wearing pressed clothes, and answering when spoken to.

The therapist had to help Jane to her feet and lead her to the playroom for the first session. She did not engage in any play during this session, choosing instead to stand and stare at the dollhouse while wringing her hands. In the last ten minutes of the session, Jane sat down and repeated "yellow" over and over. Following the session, she returned to her bed. Before the second session, the therapist found Jane at her bed getting help in dressing from a staff member. Although her appearance had not changed, the staff reported she was no longer incontinent. Jane willingly followed the therapist into the playroom and played with colors (especially yellow), the xylophone (the yellow key), and a ball. When the therapist summoned Jane for the third session, she was sitting in a corner of the room staring at the floor. The staff reported that she was voluntarily leaving her room and taking regular showers. The play routine was the same as the previous session, except that Jane made clear eye contact with the therapist at the end of the session and asked, "May I go now?"

Prior to the fourth session, Jane was found sitting in the day room reading a book. The staff reported that she had asked for the book and that she was taking more interest in observing ward activities. She did not stay in her room except at night. When the therapist greeted her, she responded and stated that things were going "pretty good." The play session again was similar to the previous one. At the beginning of the fifth session, Jane was again found reading in the day room. The staff reported that she had been overheard reading aloud around other patients. The play began with Jane coloring. When the therapist told her that the next session would be the last, she began striking the yellow key on the xylophone very hard. The therapist reflected her anger, to which Jane made eye contact, smiled, and continued her play.

Two months after completion of the play therapy, the therapist made a return visit to Jane, who was pleased to see her. Jane told the therapist that she had begun to attend school. She had achieved six out of seven of the treatment objectives, the exception being not wearing pressed clothes.

COMMENTARY

Play therapy has been demonstrated to be a safe and effective alternative in the treatment of severely impaired mental-health clients. Although regressed and schizophrenic patients are often unresponsive to traditional forms of treatment, the freedom of the play therapy process and the safety of the play therapy relationship are effective in reaching these challenging individuals. The adolescent female in this study demonstrates both the efficacy and utility of play therapy with the schizophrenic population and with adolescents. Play reaches through and beyond many of the defenses of mental illness. The profound effects of the short-term play therapy are especially noteworthy.

SOURCE

Irwin, B. L. 1971. Play therapy for a regressed schizophrenic patient. *JPN and Mental Health Services* 9:30–2.

POSSIBLE DSM-IV-TR DIAGNOSIS

295.90   Schizophrenia, Undifferentiated Type

Group Play Therapy with Psychotic Adolescent Girls

Dorian Rose, Catherine Butler, and Florence Eaton

FOCUS

Group play therapy is used with seven adolescent girls hospitalized for psychotic behavior.

INTRODUCTION

Group play therapy was used with seven adolescent females, ranging in age from sixteen to twenty, who had been hospitalized for some type of schizophrenic disorder. All of the group participants exhibited schizophrenic features and had manifested disturbances of psychotic proportions for some time prior to the intervention. A nondirective therapeutic play therapy approach was employed with the group, which met intensively for ten months.

CASE STUDY

The seven female group members were selected because they had substantial difficulty in expressing themselves verbally, were not optimally improving in their treatment, and all had shown an interest in the play materials provided. Four of the participants had been specifically diagnosed as schizophrenic, and the remaining three had been diagnosed as "mentally defective," having an "inadequate personality," and suffering from "convulsive disorder with no organic deterioration." These conditions were considered chronic.

The histories of the group participants were markedly similar. The majority had been psychiatrically referred prior to the hospitalization, were mentally ill for longer than one year, had experienced failure academically, and had no identified causes for the mental illness. Additionally, several of the following "neurotic traits" had been apparent during childhood: enuresis during puberty, aggression and discipline problems, play difficulties, and sibling rivalry. At the time the group was formed, three participants had been assaultive, and three had attempted self-injury.

INTERVENTION

For the first three months of the play therapy group, sessions were held five times a week for one hour; for the remaining seven months, sessions were held three times a week. One of the females discontinued therapy during the fourth month and another during the seventh month because they were unavailable due to a change in their home placement. The sessions were held in a special room equipped with toys and games, including dart guns, dollhouses, finger paints, playing cards, checkers, and other games. The authors pointed out that the group members had a high degree of freedom in terms of attendance and choice of activities. Due to the "destructive potentialities" of the group, two therapists were always present, with one taking a more active role than the other. Both therapists assumed the role of facilitator and were careful not to initiate any activity.

The first two months of therapy involved gunplay and war games of various kinds. The following four months were dominated by arts and crafts, and the last four months involved primarily game activity.

As the group progressed, there was a measurable decrease in assaultiveness, destructiveness, temper tantrums, and self-injury. The group members engaged in increased verbalization, group games supplanted individual activities, and they began to gather in one area in the group play therapy room.

A two-year follow-up evaluation of the group members indicated that four of the patients had "strikingly improved" over any previous level of adjustment.

Five of the six patients who had returned to the community had accepted outpatient treatment, and four of the patients were employed and were at least partially self-supporting. The authors noted that the behavior patterns that appeared to be most affected by the group play therapy process had been those involving hostility and aggression.

COMMENTARY

The social isolation prevalent in schizophrenic disorders and hospitalization can be effectively addressed in the process of group play therapy. The authors appropriately concluded that the use of play "provided a vehicle for modifying the inadequate and inappropriate social behavior" of the adolescent females in the group. Clearly, a verbally based group intervention would not have impacted this challenging group as meaningfully or effectively as the group play therapy. The participants were able to acquire a greater sense of belonging, self-esteem, and self-control in the process of the group play. Group play therapy is effective, even with a population as challenging and unpredictable as that described in this case study.

SOURCE

Rose, D. M., Butler, C., and Eaton, F. L. 1954. Playgroup therapy with psychotic adolescent girls. *International Journal of Psychotherapy* 4:303–11.

POSSIBLE DSM-IV-TR DIAGNOSES

295.90   Schizophrenia, Undifferentiated Type
298.9   Psychotic Disorder NOS

CHAPTER 9
Emotionally Disturbed Children

The behaviors of emotionally disturbed children do not differ significantly from those of well-adjusted children. What is different is the degree, frequency, and intensity of those behaviors. Emotionally disturbed children experience intense feelings of confusion, ambivalence, loss, lack of control, detachment, and poor relationship. Children cannot learn to cope or make adequate adjustments when their emotional energy is focused on defending a limited view of self. Individual and group play therapy provide for these children a safe environment, including a safe, consistent, and predictable adult—an environment in which they can play out the confusion and intensity of feeling they experience. The feelings of emotionally disturbed children are often inaccessible at a verbal level. Play is the concrete expression of children; it is their way of coping with their world. The cases in this section demonstrate the healing potential of the play therapy relationship with children who experience personal detachment and a broad range of emotional, social, and learning difficulties.

Developmental Play Group Counseling with Emotionally Disturbed Children

Jim Gumaer

FOCUS

Developmental play is used with a group of emotionally disturbed children in an elementary school setting.

INTRODUCTION

Gumaer presented the development and implementation of a developmental play group with a group of emotionally disturbed children in an elementary school class of disturbed children. Gumaer was approached by the classroom teacher, who sought a nonbehavioral intervention for the benefit of the eight students. The program was designed to "help children who are experiencing personal detachment and other emotional, social, or learning difficulties overcome these problems through the development of positive, loving interactions and attachments with important adults, who then serve as models for the children in learning how to relate to others."

RESEARCH METHODS AND DESIGN

The self-contained classroom of emotionally disturbed children consisted of four boys and four girls. The children were eight to nine years old and possessed IQ scores in the normal range. Mean behavior scores were equal to or higher than the mean scores of atypical children in residential treatment centers.

The eight children were divided into two groups for the developmental play group intervention and met once a week for twelve weeks in forty-five-minute sessions. Standardized play activities were developed for the two groups. Prior to the implementation of treatment, the children were administered the Piers-Harris Self-Concept Scale.

INTERVENTION

The plans followed in each group were specific as to objectives, description of activities, and recommended counselor responses. Within these specific plans the facilitators focused on three primary concepts of nonverbal communication that were considered key to developmental play: touching, spacing, and using facial language.

Specific activities for the twelve sessions were outlined and included having the child draw an animal and then move and act like the animal, followed by discussion of how it felt; having the child close his or her eyes and then take the hand of the child on each side ("holding the paw of the animal on each side"); having the children pair up and trace the partner's body on large paper; and expressing feelings by pantomime.

RESULTS

One week after completion of the sessions, the self-concept scale was readministered. One child failed to complete the instrument properly, but the remaining seven showed an overall score increase of 44 points, a mean increase of 6.3 points per child.

On the qualitative level the classroom teacher reported that the learning that had occurred in the group sessions generalized to the classroom. The children were more appropriate in behaviors with their peers and interactions with the teacher, and discipline problems diminished. There was an increase in displays of "warmth and caring" in the classroom, and the general environment was reported to be more relaxed.

COMMENTARY

The opportunity to develop relationship skills in a nonthreatening and accepting environment such as a developmental play group proved beneficial for this group of emotionally disturbed children. Gumaer's presentation exhibited the successful adaptation of individual play therapy to a group setting. The issues of loss, detachment, and disruption that characterize emotionally disturbed children are positively impacted by a group play experience. Developmental play groups may be one positive way for school counselors to provide relief for children and teachers.

SOURCE

Gumaer, J. 1984. Developmental play in small group counseling with disturbed children. *The School Counselor* 31 (5): 445–53.

POSSIBLE DSM-IV-TR DIAGNOSIS

Insufficient information provided in the study.

Play Therapy Treatment of Emotional Disturbance and Trichotillomania in a Child with Mild Microcephaly

John A. Perry

FOCUS

The use of play therapy and family therapy with a boy with emotional disturbance, trichotillomania, and mild microcephaly is qualitatively studied.

INTRODUCTION

Perry presented the case of Tim, a nine-year-old with a long history of emotional and physical problems. The microcephaly, considered a minor case, appeared to be a precipitating factor in considerable emotional difficulties, the most overt being the issue of trichotillomania. Perry provided considerable detail in his discussion of Tim's case, including case history and psychological theory. The treatment essentially amounted to a multimodal and multidisciplinary approach. Individual play therapy was a prominent aspect of the treatment plan. The study covered a treatment period of three and a half years.

CASE STUDY

Tim was referred for treatment by a local government clinic. He was the first of two children of a couple who had been separated for nine months prior to the commencement of therapy. The microcephaly, diagnosed by a pediatric neurologist, was reportedly minimal (below the second percentile on a standard head-circumference chart). Tim had several specific learning disabilities, including disorders of spoken and written language.

Tim's mother reported numerous emotional and behavioral concerns. She described Tim as impulsive, aggressive, and destructive; he threw temper tantrums, had difficulty socializing with peers and adults, engaged in stealing and lying, and pulled out his hair. (Tim presented in an initial evaluation with a small patch of hair beginning to grow on the crown of his head.) He had also had difficulties with enuresis, poor attention span, and low self-esteem. Prior to the treatment described in this case study, multiple medications had been prescribed, including Benadryl, Ritalin, Cylert, Melaril, Dilantin, and megavitamins. These had varying degrees of success.

INTERVENTION

The "ecological systems" approach taken by Perry in the treatment of Tim initially incorporated a child-centered approach to weekly play therapy sessions and weekly family therapy. Perry described the playroom and the therapeutic process as unstructured, with the intent of allowing Tim to feel freedom from pressure to act in any certain way and free to project his own issues in any manner he chose. Tim initially engaged in doll play, during which he processed issues of anger toward his father. Detailed discussions emerged in the doll play regarding the rejection and loss that Tim was feeling. Tim channeled considerable aggression and frustration through various media, including pounding on clay.

Tim developed a positive therapeutic relationship with Perry and soon began to look forward to the play therapy sessions. As Tim learned to verbalize feelings, his acting-out behaviors diminished outside the playroom.

COMMENTARY

Perry posited that there was a direct relationship between "losses and threatened losses" and Tim's hair-pulling behaviors. The hair pulling, as well as the other difficulties noted above, diminished as Tim was able to process issues in the play therapy and as relationships at home began to stabilize. Perry appropriately noted that "individual insight-oriented directed therapy requires specific ego strengths of the patient that Tim did not have." The projective and developmentally appropriate nature of play therapy provided Tim with an environment in which to address concerns that had previously been treated from a noneffective medical approach. The positive results noted prevented the imminent hospitalization that was the next consideration for Tim's case.

SOURCE

Perry, J. A. 1988. Reduction of trichotillomania in a microcephalic child: an ecological systems approach. Unpublished Ph.D. diss., Union Graduate School.

POSSIBLE DSM-IV-TR DIAGNOSES

312.8   Conduct Disorder
313.81   Oppositional Defiant Disorder
312.39   Trichotillomania
307.6   Enuresis
314.9   Attention-Deficit/Hyperactivity Disorder NOS

Group Play Therapy with Emotionally Disturbed Children

Mortimer Schiffer

FOCUS

Group play therapy is used with emotionally disturbed children as part of a guidance program in a public elementary school.

INTRODUCTION

Group play therapy has been demonstrated to be an effective intervention for children experiencing various difficulties. A group play therapy project for emotionally disturbed children in an elementary school setting was presented. The treatment was offered in a challenging environment, as the school was located in a slum area surrounded by industrial developments. There was a high incidence of delinquency, and children were often left unsupervised due to the difficult financial situations of the neighborhood families. The public school reflected the neighborhood, with children bringing to the classroom the effects of family discord and neighborhood tensions. Group play therapy was offered to emotionally disturbed children for whom no additional services were available.

CASE STUDY

Several play therapy groups were organized, with eight groups meeting regularly at one point. Most groups were homogeneous in terms of age and gender. Schiffer described three children in one group that had been meeting for two years at the writing of the case study. Alfred, eight years old and in the third grade, was reported to be shy, nervous, and unhappy. His behavior vacillated considerably from amenable and compliant to provocative and abusive. The school counselor's attempts to incorporate Alfred's parents in counseling proved unsuccessful as they were described as rigid and unsympathetic. Jack, age nine and also in the third grade, was a frequent truant. His father reacted with severe physical abuse, and his mother "babied" him, which the father resented intensely. Significant marital discord was reported. Jack's teacher reported that he demanded an unusual amount of attention from her and solicited overt expressions of affection. He acted out in the classroom for attention and also attacked other children without provocation. Jack's parents also refused all offers of help and denied the existence of a problem. William was seven years old when referred by his second-grade teacher. He was reported to have poor peer relationships and frequent temper tantrums, was restless and hyperactive, and required an inordinate amount of attention. The parents of all three boys, while unwilling to be involved in the intervention process, gave consent for participation in the playgroup.

INTERVENTION

A room set apart in the school building for the use of the playgroups was equipped with tables, chairs, workbenches, and a sink. The play materials provided included doll families, doll furniture, paints, easels, sand, clay, paper, toys, and games. The playgroups were led by teachers and supervised by a psychologist and social worker with Schiffer's consultation. Supervision meetings facilitated by Schiffer were held weekly. The play therapy groups met for an hour once a week.

Schiffer described the playgroups as "neither programmed nor structured; motivation stemmed from the needs of the children." The leader was permissive, accepting, and neutral. Overt aggression was permitted within acceptable limits. Schiffer noted that "identification and transference phenomena were dramatically revealed in the children's play behavior."

RESULTS

All three boys exhibited improved behavior in the classroom. Alfred's teacher reported that he related better to her and to his classmates and that he seemed happier in general. Jack also showed improvement, with decreased truancy, more security in his relationship with his teacher, and less inclination to monopolize the teacher's attention. He was also reported to be friendlier. William too exhibited improvement in his school adjustment; he was more responsive to his teacher, more amenable and compliant, and participated more in classroom activities.

COMMENTARY

Group play therapy has been demonstrated to be effective in assisting children in developing interpersonal and intrapersonal skills, as well as in facilitating the processing of emotional issues. Schiffer appropriately encouraged the incorporation of play therapy groups into the elementary school setting; although he did not promote its effects as a panacea, he did suggest that the therapeutic benefits are clear. He posited that the emotional deprivation experienced by children exhibiting some level of emotional disturbance may be addressed in the "positive surrogate identification" involved in the group play therapy process. Alfred, Jack, and William experienced this positive dynamic. Children in any treatment setting would experience the same.

SOURCE

Schiffer, M. 1957. A therapeutic play group in a public school. *Mental Hygiene* 41:185–93.

POSSIBLE DSM-IV-TR DIAGNOSES

312.9   Disruptive Behavior Disorder NOS
309.4   Adjustment Disorder with Mixed Disturbance of Emotions and Conduct
995.5   Neglect of Child

Individual Play Therapy with Emotionally Disturbed Children in a School Setting

Elaine Dorfman

FOCUS

Individual play therapy is used as an intervention for emotionally maladjusted children in the school setting and without parental involvement.

INTRODUCTION

The purpose of this study was to test the hypothesis that personality changes occur over the duration of a play therapy period that do not occur in the same child during a nontherapy period and that do not occur in control cases. The study also explored the effectiveness of individual play therapy conducted by an outsider in a school setting and the effectiveness of individual play therapy without parent therapy.

RESEARCH AND DESIGN METHODS

Subjects identified by their teachers as being maladjusted were recruited from one elementary school. The subjects met the following criteria: (1) the teacher's judgment that the child was among the five most maladjusted in the class; (2) the principal's concurrence with the teacher's judgment; (3) the consent of at least one parent; and (4) the child's being between nine and twelve years old. In a pretest/post-test design, the researcher administered three personality instruments, including Rogers Test of Personality Adjustment, Machover Human Figure Drawing Test, and Sentence Completion Test. Seventeen children were assigned to the experimental group and were observed for three periods: pretherapy (13-week period), therapy, and follow-up (1 to 1.5 years posttreatment). Seventeen children were assigned to the control group, which received no intervention. The control group was tested twice over a time interval close to the average length of therapy.

INTERVENTION

Each child participated in weekly individual play therapy conducted by the researcher at the elementary school. The sessions were facilitated according to the guidelines set forth by Virginia Axline. The children were told that they must attend play therapy at least ten times, after which they could stop or continue as they wish. All cases terminated at the end of one school year. The average number of sessions was nineteen.

RESULTS

On the Rogers Test, results indicated that the experimental group significantly improved over the pretherapy period and over the separate control group. Significant change did not occur at follow-up, but the gains of therapy were maintained. The Sentence Completion Test showed significant gains during therapy that were reliably greater than those of the pretherapy interval and the separate control group. The therapy gains were maintained during the follow-up period, but no significant improvements occurred once therapy had stopped. The Machover Human Figure Drawing Test was not analyzed because it lacked an objective scoring system. Follow-up letters indicated that participants reported favorable memories of the therapy experience.

COMMENTARY

Individual play therapy appeared to be effective in moving emotionally maladjusted children toward healthy adjustment. Because of the era in which this research was conducted, the author's definition of maladjustment is unclear. In the manuscript, the children are referred to as "maladjusted" or "emotionally disturbed." Behavioral terms are not addressed. The author made several conclusions, which include the following statements. Despite emotional dependence of children upon parents, therapy improvement occurred without parent counseling. Projective test improvements appeared greater than those of an objective test that offered problems with validation. Effective therapy can be done in a school setting. Therapy improvements were not correlated with gender differences or number of sessions.

SOURCE

Dorfman, E. 1958. Personality outcomes of client-centered child therapy. *Psychological Monographs: General and Applied* 72 (3): 1–22.

POSSIBLE DSM-IV-TR DIAGNOSIS

Insufficient information provided in the study.

CHAPTER 10

Enuresis and Encopresis Problems

Toilet training may be one of the most difficult tasks of childhood and may easily be one of the most trying and stressful experiences for parents with young children. Fortunately, most children progress through this developmental task quite rapidly. However, some children relapse. Enuresis, or wetting, is common in preschool-age and early school-age children; some estimates claim that 15 to 20 percent of five-year-olds experience nocturnal enuresis. Encopresis is usually defined as voluntary or involuntary fecal incontinence that results in soiled clothes and usually occurs more often in boys than girls. Enuresis and encopresis problems may not occur in the presence of other children but are usually made known to other children by the smell and because such information readily passes from one child to another as interesting information. Consequently, the resulting peer difficulties may have drastic consequences on a child's self-esteem, and other psychological problems secondary to the wetting or soiling problem may develop. Play therapy provides children with a safe place to act out the accompanying frustration, anger, and helplessness and to restore a sense of personhood.

Play and Drama Therapy for Enuresis and Acting-Out Behaviors

Caroline Burton

FOCUS

Hide-and-seek and peek-a-boo games are used within play therapy to treat a boy with enuresis, social withdrawal, and acting-out behaviors.

INTRODUCTION

Burton presented the case of Tommy, a seven-year-old boy who was referred by his school and local child welfare. The presenting problems included enuresis, disruptive behavior, social withdrawal, and conflict with his foster mother. As background for the case study presented, various theoretical models of hide-and-seek play were discussed, along with developmental considerations for peek-a-boo games. It was hypothesized that these games, typical of most children's play in early development, address many of the emotional and attachment issues of children in crisis.

CASE STUDY

Tommy had a long history of emotional difficulties. A psychological report described him as "very regressed," stating that the "intrusion of primitive thinking was interfering with his learning and social interaction." Tommy's play was described as infantile and fragmentary, absent of themes or sequencing. His foster mother reported considerable noncompliance and oppositional behavior. Tommy's history included early neglect and abuse, as well as four previous foster placements. He had been diagnosed as having "psychogenic mental retardation," as well as an organic learning disability. Tommy was referred for therapy while a new foster placement was sought for him.

INTERVENTION

Tommy's foster mother brought him to his first play session. In the office, Tommy was able to play only with clay, which involved hitting it and throwing it against the wall, with accompanying sounds of "kaka" and "peepee." The therapist attempted to lead Tommy into less regressive play, to which Tommy responded by banging his head against the wall. The second session began much like the first, with Tommy attempting to remain out of sight of the therapist, which she first identified as withdrawal; she then redefined it as "hiding" and commenced a game of peek-a-boo. Burton reported that Tommy was quickly engaged and spent the next year and a half in therapy playing progressively more advanced forms of hide-and-seek and peek-a-boo.

By the fourth month of treatment, Tommy began introducing more fantasy and drama into his hide-and-seek games. He created elaborate stories and scenes and invented all of the roles in these stories. Throughout this phase, he was essentially nonverbal. By the sixth and seventh months, Tommy was playing out specific and "traditional" roles and themes in the play. These included interactional games of burglar and victim, and doctor and patient, as well as other games involving aggression, rescue, and self-defense in which he played both sides of the issue. After the seventh month, Tommy began to use the puppet theater, and his final sessions included large dance dramas. Themes that developed dealt with feelings of abandonment and fear of parental loss. Tommy also expressed fear that his acting-out behaviors might cause his new foster parents to reject and abandon him.

RESULTS

In addition to the many positive strides in the play therapy, Tommy's social worker, foster mother, and teacher noted many important changes. He reportedly had improved impulse control, increased ability to delay gratification, and the ability to behave appropriately within stimulating settings in which he had previously been out of control. Tommy also exhibited improved peer interactions, had a more positive affect, and experienced improved cognitive skills. Surprisingly, although the enuresis was a primary presenting issue, the outcome of this concern was not addressed in the case presentation. The assumption is that there was substantial amelioration of this problem.

COMMENTARY

Play therapy has been effective with children experiencing issues of rejection and abandonment. The presenting concern of enuresis was not identified as a physiological issue and was likely a somatic side effect of the multiple emotional issues. Within play therapy, Tommy was given the experience of playing games in which he set up the rules. Burton noted the importance of Tommy being "in control of the interaction" and feeling "understood." She further suggested that the symbolic nature of the play could be viewed in terms of object constancy and as reflecting Tommy's developing progress toward a sense of personal identity. The opportunity for self-expression led to the benefit of self-validation. Although Burton suggested that Tommy did not have the opportunity to process important issues as he did not remain in therapy long enough, the therapeutic benefit of his play therapy experience is clear.

SOURCE

Burton, C. 1986. Peekaboo to "All the all the outs in free": hide-and-seek as a creative structure in drama therapy. *The Arts in Psychotherapy* 13 (2): 129–36.

POSSIBLE DSM-IV-TR DIAGNOSES

307.6   Enuresis
313.81   Oppositional Defiant Disorder
313.89   Reactive Attachment Disorder of Infancy or Early Childhood
319.0   Mental Retardation, Severity Unspecified
V61.20   Parent-Child Relational Problem

Cognitive-Behavioral Play Therapy in the Treatment of Encopresis

Susan Knell and Douglas Moore

FOCUS

Cognitive-behavioral play therapy is used with primary encopresis and language deficits.

INTRODUCTION

Knell and Moore presented the case of a five-year-old male triplet with primary nonretentive encopresis as well as a language disorder. The treatment included a structured, focused, cognitive-behavioral play therapy program in combination with a behavioral management program implemented by the parents.

CASE STUDY

The child was reported to be the quietest and most passive of a set of male triplets. He reportedly did not want to be like his brothers and became angry when adults could not tell them apart. Psychoeducational testing noted an average intellectual range but indicated evidence of developmental expressive and articulation language disorders. The child's parents reported that he soiled several times daily and would remain in soiled clothing unless changed by an adult. He had been toilet trained for urination at the age of three but resisted all attempts at training to use the toilet for bowel movements. He denied any phobia about the toilet but stated that he did not want to learn to use the toilet like his brothers.

INTERVENTION

Baseline data were collected for twelve days prior to any treatment intervention. During this time, the parents recorded the number of soiling incidents, as operationally defined by the authors. The therapist then employed cognitive-behavior play therapy with the child and worked with the parents in the behavioral management of the child's encopresis. According to the authors, cognitive-behavioral play therapy differs from other behavioral treatments of encopresis in that it helps the child incorporate "positive self-statements and more adaptive coping skills." Additionally, this approach incorporates cognitive interventions that reportedly directly address the "child's distortions and misperceptions about the presenting problem."

The child initially engaged in play that exhibited the themes of his toileting struggle and competition with his brothers. The cognitive-behavioral intervention was developed following the emerging theme of a stuffed bear being repeatedly "flushed away." The following treatment situation was given as an example of the developed intervention: "The therapist acknowledged the repetition of this theme (identification of irrational belief), gradually had the bear sit on the toilet (shaping) without getting flushed down (exposure, response prevention), and stated that the bear would not get flushed away (changing an irrational belief)." This led to the child's beginning to "compete" with the bear, expressing a desire to "beat the bear" in the acquiring of stars in a contingency management program similar to the one being established with the parents.

The behavioral management program implemented by the parents began simultaneously with the play therapy. The program consisted of a sticker program in which the child was reinforced for appropriate toilet use and not soiling his pants.

Positive results were reported. The child was soiling during the baseline period approximately 77 percent of the time. After the twelfth session the child spontaneously and regularly used the toilet for bowel movements. Following the fourteenth session, appropriate toileting without soiling accidents was reported. Follow-up at eight and forty-five months noted a continuation of this pattern.

COMMENTARY

Knell and Moore suggested several benefits of the cognitive-behavioral play therapy intervention in their discussion of this case. They proposed that the soiling behavior provided the child with a way to be different and gave him identity. Play therapy in turn provided the opportunity for cognitive self-perceptions and self-statements to be addressed; the cognitive-behavioral elements of the play therapy provided the child with the opportunity to address his anger and "modify the cognitive distortions associated with it." Additionally, the authors suggested that the child's language deficits made aspects of the play therapy, such as "symbolic modeling," more useful to him than a more verbal approach to treatment. Certainly, it appears that this child benefited from the opportunity to express his behaviors and emotions in the play modality, and he was the primary choreographer of the behavioral intervention designed. The concurrent work with the parents appeared to facilitate the translation of learned experiences in the play to the soiling situation at home. The significant positive results attest to the child's taking control of his issues, both in the play and at home.

SOURCE

Knell, S. M., and Moore, D. J. 1990. Cognitive-behavioral play therapy in the treatment of encopresis. *Journal of Clinical Child Psychology* 19 (1): 55–60.

POSSIBLE DSM-IV-TR DIAGNOSES

307.7   Encopresis
315.31   Expressive Language Disorder
315.39   Phonological Disorder

Psychodynamic Play Therapy with an Encopretic Child

Samuel Warson, Marilyn Caldwell, Alice Warinner, A'Lelia Kirk, and Reynold Jensen

FOCUS

Psychodynamic play therapy is used with a young girl with primary encopresis since infancy.

INTRODUCTION

M. J., a six-year-old girl who had exhibited encopresis since infancy, was referred for psychotherapy following several unsuccessful medical interventions. She was described as having "psychogenic" encopresis, including the comorbid symptoms of temper tantrums, fears, and excessive thumb sucking. Psychodynamic play therapy was chosen as the treatment modality.

CASE STUDY

M. J. was the second of three children in an upper-middle-class family. Her parents were described as highly intellectual, compulsive, and exhibiting very little warmth. The mother was reported to be emotionally disturbed and preoccupied with feelings of failure as a parent. Both parents were reportedly disgusted with M. J.'s condition, and the father was described as angry with her for not responding to the various treatment applications attempted. He was also angry with the physicians for their lack of success in treating her.

M. J. was described by her mother as a happy infant until the age of two, when her brother was hospitalized. She was frequently cared for by neighbors and babysitters at this time. The family also had to sell their house and move as the father had transferred to a new job and was available only on weekends for three months prior to the move. M. J. received scant attention during this period and changed from a contented child to a whiny and demanding one. Between the ages of two and three, M. J. was reported to purposefully restrain her bowel movements. The encopretic behavior began at this time. She exhibited indifference to the problem, refusing to "cooperate with the mother who spent a lot of time keeping her clean." Interventions by the family pediatrician were unsuccessful.

INTERVENTION

M. J. was seen in a nondirective and interpretive form of play therapy for forty-two sessions over fourteen months. During the initial play therapy sessions, she moved restlessly from one play activity to the next and called the toys "dirty, black, nasty brown, or broken." If she touched any of these "condemned" toys, she immediately ran to the sink to wash her hands. She seemed afraid of finger paint and clay and apparently soiled frequently during the play sessions.

M. J.'s play progressed to smearing the finger paints while she verbally attacked her siblings. Although initially this caused considerable anxiety, she progressed in this play through one session where she spent the hour aggressively pushing the "brother" doll through a mound of brown finger paint. M. J. gradually moved to expressing hostility toward her mother through doll play, with "mother" dolls being described as angry and punishing. She eventually began engaging in nurturing activities with the dolls and introduced play in which the dolls had bowel movements using clay and finger paints. During the final sessions, M. J. began to use the paints and clay in a constructive manner and expressed the desire to terminate therapy since she was no longer soiling.

The mother was also seen separately in therapy. In follow-up visits two and twelve months after termination, M. J. continued to be symptom free and was described by her mother as a "changed" child. M. J. and her mother exhibited increased confidence and positive affect.

COMMENTARY

The authors suggested that both M. J. and her mother benefited from the acceptance and support of psychotherapy and the removal of the stigma of an inadequate mother and a nonconforming child. They offered the psychodynamic interpretation that the "emotional disturbances in mother and child were similar (resentment and hostility, fears of rejection and abandonment)." Play therapy offered M. J. the opportunity to process anger and hostility in the safety of the playroom, instead of through the encopresis. The tactile play with the clay and finger paints gave expression to intrapsychic needs that previously had no outlet for expression. In addition to addressing relationship concerns in the play, the encopretic child has the opportunity to process the self-esteem and control issues inherent to this childhood challenge.

SOURCE

Warson, S., Caldwell, M., Warinner, A., Kirk, A., and Jensen, R. 1954. The dynamics of encopresis. *American Journal of Orthopsychiatry* 24:402–15.

POSSIBLE DSM-IV-TR DIAGNOSES

787.6   Encopresis with Constipation and Overflow Incontinence
V61.20   Parent-Child Relational Problem
313.81   Oppositional Defiant Disorder

CHAPTER 11

Fear and Anxiety

A commonly expressed concern of parents and teachers is how to cope with children's anxieties and fears. Anxiety over separation from parents is frequently identified in initial referral sessions and in parent training groups. Play therapy provides an accepting and nonthreatening environment in which children are able to express their fears and anxieties through the safety of symbolic play. What cannot be talked out can be played out in a manner that allows the child to move at his own pace as his level of comfort dictates. In the process of playing out frightening experiences, children experience being in control of the frightening experience because they are in control of the play and can thus determine the outcome. This chapter illustrates the effectiveness of play procedures in alleviating school phobia, anxiety attacks, self-injuring, hair pulling, and fear of pain. The demonstrated effectiveness of play therapy leads us to recommend the use of this approach in hospital settings where children often experience severe stress brought on by a strange and threatening environment over which they have no control.

Extreme Anxiety in a Primary-Grade Child

Eugene D. Alexander

FOCUS

Play therapy is studied in an elementary school setting with a highly anxious, withdrawn child who would shake his hands as though they were foreign objects.

INTRODUCTION

The emotional healing power of the play therapy relationship is demonstrated in this case of Chucky, an extremely anxious, seemingly detached child, whose elementary school teacher described him as having a faraway look in his eyes and as sometimes not responding when spoken to; at other times, he would respond in irrelevant, unrelated sentences. The teacher reported times when Chucky would cling desperately to her. This case report is unique in that the play therapy took place in an elementary school building. The play therapist utilized any available quiet place, and the toys and materials were carried in a suitcase. The approach to play therapy was child centered, with an emphasis on the importance of the relationship and a willingness to trust the child.

CASE STUDY

Chucky began his once-a-week play therapy experience by standing in the corner of the room, shaking his hands in the air. He briefly examined the toys and then spent most of the remainder of the session rooted to one spot in the room checking out the therapist with sidelong glances. In succeeding sessions, Chucky began to talk a little about things that raised his anxiety—walls of the building, storms, big animals, time—but he played very little, seeming to prefer just to sit and stare at the clock or the therapist's watch and call out the time. Slowly, he began to verbalize his anxieties that the walls would fall in, that the next minute would not come, or that a big snake would come in and eat him. Chucky was then able to hold the therapist's hand and look at his watch. This physical contact seemed to provide the security Chucky needed to become actively and expressively involved with the toys. Chucky became aggressive and destructive with the toys, even struck the therapist, and limits had to be set.

An interesting development was Chucky's loss of interest in the toys and his complete focus on making physical contact with the therapist, seeming to need to touch all parts of his body and to sit on his lap. In later sessions, Chucky verbally expressed anger toward his father. Alexander reported that much of Chucky's anxiety seemed to be related to his father's attempt to control and mold him. Chucky's attitude toward his father changed gradually, and his conversation during play therapy indicated he was having more of a mutual sharing relationship with his father. Alexander reported that Chucky developed new confidence in himself and was able to accept the love that his father had for him.

COMMENTARY

This case amply demonstrates the power of the play therapy relationship and the value of allowing the child to choose the communication medium he or she feels comfortable with at the moment. As is often the case, Chucky needed to be accepted on his own terms when he said nothing and did nothing. That kind of total acceptance is freeing to children and facilitates their movement toward expressing and exploring those parts of their lives they may find frightening. This case study suggests the importance of being patient and understanding with the child in play therapy.

SOURCE

Alexander, E. 1964. School-centered play therapy program. *Personnel and Guidance Journal* 43:256–61.

POSSIBLE DSM-IV-TR DIAGNOSES

300.02   Generalized Anxiety Disorder
300.14   Dissociative Identity Disorder
V61.20   Parent-Child Relational Problem

Play Therapy with a Child Who Had Pulled Out All of Her Hair

Karen Barlow, Garry Landreth, and JoAnna Strother

FOCUS

Child-centered play therapy is facilitated with a young girl suffering from Trichotillomania.

INTRODUCTION

The authors suggest a parallel between early emotional development in the family and emotional growth in play therapy. Nancy lived with her mother, father, and sister, aged four months. Her mother was overprotective of the four-month-old infant and seldom had any time for Nancy. In addition, the mother suffered from an illness that resulted in frequent hospitalization for periods of several days. It seemed likely that Nancy's fear was associated with her perception of the lack of anything permanent in her life. In addition, Nancy's mother and grandmother were overcontrolling and placed limits on almost all of her behavior. Nancy reacted by rebelling. In the once-a-week sessions in the playroom, the therapist took a child-centered approach.

CASE STUDY

In the first session, Nancy tentatively explored the room. By the middle of the second session, she was playing with the sand and water. In the third session, she shoved two baby dolls into the stove and took their place in the baby bed where she sucked on a bottle. Baby play continued as the primary act in the next three sessions. Nancy further released her emotions by crumbling play dough and walking in it and spilling paint. In the fifth session, she had an angry outburst, threw the baby dolls out of their bed, got into their bed, sucked on the bottle, and then climbed into the therapist's lap with the baby bottle and wanted to be rocked. In this fifth week, the therapist noticed wisps of fine baby hair covering Nancy's head. Baby play became a thing of the past after the fifth session.

In the seventh session, the therapist noted that Nancy's head was covered with short blond hair. Painting, cutting up play dough, sticking her hands into the paint, and using lots of glue and paper became the primary play activities. During a role-play episode in the seventh session, Nancy indicated her awareness of her hair-pulling habit by saying, "When Mother says 'No,' you suck your thumb and pull your hair and eat it." Nancy's therapy was terminated after eight sessions.

COMMENTARY

The play therapy experience provided Nancy with a way in which to organize her experiences, express her feelings, and explore relationships. The authors concluded that the atmosphere created by the play therapist was the single most important factor of the therapeutic procedure and enabled Nancy to feel a freedom to express herself that she had never felt before. Nancy's play with babies, bottles, and baby bed provided her a unique experience through which she experimented and began to resolve her inner conflict. As in this case, sometimes important actual events in children's lives fail to enter either into their play or into their associations. Nancy never pulled out her hair in the playroom or acted out this procedure. She did refer verbally to the behavior once. The regrowth of Nancy's hair is dramatic evidence of the effectiveness of play therapy.

SOURCE

Barlow, K., Landreth, G., and Strother, J. 1985. Child-centered play therapy: Nancy from baldness to curls. *The School Counselor* 34 (1): 347–56.

POSSIBLE DSM-IV-TR DIAGNOSIS

312.39 Trichotillomania

Use of Structured Play to Discover the Cause of the Fear of Being Kidnapped

Jacob Conn

FOCUS

The use of structured play therapy assists a child in coming to terms with the cause of her fears.

INTRODUCTION

A structured play situation has been found useful in the intervention of many children's problems, such as somatic complaints, sibling rivalry, car sickness, tics, and parental neglect. The case study provided as an example of this intervention is a child who was afraid of being kidnapped. The procedure outlined allows the parent to provide information regarding the child's problem, thereby reducing the parent's tension and overconcern. It also provides the clinician an opportunity to ascertain what, if any, role the parent may play in the child's presenting problem.

CASE STUDY

For approximately two years, nine-year-old Harriet had been afraid of the dark. She believed there might be kidnappers in the dark and, consequently, could not tolerate bedtime unless her father lay down with her until she fell asleep. After hearing about the kidnapping and killing of three children, she was unable to sleep without someone near and, even then, often cried in her sleep. Harriet told her father she was afraid the kidnappers would take her younger sister away.

INTERVENTION

Harriet's mother was interviewed first to obtain Harriet's and the family's background information. After it was discovered that financial problems were causing the mother severe anxiety, she was referred for her own therapy. During testing, Harriet was found to have a reading problem and was referred to a special remedial class. It was also learned that Harriet never went into a dark room alone, was afraid of strangers, and cried easily.

In the playroom, Harriet was allowed to explore the various toys. The therapist gave no formal information regarding what was to happen in the playroom or what her mother had said about her problem. Harriet was put at ease and shown acceptance. After a few minutes, she was asked to come and sit next to the dollhouse. The therapist proceeded to illustrate Harriet's problem by using dolls and doll furniture. Allowing children to speak through dolls enables them to present their view of a problem and their role in it.

In the first session, Harriet said she was afraid of the dark and hid under her covers. She also volunteered that she was afraid a kidnapper might come and take her younger sister but then confided that it was only the doll who said that, and it wasn't really true. The second session began with the therapist again selecting the specific toys for the specific scenario and asking Harriet to summarize what they had learned. Harriet responded that the two dolls had been kidnapped, and it was all in the big girl's thoughts. The therapist then added another doll and had Harriet speak for each doll. In this way, Harriet was able to share that she hated her little sister because she "got everything" and was "a lot of trouble," and she wished she could get rid of her. The therapist added a male adult doll as the kidnapper and asked Harriet several questions. During this interchange, Harriet admitted she felt she had lost her father's love to her little sister, and she wanted a kidnapper to come and take her sister away. The therapist did not stay within the fantasy of the play situation but had Harriet identify the bigger girl doll as herself and state she had made up the fear of the dark and the kidnapper in her own mind.

At the beginning of the third session, the therapist asked Harriet what she wanted to play. Harriet responded that she wanted to play what they had done before. Again, through the use of the dolls and the therapist's carefully worded questions, Harriet was able to realize she had thought about the fear of the dark and the kidnappers so long that she had made herself scared. She also acknowledged that she wasn't thinking those thoughts anymore and was able to go to bed without being afraid of either the dark or kidnappers. Her mother reported after the third session that there had been marked improvement. Harriet could now enter dark rooms and turn on the lights and go to bed without crying or needing her father to stay with her. Her mother also noted that Harriet was able to interact with strangers more easily.

In the fourth and subsequent sessions, Harriet and the therapist continued to work through her feelings of having to share her father with her sister. Harriet continued to acknowledge how she had made up the stories and had ended up frightening herself. The seventh and eighth sessions were two months apart, with the ninth and final session five months later. "At the ninth session the child was asked: How are you? A: All right. Q: Are you scared any? A: No. Q: Why? A: I learned there was nothing in the dark to be afraid of. Q: Who was scaring you? A: It was myself" (Conn 1941, 749).

Harriet's mother continued to report improvement. Harriet was playing with children her age rather than dominating younger children, and she was doing better in reading. The mother's own therapy was helping her reduce her anxiety attacks, resulting in less stress in the home. It appeared the intervention in this family brought about lasting and positive results.

COMMENTARY

This form of structured play intervention places the emphasis on the child's ability to express feelings and sort out the cause of the problem. It provides for reorientation and then synthesis of the child's experiences. All this occurs with the setting up of specific play scenarios consistent with the child's reality by a caring, accepting, and insightful therapist. The vehicle of play with the dolls provides enough emotional distance for the child to allow this to occur. As this case shows, the child is the one who reveals the root cause of the fears and is skillfully guided to further self-realization.

SOURCE

Conn, J. 1941. The treatment of fearful children. *American Journal of Orthopsychiatry* 11:744–51.

POSSIBLE DSM-IV-TR DIAGNOSES

300.02   Generalized Anxiety Disorder (Overanxious Disorder of Childhood)
309.24   Adjustment Disorder with Anxiety

V61.20 Parent-Child Relational Problem
V61.08 Sibling Relational Problem
315.00 Reading Disorder

Home Play Therapy and Toilet Training

Natalie Rogers Fuchs

FOCUS

Play therapy is used at home by a mother to alleviate a child's fear of pain during bowel movements.

INTRODUCTION

Despite efforts by her parents and pediatricians, one-and-a-half-year-old Janet would not allow herself to have a bowel movement because she was afraid of possible pain. Through the use of play therapy at home, provided by her mother, Janet was able to overcome this fear.

CASE STUDY

Janet was constipated as an infant and occasionally experienced pain during elimination. Some rectal fissures that probably also caused pain were discovered on two or three other occasions while she was still an infant. Now one-and-a-half years old, Janet cried during diaper changes and avoided the new potty-chair. As medical exams found no physical reason for the current problem, the mother sought a psychological solution.

Janet's mother was instructed to provide play therapy for her daughter in the home. The mother-therapist introduced specific toys for these sessions: dolls, furniture, a potty-chair, toilet paper, and brown clay. In the initial session, Janet surprised her mother-therapist by attempting to sit on the toy toilet. She did so playfully and without any expression of fear. Janet then moved on to dollhouse play, which continued for several sessions. The mother-therapist then added brown plasticine to the selection of toys, and play for the next few sessions focused on Janet's making brown cakes for her parents. She made more and more cakes but did not overtly communicate any connection between the cakes and fecal material. Next, Janet put diapers on the doll and instructed the doll to say repeatedly, with increasing emotion, "B.m. hurt you." The mother-therapist continued to reflect Janet's feelings: "The baby thinks the b.m.'s hurt too much." Janet next relabeled the cakes as b.m.'s and began putting them in the play toilet and around the dollhouse. She asked her mother to eat one, her mother-therapist responded that it would give her a tummy ache but that she would pretend to eat it. Janet was delighted with this response and continued to be preoccupied with the idea of b.m.'s in her mother's tummy.

RESULTS

Janet stopped displaying negative behaviors or emotions about her bowel movements and returned to being a pleasant child. She began using her potty-chair without any further problems. Two years later, at the age of three-and-a-half, she still had no problems with bowel movements. Her development continued to be normal and typical. These special playtimes were used to assist Janet through two additional stressors during these two years: the emergency departure of her mother to the hospital for an appendectomy and the arrival of a baby sister.

The mother-therapist indicated that she also noted changes in herself. She stated that she experienced increased patience with Janet and a willingness to listen to her. As the mother's ability to accept Janet's feelings grew, she found it easier to express her own attitudes to her daughter. The mother-therapist believed that accepting her daughter's feelings without judging them was the key to the successful outcome of the play therapy at home.

COMMENTARY

Janet clearly played out the fears of her situation through the use of the brown plasticine. Assisted by her mother's acceptance of her feelings, Janet mastered her anxiety and put herself back on a normal developmental track.

The mother-therapist and author of this case, Natalie Rogers Fuchs, is the daughter of Carl Rogers. Her father recommended that she read Virginia Axline's *Play Therapy*[1] to build on her previous experience with children in therapeutic settings. This may well have been one of the first forms of filial therapy as later developed by Bernard Guerney.[2] As professional play therapists, we must remember to utilize the power of an effective parent-child relationship. With

---

1. Virginia Axline, *Play Therapy* (Boston: Houghton Mifflin, 1947).
2. Bernard Guerney, Filial Therapy: Description and Rationale, *Journal of Consulting Psychology* 28 (1964): 304–60.

proper training, parents are able to be competent and effective therapeutic agents in their own home and with their own children.

SOURCE

Fuchs, N. R. 1957. Play therapy at home. *Merrill-Palmer Quarterly* 3:89–95.

POSSIBLE DSM-IV-TR DIAGNOSIS

300.29   Specific Phobia, Situational Type

Brief Play Therapy for Stammering

David M. Levy

FOCUS

Form of brief play therapy is used with a two-year-old boy who began stammering after being hit and scratched by another child in day care.

INTRODUCTION

Continuing problems often result after a child has had a specific traumatizing experience. In this case, Paul was attacked by a child and responded with high anxiety. Initially, that anxiety was manifested by withdrawal, but additional reactions of stammering and a general fearful demeanor also developed.

CASE STUDY

Paul, a two-year-old child, had developed speech rapidly and had a larger than typical vocabulary without any history of speech problems. Within the span of a week, another child had hit and scratched Paul on two occasions. This was reportedly the first time he had experienced this kind of behavior. He did not hit back and appeared to respond to the initial incident with indifference. After the second incident, however, Paul began stammering and developed a generally fearful demeanor. He was referred to play therapy approximately one week after his stammering began.

INTERVENTION

Paul's stammering was considered to be the result of anxiety due to the two attacks. To provide Paul with the opportunity to release his anxiety, the attacks would be reenacted through the use of toys within the play therapy milieu. This reenactment would be repeated until Paul was able to discharge his anxiety by being aggressive. This was accomplished in four play therapy sessions.

Paul's first session was typical. He explored the room, touching and naming toys. Clay, often used in this form of brief therapy, was introduced, and Paul manipulated it in a tentative manner. The second session began with spontaneous, child-directed play. Paul then asked the play therapist to break off some clay and initiated interactive play, using the clay, with the therapist. Once this interaction had been established, the play therapist asked Paul what the boy at school did to him. Paul responded by making a slapping movement at both cheeks. The play therapist picked up two dolls, labeling one as Paul and the other as the other boy. Reenacting the slapping incident, the therapist asked, "Then what does Paul do?" Paul moved to hit the doll, stopped mid-move, and asked to leave the room. After being redirected to other play, Paul was able to remain in the playroom until the end of the session.

During initial spontaneous play in the third session, Paul exhibited short displays of aggression. After about thirty minutes, the play therapist again introduced the slapping incident through the doll play. This time Paul hit the doll out of the therapist's hands and onto the floor, then stomped on it. He immediately asked for his nanny (who brought him to play therapy) but made no attempt to leave the playroom. Paul was then able to engage in other play, some of it aggressive, including aggression toward the play therapist.

Following this session, Paul's mother reported a cessation of the stammering and fearful attitude. Follow-up one and two years after play therapy indicated Paul had no recurring problems with stammering. His parents and school personnel reported normal, healthy development.

COMMENTARY

Paul's ability to deal so rapidly with the anxiety may have been due in part to the quick referral for play therapy after the onset of his stuttering. The decision to select this form of brief therapy, release or abreactive play therapy, was based on awareness of the connection between the attacks by the other child and Paul's maladaptive response.

During Paul's second and third sessions, his anxiety disruptions were clear. The play therapist using this approach must be able to identify the appropriate time to introduce the abreactive play. The child must be able to tolerate a certain amount of anxiety. Paul displayed this ability by being able to remain in the play-room and engage in other play. It should also be noted that acting out the anxiety reactions in play enabled Paul to discharge the anxiety through aggressive play.

This approach to play therapy would be applicable to many children who have various maladaptive responses to a specific, disturbing experience.

SOURCE

Levy, D. 1939. Release therapy in young children. *Child Study* 16 (1): 141–43.

POSSIBLE DSM-IV-TR DIAGNOSIS

307.0   Stuttering

Focused Play to Resolve Separation Anxiety

Mary Ellen Milos and Steven Reiss

FOCUS

Separation-relevant play is used effectively to reduce separation anxiety in young children.

INTRODUCTION

Play has long been understood from the child development view as a way children develop mastery. A basic assumption of play therapy is that play can reduce anxiety associated with many psychological problems. This study explored the effectiveness of nondirected and directed play with young children experiencing separation anxiety as they played with toys directly related to the anxiety-producing experience.

RESEARCH METHODS AND DESIGN

The Hall Inventory was used by teachers to rate the level of difficulty children had in separating from their parents. The thirty-two boys and thirty-two girls, two to six years of age, were randomly assigned to one of four groups: free play, directed play, modeling, and the control group. Pre- and postmeasures of speech disturbance were also taken to assess the child's anxiety level. The speech disturbance measure was used to identify the level of speech disturbance evident in each child's response to six anxiety-relevant and four non-anxiety-relevant questions.

INTERVENTION

Each of the three treatment groups was presented with the same toys: a dollhouse, furniture, and flexible dolls arranged to look like the nursery school. The children in the control group were provided with several wooden puzzles, blocks, crayons, and coloring books. The children in all four groups received three individual, ten-minute play sessions with two to three days between sessions. All sessions for the children in the treatment groups were conducted by the same adult female. This adult was unaware of the purposes of the study but was given specific instructions to use with each type of group. Children in the free play group were told they could play with any of the dolls and toys they wanted. The directed play group was shown the dollhouse and teacher's desk and other elements that served to identify the dollhouse specifically with the nursery school. The children were also instructed to identify the dolls as teacher, child, and mommy. A scenario was then described, such as "Mommy brings the child to school and then. . . ." In the modeling group, the adult controlled the behavior of the children by playing out make-believe scenes of parents bringing children to school, focusing on separation scenes, feelings of fear and anger, and then the possible positive feelings of the child. The control group children were simply allowed, without input, to use the toys and materials in any way they liked.

RESULTS

The opportunity for children to play with anxiety-relevant toys in the presence of a nonjudgmental adult resulted in a dramatic reduction of anxiety. There was no significant difference in the results between the three treatment groups.

The results appeared to be tied to factors about the play itself. As might be expected, there was more separation-relevant play in the directed play sessions than by children in the free play sessions, but there was no significant difference in the reduction of anxiety in the respective children. Apparently, the most important factor was the quality of separation-relevant play. Higher quality of play was directly related to lower anxiety levels in the children. High and low quality of play, however, was not found to be tied to whether the children were in the free play or directed play sessions. This indicates it is the individual child's level of emotional involvement in the play and not the setting in which this play occurs that influences the quality of play.

The authors acknowledge that while this study was not meant to be a clinical-outcome study comparing types of play therapy, the point is made that the free play was an analog of child-centered play therapy, the directed play was an analog of structured play therapy, and the modeling reflected modeling procedures used by many play therapists.

COMMENTARY

This study again supports the basic belief of play therapists that children are able to work out their problems through play given an accepting atmosphere in which they sense the freedom to explore their feelings. The specifically selected toys focused the children's work on a specific issue, much like structured play therapy. It is quite possible these children may have worked on other issues if given the wide variety of communicative possibilities available with a fully equipped play therapy room and a trained play therapist.

SOURCE

Milos, M. E., and Reiss, S. 1982. Effects of three play conditions on separation anxiety in young children. *Journal of Counseling and Consulting Psychology* 50 (3): 389–95.

POSSIBLE DSM-IV-TR DIAGNOSES

309.21 Separation Anxiety Disorder
309.24 Adjustment Disorder with Anxiety

CHAPTER 12

Grief

Contrary to what many adults think, very young children do experience grief. Even infants have been shown to experience sadness. The experience of grief is not dependent on a person's mental facility or ability to understand but rather on the person's capacity to feel and ability to experience. Thus, all children can be assumed to grieve and should be dealt with accordingly, that is, through their most natural medium of expression and communication, play. Separation from an object of love can be considered a loss for very young children and can precipitate the experience of grief, which should be considered a process rather than a specific emotion and can be expressed in a variety of ways, often undetected by the significant adults in their lives since children do not express grief in the same way as adults. Children do not generally experience acute pain for lengthy periods; rather, they experience it in short bursts, almost as though their attention span for pain is short. They deal with their feelings through play, often in a kind of symbolic distancing that allows them to feel safe in the midst of acting out the experience.

Sand Play Therapy with a Grieving Child

Lois Carey

FOCUS

Sand play therapy is used as a treatment for a nine-year-old child grieving over the loss of a parent.

INTRODUCTION

Jack was referred to therapy for multiple symptoms surrounding his response to the death of his father. The discussion of the process of sand play with Jack included detailed descriptions and several photographs of individual sand trays created during therapy. Jack displayed several themes in his sand play that were indicative of his emotional problems.

CASE STUDY

Jack experienced two primary losses ("double abandonment") before entering treatment: the sudden death of his father the previous year and the ensuing full-time employment of his mother. Jack was referred by the school psychologist, who reported evidence of enuresis, encopresis, pica, and a general deterioration in affect and behavior. Jack was in a class for neurologically impaired children and had been making continual progress until his father's death and his mother's return to work.

The psychologist was also concerned that Jack might have been sexually molested. This was not found to be true, but it was discovered that Jack had been viewing pornographic movies with his older brothers (Jack was the youngest of four boys).

INTERVENTION

In the first sand play session, Jack entered the room with wide eyes and a sense of wonder as he viewed the substantial display of sand play miniatures. After receiving minimal instructions, Jack created a sand picture in the dry sand tray. Carey noted that the initial selection of dry (versus wet) sand is typical of children with learning disabilities as well as those with enuresis and encopresis. Jack's speech was difficult to follow as he spoke in a monotone with little affect, and he became angry when asked to repeat a word or phrase. Several themes emerged in the first tray, including a struggle for autonomy, depression, and "magical thinking" (including the belief that he had caused his father's death and might undo it as well).

One of the themes addressed in the early sessions was Jack's fantasy that if he used the bathroom, he might have a heart attack. Jack told Carey that on the night his father died, his father had gone to the bathroom, and that was why he had died. Jack began to cry during this exchange and said that if he (Jack) was not so "stupid," his father would not have died. The encopretic episodes stopped almost immediately following this session.

Jack constructed multiple trays that were chaotic representations of his own chaotic world and the creation of which included burying and unburying objects (representative of loss, buried rage, and protection of self). Eventually, the sand tray themes were organized as Jack attempted to make sense of his life. He eventually began using the wet sand, which Carey suggested indicated his willingness to move to deeper psychological issues. Shortly after this move, Jack's mother reported that he had become increasingly outspoken and displayed some temper outbursts ("positive growth"). His nightmares had apparently stopped, he no longer requested a night-light, and no recurrences of enuresis were reported. The pica had not continued past the second session. Carey reported that during the six months of treatment, Jack achieved "significant relief from his presenting symptoms, made a better ego adaptation, and was far less depressed."

COMMENTARY

Sand play therapy provided Jack with the opportunity to illustrate and process issues of low self-esteem, abandonment, and lack of control over his father's death and mother's return to work, as well as to resolve grief issues and confront guilt and rage. The many issues that grieving children present are effectively addressed in the projective nature of play therapy approaches. Integration of losses and relationship issues can be processed symbolically through the safety of play, which Carey demonstrated through Jack's case. Sand play has been shown to be an effective modality with many issues, including grief, and has been used with all age groups.

SOURCE

Carey, L. 1990. Sand play therapy with a troubled child. *The Arts in Psychotherapy* 17 (3): 197–209.

POSSIBLE DSM-IV-TR DIAGNOSES

V62.82   Bereavement
307.6   Enuresis
307.7   Encopresis
307.52   Pica
309.4   Adjustment Disorder with Mixed Disturbance of Emotions and Conduct

Puppets in the Treatment of Traumatic Grief

Stephanie R. Carter

FOCUS

Puppets are used in nondirective play therapy with a ten-year-old child experiencing traumatic grief.

INTRODUCTION

Steven had witnessed his father's murder two years before entering treatment. His behavior at school and home had deteriorated following the event, and he was referred for therapy by his teacher. In the nondirective treatment approach, Steven selected puppets to process his previously denied traumatic grief.

CASE STUDY

Before witnessing the murder of his father, Steven was described as a "normal boy" who functioned well academically, socially, and behaviorally. Afterward, the child became aggressive, frequently hit teachers and other children, used profanity, and destroyed property. His mother reported similar behaviors at home. Steven's academic progress virtually stopped at the time of the trauma, and within two years, he was placed in a class for emotionally disturbed children. He would not talk about his father, the murder, or his feelings.

INTERVENTION

Carter described her rationale for employing nondirective play therapy and suggested that "Steven freely chose puppets in a neutral play atmosphere that was unstructured and nondirective and began to break through his defenses of traumatic anxiety, to understand his feelings, and finally to experience the full range of grief and its accompanying anger." Steven began weekly therapy as a ten-year-old fifth grader and continued the one-hour sessions for two years. An important issue that Carter noted was that during these two years, three additional people close to Steven also died, which he processed in the play.

The treatment process began with Steven covering his head with a towel and turning his back on the therapist. He informed the therapist that talking about his father made him angry and that he would refuse to talk about anything related to his father. By the third session, Steven had chosen the puppets to focus on and continued to use them throughout treatment. Eventually, the father puppet was shot, and Steven staged the funeral and burial. The following sessions included the puppets engaged in numerous fights and the themes of violence, his father's death, and the little boy puppet narrowly escaping death. During session eight, there appeared to be a breakthrough as Steven grieved for the father puppet, dropped the boy puppet, and cried out, "My daddy died. . . . Oh no, my daddy died. Don't let him die. What am I going to do? My daddy died."

Following this session, positive changes began to occur outside the playroom. Steven's teacher reported academic improvement. His social skills improved, and his anger was expressed more appropriately. The teacher also reported that Steven was much more "joyful," and his mother reported fewer incidents of misbehavior at home. By the termination of treatment, Steven was in junior high school and was being taken out of the special academic program and returned to the mainstream population. In addition to the reduction in acting-out behaviors, Steven talked about his future, visualized himself as successful, and displayed personal confidence.

COMMENTARY

Play therapy is effective for children dealing with traumatic grief since it gives them the opportunity to have control over the issues, to proceed at their own pace, and to experience the safety of projection and communicating in the language of play. In summarizing Steven's puppet play, Carter says, "He used [the puppets] to test reality, to express his needs symbolically, and to relieve the pressure of his traumatic anxiety." The play clearly provided Steven with a safe outlet through which to express and ultimately experience his grief and anger. Grieving children need the safety of play therapy to process their pain.

SOURCE

Carter, S. R. 1987. Use of puppets to treat traumatic grief: a case study. *Elementary School Guidance & Counseling* 21 (3): 210–15.

POSSIBLE DSM-IV-TR DIAGNOSES

V62.82 Bereavement
312.8   Conduct Disorder
313.81 Oppositional Defiant Disorder

Group Play Therapy with Bereaved Children

Donna Casey Tait and Jo-Lynn Depta

FOCUS

Group play therapy is used with children experiencing emotional and behavioral difficulties following the death of a parent.

INTRODUCTION

The planning of a bereavement group and the rationale for using a group play therapy approach to treating this population are explored. Cofacilitators were used for the group, which consisted of ten children who had experienced the loss of a close family member. In addition to a discussion of the group process and summary of the sessions, guidelines for bereavement group facilitators and discussion questions are provided.

CASE STUDY

The ten children ranged in age from seven to eleven years. The family deaths had occurred eighteen months to three years before the group therapy. Two of the children had observed the death of a parent following a prolonged illness, while the remaining eight had had no warning of the death of their relative. Nine of the ten experienced the death of a parent.

The children were described as experiencing nightmares, anger outbursts, academic and social difficulties, withdrawal, hypervigilance, abandonment, and depression. Their families described them as having difficulty expressing anger and being withdrawn and depressed. Additionally, most of the surviving parents had considerable difficulty talking objectively about the death.

INTERVENTION

The treatment consisted of eight sessions. Each session's focus, together with corresponding play activities, was planned before the group began therapy. Some of the play activities included were drawing, clay work, charade games, family sculpting, storytelling, and puppet play. Most of the sessions began with fifteen minutes of free play prior to the structured activities.

The facilitation of normalization and the benefit of peer support in group therapy became quickly evident in session two, when one of the children (Justin) fashioned a train out of clay—the train that hit his mother and sister and killed them. He started to cry, and in addition to the reflection and support of one of the group facilitators, Justin received the support and comforting of the other children. Session seven included a symbolic activity developed to assist the children in letting go by asking them to write a message to the deceased family member. The message was placed inside a helium balloon with an attached string, and the balloons were released outdoors as a group. Session eight consisted of a formal goodbye and included a "graduation party" with pizza, certificates, and picture taking. Pre- and post-assessments were given to the parents, and a post-test questionnaire was given to the children. Positive results were reported.

COMMENTARY

Group therapy provides participants with a safe place to share difficult issues; it breaks the sense of isolation, normalizes the recovery process, and provides peer support. The combination of group work and play therapy procedures provided these grieving children with the opportunity to process their sense of being in an out-of-control situation. They were able to bring some sense of empowerment and control to their lives, which were marked by the opposite feelings. The authors acknowledge that group play therapy with grieving children is a recent innovation and that limited guidelines are available. At the same time, the potential benefits for this challenging population are limitless.

SOURCE

Tait, D. C., and Depta, J. 1994. Play therapy group for bereaved children. In *Helping Bereaved Children: A Handbook for Practitioners*, ed. N. B. Webb, 169–85. New York: Guilford.

POSSIBLE DSM-IV-TR DIAGNOSIS

V62.82 Bereavement

Child-Centered Play Therapy with a Grieving Child

Jane LeVieux

FOCUS

Child-centered play therapy is used with a five-year-old girl grieving over the death of her father following a terminal illness.

INTRODUCTION

Celeste was referred for treatment six months after the death of her father. She was described as being uncooperative, defiant, and depressed. Child-centered play therapy was the chosen treatment modality.

CASE STUDY

Celeste was the oldest of three children. Her mother explained that the father's illness (cancer) involved multiple short hospitalizations and rounds of chemotherapy. From December through February of the year he died, the majority of the father's time was spent in the hospital. The children saw little of him in the weeks prior to his death because the father did not want them to see him in such pain. He died at the hospital. Memorial services were held, which the children attended.

Her mother reported that Celeste was moody and irritable since her father's death. There were also increased incidents of uncooperative and defiant behaviors, which were not previously evident. Celeste presented as periodically depressed and had become increasingly impatient with her younger siblings. Over the following summer, Celeste's preschool teacher had given birth to a new child, which precipitated crying and concern by Celeste about the upcoming school year. Her mother then decided to request treatment.

INTERVENTION

The treatment process began with a family intake session in which LeVieux gathered background information and introduced Celeste and the rest of the family to the playroom. The initial session with Celeste was typical of the entire treatment process, which was child centered and, thus, led by Celeste. The treatment plan included providing Celeste with "opportunities for her to express feelings, either verbally or symbolically through her play." The objective was to help Celeste to integrate her father's death into her own life and to process the grief and anger issues through play, which in turn would lead to a reduction in aggressive and noncompliant behaviors in the home.

Given the lead in the play therapy process, Celeste began to talk about her father, play with the toys, and do artwork. Celeste repeatedly buried items in the sand and drew pictures of her sadness and of her father. In one session, she drew a picture of her father with big hands and verbalized that she remembered how safe she had felt with him, especially when they held hands. By session seven, Celeste's mother reported that she was able to talk more easily with Celeste about her father. LeVieux was still seeing Celeste in treatment at the writing of the case study and noted considerable progress in her integration of her father's death and the processing of grief and anger issues. LeVieux noted the importance of working with the surviving parent, as well as the importance of allowing the child simply to play (to be a child) as opposed to focusing constantly on the presenting grief issue.

COMMENTARY

Play therapy is effective in assisting grieving children to process the out-of-control issues of loss and anger in a safe and empowering environment. Celeste was able to address previously unprocessed grief concerns and to begin to make sense of a situation, life without her father, that was frightening and produced powerlessness. The therapeutic approach of child-centered play therapy provided Celeste with an opportunity to manage what seemed unmanageable. As LeVieux summarized, "Perhaps during those moments of play where freedom is granted and creativity abounds, Celeste feels safe and comfortable."

SOURCE

LeVieux, J. 1994. Terminal illness and death of father: case of Celeste, age 5 1/2. In *Helping Bereaved Children: A Handbook for Practitioners*, ed. N. B. Webb, 81–95. New York: Guilford.

POSSIBLE DSM-IV-TR DIAGNOSES

V62.82 Bereavement
313.81 Oppositional Defiant Disorder
309.4   Adjustment Disorder with Mixed Disturbance of Emotions and Conduct

CHAPTER 13

Hospitalization

Hospitalization can be a frightening experience for children. They are suddenly uprooted from what is familiar (home, parents, siblings, school, peers) and predictable, and placed in an environment that is neither familiar nor predictable. In addition, children no longer have personal freedom, privacy, or control. They are suddenly thrust into a new, strange, and bewildering environment in which they are poked, looked at, made to swallow weird substances, and subjected to mysterious machines and procedures. Is it any wonder that these experiences may contribute to severe stress in children that may be manifested in behavioral changes? Behavioral changes that occur as a result of hospitalization may persist well beyond the time of discharge from the hospital if there is no systematic intervention. Play therapy provides children with an opportunity to experience a familiar activity and, thus, reconnect with life outside the hospital. Through play, children can construct their lives to be the way they want them to be and, in that process, experience being in control. The most important factor in this process, however, is the establishment of a consistent relationship with a play therapist who is understanding, accepting, and completely trustworthy.

Treating Hospital Fear Reactions with Play Therapy

Pauline H. Barton

FOCUS

Play therapy is used as treatment for a five-year-old child exhibiting an inability to trust and significant fear regarding open-heart surgery.

INTRODUCTION

Kathy was hospitalized twice for open-heart surgery. The second hospitalization included a play therapy experience, using the child-centered approach of Clark Moustakas.[1] Situational hospital doll play was employed to help Kathy express her feelings of fear and anxiety.

CASE STUDY

Kathy was an intellectually superior child, and her home environment stimulated this aspect of her development. During a previous hospitalization for heart catheterization, Kathy had demonstrated high levels of distrust and hostility, yelling at hospital staff, calling them names, and accusing them of lying about medical procedures. Before her second admission for surgery, the hospital staff arranged for play therapy utilizing situational hospital doll play as a means to assist Kathy in dealing with her fears about the surgery and her distrust of the staff.

INTERVENTION

Presurgery: The first play therapy sessions were held in a "play hospital," an exact replica of a two-bed hospital ward with all the appropriate and expected equipment. Dolls were dressed to represent patients, nurses, doctors, and parents. After a cursory examination of the room, Kathy picked up the hypodermic syringe and needle and asked how to attach the two. She then gave the girl doll an injection. After being shown how to fill the syringe with water, Kathy shot the fluid into the air. Consistent with children who are extremely anxious, Kathy's expression remained stony and impassive.

The therapist was then called from the play/hospital room for a few minutes. She remained in the hall where she could observe Kathy without being seen. Kathy quickly picked up the mother doll and gave her repeated injections. Although Kathy's body posture remained rigid and tense, she displayed a wider range of emotions during this play, including joy, intense concentration, and considerable anger. When the therapist returned to the playroom, Kathy left the play with the mother doll but continued to play with the syringe.

To assist in developing Kathy's trust of the hospital staff, the therapist took her on a tour of the recovery room, where she met the nursing staff who would

---

1. Clark Moustakas, *Children in Play Therapy* (Northvale, NJ: Jason Aronson, Inc., 1973).

provide her care following surgery. In addition, the therapist and the nurses walked Kathy through the complete surgical procedure, from preparation through recovery.

During the next play therapy session, Kathy's mother was present. The therapist suggested that they get the doll hospital and play out what would happen when someone has surgery. Initially, Kathy wanted the mother doll to undergo surgery but then changed to the girl doll, which she identified as herself. Kathy included the therapist in the play as her assistant and was able to play through the entire procedure. This included Kathy bandaging the girl doll and pushing a large needle into the doll's chest to represent the stitches. Despite Kathy's mother's request to be a part of the play, Kathy chose not to include her.

Postsurgery: The recovery nurses reported that Kathy was one of the best-behaved children they had worked with in postoperative care. She was cooperative and did not appear frightened of any of the procedures, and her doll play reflected the change the staff had seen in Kathy. The doll play was focused on routine daily events, including bath time, bed making, stitch removal, injections, and playing. She identified one doll as "Kathy" and often talked through the doll: "Kathy, you have to have a shot now. It will hurt just a little, but not very long. Now, now, it's all over. You have just three shots more today." Kathy's play appeared self-comforting and reassuring. It was also relaxed and cheerful.

Follow-up hospital visits: Kathy continued to be cheerful and happy to see the hospital staff. One visit took place primarily because Kathy begged her mother to let her visit her hospital friends. Kathy's family reported she was taking greater responsibility in her own care, including remembering to take her own medications and following guidelines regarding exercise and avoiding overexertion. Kathy was also seen as being more mature and considerate, having greater ability to concentrate on tasks, and more attached to her mother.

COMMENTARY

Play therapy is a proven and effective procedure for helping children release anxiety and develop a sense of mastery and self-control in a hospital environment. Kathy was able to process some feelings toward her mother in the first play session (her repeated injections of the mother doll), including anger toward her for allowing Kathy to be placed in a frightening and painful situation. Kathy also developed trust in the staff (talking with the doll about the number of shots to be given), believing, as she had been told, that there would be only four shots that day in the recovery room. The directed play experience allowed Kathy not only to express a variety of feelings, but also to clarify her perceptions of the medical procedures, her mother, and herself. As in this case with Kathy, many children are able to apply this new sense of self in hospital situations to other areas of their lives.

SOURCE

Barton, P. H. 1962. Play as a tool of nursing. *Nursing Outlook* 10:162–64.

POSSIBLE DSM-IV-TR DIAGNOSES

293.89   Anxiety Disorder Due to a General Medical Condition
309.81   Posttraumatic Stress Disorder

Brief Puppet Therapy for Children Facing Cardiac Catheterization

Sylvia Cassell

FOCUS

The effect of brief puppet therapy on the emotional responses of children hospitalized for cardiac catheterization is investigated.

INTRODUCTION

Previous research has shown that children can express emotions more easily through a "third person" (such as a puppet or doll) than they can directly. The research hypotheses were that children who received puppet therapy would be (1) rated by the cardiologist as less disturbed, (2) rated as showing less emotional disturbance on the hospital ward following the catheterization, and (3) more willing to return to the hospital for further treatment.

RESEARCH METHODS AND DESIGN

The subjects for this study included forty children, ages three through eleven, admitted to a children's hospital for cardiac catheterization. Twenty children were randomly assigned to each of the experimental and control groups.

The play materials consisted of a miniature mock-up of the catheterization facilities, including puppets representing a doctor, nurse, boy, girl, mother, and father. Miniature hospital equipment was also used. The children in the experimental group were given two sessions of puppet therapy, one before and the other after the catheterization. The children in the control group received routine hospital services.

Three measures of the children's emotional responses were employed with both groups: parental questionnaires, ward observations, and catheterization observations.

INTERVENTION

During the puppet therapy sessions, the child and the therapist acted out the catheterization procedure. In the initial phase of the first session, the therapist played the role of the cardiologist, explaining as many of the medical procedures as possible. Play included giving injections, changing into hospital gowns, and placement on the examining table. Following this initial enactment of the hospital procedure, the patient-doctor roles were reversed, and the child played the medical role(s). After the puppet play, the child was encouraged to discuss aspects of the role plays and to use any of the puppets in a free manner.

RESULTS

Children participating in puppet therapy showed less emotional disturbance during the cardiac catheterization and expressed greater willingness to return to the hospital for further treatment. These results were attributed to two assumptions: (1) that understanding of the staff's empathy reduced the child's need to communicate his or her feelings, and (2) that the puppet therapy offered a combination of mastery, acceptance of professional empathy, and release of emotions.

COMMENTARY

The healing power demonstrated in two sessions of play therapy is amazing. By projecting fear and anxiety related to hospitalization onto the puppets, children are able to make sense of a situation that seems out of control. When given the opportunity to process emotional issues and release anxiety through the day, children can build some level of mastery of and control over an experience that is otherwise unmanageable, leading to the development of emotional coping mechanisms.

SOURCE

Cassell, S. 1965. Effect of brief puppet therapy upon the emotional responses of children undergoing cardiac catheterization. *Journal of Consulting Psychology* 29 (1): 1–8.

POSSIBLE DSM-IV-TR DIAGNOSES

293.89   Anxiety Disorder Due to a General Medical Condition
309.24   Adjustment Disorder with Anxiety

The Effects of Play Therapy on Hospitalized Children

Stephanie Clatworthy

FOCUS

Play therapy is demonstrated to be an effective treatment of hospital-induced anxiety in children.

INTRODUCTION

The effectiveness of play therapy in the treatment of children experiencing hospital-induced anxiety was investigated in this study. The stabilization or reduction of anxiety levels in hospitalized children has been determined to be associated with a greater degree of cooperation with medical staff and treatment procedures. The effect of therapeutic play on hospitalized children was investigated at two large hospitals over the course of several years, focusing on levels of anxiety.

RESEARCH METHODS AND DESIGN

The study involved a total of 114 children in three phases. Phases I and II were conducted in the general pediatric unit of a private hospital in a large metropolitan area and consisted of twenty-three and twenty-six children, respectively.

Phase III was conducted in a large university hospital and consisted of sixty-five children. All children between the ages of five and twelve years were considered candidates for the study. The length of the anticipated hospital stay (two to four days) and number of previous hospitalizations (no more than three) were controlled in the first two phases. Parental reports of previous "good" mental health and normal intelligence were required for all participants.

The total study was conducted over a four-year period and consisted of fifty-five children in the treatment group and fifty-nine in the control group. All groups were homogeneous in relation to family size, economic status, previous hospitalizations, experience with separation, and preparation for this specific hospitalization. The mean age for children in the study was 7.4 years for the experimental group and 8.53 years for the control group.

Upon admission and on the last or seventh day of hospitalization, the children were given the Missouri Children's Picture Series (MCPS) to assess levels of anxiety. This test instrument consisted of 238 cards with line drawings depicting children in daily activities.

INTERVENTION

The experimental group received daily individual play therapy conducted by a nurse play therapist. Play materials considered conducive to hospital and family role play were provided, including fantasy play through dolls, puppets, and storytelling; art with paints and crayons; and aggressive play with punching bags, clay, cars, and balls. The play was directed primarily by the child, with the therapist providing reflection and some interpretation of feelings.

RESULTS

The children's current level of anxiety was measured with the MCPS during the first twenty-four hours of hospitalization and again at discharge and/or on the seventh day. In Phase I of the study (children who were hospitalized for four days), the children in the experimental group exhibited a significantly lower level of anxiety at the conclusion of the intervention. The statistical analysis indicated that the intervention did not decrease the anxiety of the children in the experimental group but rather prevented them from developing as much anxiety as the children in the control group. In Phase II of the study (children who were hospitalized for two days), similar results were attained. For children experiencing longer hospitalizations (Phase III), the same significant, positive results were reported. Children in the experimental group continued to exhibit less anxiety as measured by the MCPS.

COMMENTARY

This research demonstrated significant differences in the anxiety levels of hospitalized children who received regular play therapy, regardless of setting, age, gender, or diagnosis. In general, the play therapy appeared to act as a deterrent to anxiety in children in an environment in which anxiety routinely manifests. The authors suggested that play therapy should be routinely included in the treatment program for pediatric patients. Children who experience less anxiety during the hospitalized experience are more amenable to medical treatment and more cooperative with family and hospital staff. The positive effects of play therapy with hospitalized children appears experientially clear—this study offers empirical evidence in support.

SOURCE

Clatworthy, S. 1981. Therapeutic play: effects on hospitalized children. *Journal of Association for Care of Children's Health* 9 (4): 108–13.

POSSIBLE DSM-IV-TR DIAGNOSES

293.89 Anxiety Disorder Due to a General Medical Condition
309.24 Adjustment Disorder with Anxiety

Helping Young Children Master Intrusive Procedures through Play

Mary-Lou Ellerton, Suzanne Caty, and Judith Ritchie

FOCUS

Analysis of play interviews with chronically ill, two- to six-year-old, hospitalized children revealed that nine of the ten children were able to use clinical equipment to express their concerns about intrusive medical procedures.

INTRODUCTION

Young, chronically ill children who experience repeated or prolonged hospitalization struggle not only with developmental stress but also with the anxiety of the illness and hospitalization. These children have been found to be at considerably increased risk for social and emotional difficulties. A series of play interviews was implemented to determine differences in the expression of issues of healthy children, acutely ill children, and chronically ill children. The play of the chronically ill children focused on issues of intrusion.

RESEARCH METHODS AND DESIGN

The research sample included six boys and four girls who had been diagnosed with a chronic illness and whose hospital stay had a duration of at least twenty-one days. The children had had several previous hospitalizations, and seven had had previous surgeries. Six of the children were between two and four years of age, and four were in the four- to six-year age range.

Play interviews were conducted every five to seven days with each child until his or her discharge from the hospital or a maximum of six interviews was reached. A total of forty-nine interviews were conducted. Data were collected using a specific play interview procedure and specific materials. The children were presented with a suitcase containing a variety of toys, including familiar toys, family figures, and medical/hospital equipment. They were free to take the lead and play, while the researcher took notes.

INTERVENTION

In the initial play interview, the researcher picked up and identified each toy in the suitcase. The child was then permitted to play with the toys, while the researcher took notes. The play session was nondirective, and requests by the child for the researcher to participate were declined. Each play interview lasted for forty-five minutes, and the child was free to refuse to play. All behaviors identified as intrusive constituted the data base for the study and were content-analyzed.

RESULTS

Nine of the ten chronically ill children played out intrusion themes during the play interviews. For five children, more than 25 percent of the total play was related to intrusion. Four types of intrusion behaviors were identified in the content analysis: (1) injection play (55% of the intrusive play), (2) giving medications (23%), (3) temperature taking (17%), and (4) tube-feeding (4%).

Playing out injections was clearly a major concern for the children. The level of injection play appeared to parallel the children's experience in the hospital: 33 percent of the children's play with the syringe was exploratory, learning how the materials operated. The children's play was an accurate replication of the intrusion experience in the hospital 93 percent of the time during the first interview; 78 percent of their play activities were accompanied by verbalizations.

COMMENTARY

All nine of the children playing out intrusion themes played with the injection materials. Receiving injections continues to be a significant issue for hospitalized children. Some 40 percent of the intrusion behaviors displayed represented temperature taking and giving medications. This suggests that although these procedures are routine for hospital staff, they can be potentially devastating for the pediatric patient. It is imperative that hospitalized children have the chance to express their fears, especially those related to intrusion. This study amply demonstrates children's willingness to communicate their concerns through play.

SOURCE

Ellerton, M. L., Caty, S., and Ritchie, J. A. 1985. Helping young children master intrusive procedures through play. *Children's Health Care* 13 (4): 167–73.

POSSIBLE DSM-IV-TR DIAGNOSIS

Insufficient information provided in the study.

Play Therapy in a Pediatric Hospital Department

K. Zilliacus and S. Enberg

FOCUS

The effectiveness of a hospital-based play therapy program is evaluated through survey research.

INTRODUCTION

Children who experience hospitalization must deal with concomitant fears and anxiety. While the efficacy of play therapy interventions with children who have already been admitted to the hospital has been determined, bringing a therapeutic play experience to children in the hospital waiting room is an innovative treatment intervention. The effectiveness of a play therapy program based in the outpatient department waiting room of the Children's Hospital in Helsinki, Finland, was investigated.

RESEARCH METHODS AND DESIGN

The subjects involved in the survey research included one hundred parents whose children had participated in the organized play therapy program at the hospital and twenty-one members of the hospital staff. Interviews were conducted to assess the effectiveness of the program by studying the respondents' attitudes. The age range of the children whose parents participated in the study was 2 to 16 years, with a mean of 6.8 years.

INTERVENTION

The play therapy program consisted of a well-supplied play area in the waiting room of the pediatric section of the hospital. A trained adult "play leader" was present during the day. In addition to the waiting room play therapy, the authors noted that there were six play leaders working on ten wards with an average of twenty patient beds. Children visiting the hospital for outpatient services or children being admitted to the hospital were able to take advantage of the play activity.

A variety of play materials was offered, including a kitchen set, dolls, cars, and building modules. Games, books, and music were available for the older children. Art and craft materials were also provided. The play leader provided direction for the play activity, but the children were free to participate or not or to choose an alternate activity. Play therapy was conducted in a corner of the waiting room, with the intent of involving the children and their parents in the process. Interested parents were informed about the process and encouraged to continue play activities at home. Siblings were also encouraged to be involved.

RESULTS

Both parents and hospital staff responded to the interviews with positive feed-back for the play therapy program. In response to a question about whether the play activity reduced the children's tension, 35 percent of the parents answered "very much," 47 percent answered "somewhat," and 18 percent saw no reduction in tension. Thus, 82 percent of the parents considered the play therapy to be effective in reducing fear and anxiety. Also, of the parents asked, "How do you feel when your child is taking part in the play activity?" 91 percent answered "more relaxed," and 9 percent reported "no change." To the question about whether the parents themselves received ideas from the play activity, 88 percent answered positively. An examination of what the children involved in the play therapy program talked about both before and after the hospital visit found that they talked twice as much about the play as about the waiting and treatment and nearly five times more about the play than about the pain.

The hospital staff noted that the children appeared more relaxed and that making contact with the parents was easier, and 90 percent of the staff respondents noted that the play therapy influenced their work (from "very much" to "some extent"). To the question "Is there any difference between children who have been occupied at the play table compared with those who have not?" 19 percent answered "yes, very much," 33 percent answered "yes, a lot," and 43 percent answered "yes, to some extent"; 5 percent saw no difference.

COMMENTARY

The authors suggested that organized play in the hospital should be tension relieving and fear reducing and give the child an opportunity to live out feelings. Providing children with the opportunity to express their emotional and behavioral needs and concerns in such a challenging setting has been demonstrated to be effective with hospitalized children in many settings. The play therapy program in the waiting room facilitates both the treatment process for outpatient children and the admitting process for children to be hospitalized. The authors appropriately asserted that as more sick children are being treated at a hospital on an outpatient basis, organized play therapy activities in the waiting room and in the outpatient department are crucial additions to the overall treatment program.

SOURCE

Zilliacus, K., and Enberg, S. 1980. Play therapy in the pediatric out-patient department. *Paediatrician* 9: 224–30.

POSSIBLE DSM-IV-TR DIAGNOSES

309.24   Adjustment Disorder with Anxiety
293.89   Anxiety Disorder Due to a General Medical Condition

Puppet Therapy for Children Undergoing Hospital Surgery

Patricia Johnson and Dahlia Stockdale

FOCUS

The effects of one session of puppet play on the anxiety level of children undergoing hospital surgery are studied.

INTRODUCTION

Children who are admitted to the hospital for surgery may experience significant emotional trauma. One approach to alleviating anxiety for children is to provide psychological preparation for surgical patients. The purpose of this study was to investigate the effects of a puppet play session on the anxiety levels of hospitalized children.

RESEARCH METHODS AND DESIGN

Subjects were forty-three children, ages five to eight years, who were admitted to a children's hospital for surgical procedures including adenoidectomy with or without tonsillectomy, herniorrhaphy, myringotomy with or without placement of polyethylene tubes, and dental restoration or extraction. Subjects were randomly assigned to treatment or control groups. The researchers determined anxiety levels according to a Palmar Sweat Index (PSI) measured through fingerprints. PSI levels were measured four times: prior to puppet play session at admission, following puppet play session (fifteen minutes following first observation for control patients), on the evening prior to surgery, and on the evening following surgery. Three judges scored the prints blindly, and a mean score for each measure from each subject was calculated.

INTERVENTION

The experimental group participated in one puppet play session facilitated by hospital volunteers trained in the puppet intervention. The puppet show was designed to familiarize the patient with the procedure to be used for his or her specific operation. Equipment used in the presentation included a puppet doctor and nurse, surgical gowns and caps, surgical masks, an anesthesia mask, a syringe, intravenous equipment, and material for bandages. The patients were allowed to interact, manipulate puppets, and ask questions during the puppet demonstration. The sessions varied from nine to twenty minutes. The control group received no intervention. Control group PSI levels were measured at admission and then fifteen minutes later to approximate the time of the puppet intervention for the experimental group.

RESULTS

The data on average change in PSI scores from the first measurement to second measurement (before and after the puppet session) indicated that the puppet session was associated with a significant reduction in anxiety. The direction of change in difference scores from following the puppet session to directly before surgery favored the control subjects. The researchers commented that Palmar sweating may have increased among experimental subjects because they had more knowledge about the hospital operative procedures that they would encounter than did the control subjects. Experimental subjects again showed a significant reduction in anxiety when difference scores from the first to final measurements were compared. Children who had been exposed to puppet therapy were less anxious than control subjects, even after the operation had been performed. This finding indicated that there is some positive carryover effect for experimental subjects from posttreatment to postsurgery.

COMMENTARY

This study demonstrated that one puppet play session was effective in reducing the anxiety of children undergoing surgery. Many children do not have the experience to help cope with fears about hospitalization. The puppet intervention helped them to prepare for and understand their upcoming procedures, thereby reducing their anxiety.

SOURCE

Johnson, P., and Stockdale, D. 1975. Effects of puppet therapy on Palmar sweating of hospitalized children. *The Johns Hopkins Medical Journal* 137: 1–5.

POSSIBLE DSM-IV-TR DIAGNOSES

293.89   Anxiety Disorder Due to a General Medical Condition
309.24   Adjustment Disorder with Anxiety

Impact of Therapeutic Play on Hospitalized Children

William Rae, Frances Worchel, Jan Upchurch,
Jacqueline Sanner, and Carol Daniel

FOCUS

The impact is studied of therapeutic play on the psychosocial adjustment of forty-six children hospitalized for acute illness.

INTRODUCTION

Frequently, therapeutic play is used as an in-hospital intervention to ameliorate coping problems. In the hospital setting, therapeutic play is credited with helping children to regain control, express feelings of anxiety, gain information about hospital procedures, prepare for medical events, and transform from passive sufferers to active agents in their care. Although therapeutic play is considered an effective psychosocial intervention for hospitalized children, little empirical evidence exists for its efficacy. The purpose of this study was to assess the effects of two different types of play and verbal support on the psychological adjustment of hospitalized children.

RESEARCH METHODS AND DESIGN

The subjects were sixty-one children, ages five to ten, who were admitted to the pediatric ward of a hospital. Children were admitted for a variety of illnesses requiring hospitalization for fewer than two weeks, including brief surgical intervention and treatment for acute, non-life-threatening, infectious diseases. Patients were stratified based on age, sex, and number of hospitalizations, then randomly assigned to one of four experimental groups. Within twenty-four hours of admission, children completed the Missouri Children's Picture Series, the Fear Thermometer, a human figure drawing, and a hospital drawing. Parent pretesting consisted of the Stress Inventory and the Zuckerman Adjective Checklist. Nurses also completed the Zuckerman Adjective Checklist. Post-testing was completed on every third day and the last day of hospitalization. A follow-up measure, the Vernon Post-Hospitalization Behavior Questionnaire, was completed by parents at one month postdischarge. Chi-square analyses were used to verify the effectiveness of the stratified random sampling. Change between pre- and posttreatment measures was analyzed for each outcome measure using analysis of variance, with age, sex, and treatment assignment as independent variables and the difference between each child's pre- and post-treatment values as the dependent variable.

INTERVENTION

Children were randomly assigned to one of four groups. The verbally oriented support condition consisted of a verbal discussion of children's concerns, anxieties, and fears within a supportive, nurturing, interpersonal relationship with the research assistant. The diversionary play condition provided that children were allowed to play with toys, but fantasy play was discouraged. Activities included board games, card games, and puzzles. The research assistant talked about superficial, non-hospital-related information. In the therapeutic play condition, children were involved in nondirective, child-centered play therapy that included reflection and interpretation of feelings. Children in the three treatment groups received two thirty-minute sessions, which were administered individually in the child's room without interruption. The control condition received no contact with the research assistant other than the pre- and post-assessment sessions.

RESULTS

The results revealed a significant reduction in children's self-reports of hospital fears following two thirty-minute sessions of nondirective, child-centered play therapy. A reduction in fears was not evidenced for diversionary play, verbally oriented information and support, or for the control group. Parent and nurse ratings of children's anxiety were not differentially affected by treatments. Parents in all four groups rated their children as less anxious from pre-testing to post-testing following treatment.

COMMENTARY

One of the goals of this study was to examine the differential effect of information giving, therapeutic play, and diversionary play. Many investigators have shown benefits from multimodal programs without documenting whether or not all the components are necessary. This study suggested that play therapy yields benefits not evidenced by alternative methods.

SOURCE

Rae, W., Worchel, F., Upchurch, J., Sanner, J., and Daniel, C. 1989. The psychosocial impact of play on hospitalized children. *Journal of Pediatric Psychology* 14: 617–27.

POSSIBLE DSM-IV-TR DIAGNOSES

293.89 Anxiety Disorder Due to a General Medical Condition
309.24 Adjustment Disorder with Anxiety

CHAPTER 14

Learning-Disabled Children

Children with learning disabilities may be found in almost any group of children, and such difficulties are not likely to exist in isolation. Children's problems must always be viewed from a global perspective. Although causality cannot always be established, we do know that such problems typically exist in an interrelated nature. Just as ripples travel the entirety of the pond, disturbances reverberate throughout the child's organism, especially impacting the emotional state of the child. This in turn exacerbates the identified learning difficulty, resulting in a vicious cycle. Published accounts in the literature indicate that play therapy is a viable approach for intervening in this cycle in a manner that frees the child to focus internal resources on correcting the problem. Play therapy, in fact, may be the only experience that allows these children to experience the emotional success that is necessary for them to begin the process of correcting identified problems. Success of any kind has usually been lacking in the lives of these children, and in the playroom, they can create their own success.

Play Therapy for Children with Learning Disabilities

Claire Lynn Fleet Siegel

FOCUS

Play therapy and parental counseling with learning-disabled children are studied.

INTRODUCTION

Serving learning-disabled children in the educational setting is an important and often difficult task. It includes finding ways to increase a child's cognitive, affective, psychomotor, and environmental dimensions. In this study, combinations of play therapy and parental counseling were found to significantly impact children's educational dimensions, as well as parents' attitudes and the parent-child relationship.

RESEARCH METHODS AND DESIGN

Forty-eight second- to fifth-grade children with learning disabilities participated in this yearlong study. The children were randomly placed in two educational settings: twenty-four children in a special class and twenty-four in regular classes with tutorials, forty minutes a day, five days a week. Twelve children in each class received therapeutic intervention and twelve served as the control group, with no treatment.

Pre- and post-tests were given to measure changes in the areas of cognitive, affective, psychomotor, and environmental dimensions. Three constructs derived from factorial analysis of the foregoing dimensions were also analyzed: (1) interaction between parent attitude and child achievement, (2) interaction between child and parent adjustment, and (3) interaction between psychomotor functioning and intelligence. The study ran for a full school year.

INTERVENTION

The treatment group in each class was divided into three groups of four children each. The first group received play therapy, the second group's parents received parental counseling, and the third group received play therapy with parental counseling. All of the parents agreed to a minimum of ten counseling sessions.

RESULTS

This yearlong study found that learning-disabled children who received therapeutic interventions significantly improved in all four dimensions: cognitive, affective, psychomotor, and environmental. The children also improved at a statistically significant level in the three constructs, which included the four dimensions identified above: (1) interaction between parent attitude and child achievement, environmental and cognitive (p = .001); (2) interaction between child and parent adjustment, affective and environmental (p = .001); (3) interaction between psychomotor functioning and intelligence, psychomotor and cognitive (p = .05). The children who received none of the therapeutic interventions actually had a decrease in post-testing scores in the psychomotor and cognitive areas, while those receiving therapeutic intervention had increased scores.

There was no significant difference in whether the children were in the special classroom of all learning-disabled children or in a regular classroom receiving additional tutoring.

COMMENTARY

It is apparent that learning-disabled children benefit greatly with the addition of therapeutic interventions to their classroom experiences, regardless of the type of classroom setting. One might expect play therapy and/or parental counseling to improve child-parent interactions, but the added growth and development in areas of cognitive and psychomotor skills is an exciting finding.

SOURCE

Siegel, C. L. F. 1970. The effectiveness of play therapy with other modalities in the treatment of children with learning disabilities. *Dissertation Abstracts International* 31 (08): A3970.

POSSIBLE DSM-IV-TR DIAGNOSIS

Insufficient information provided in this study.

Effectiveness of Self-Directive Play with Educationally Handicapped Children

Mary Jane Wall

FOCUS

The effect is studied of self-directive play therapy on the self-concepts of children who are labeled as educationally handicapped.

INTRODUCTION

Children who are labeled educationally handicapped often display feelings of anxiety, frustration, and social and personal maladjustment and suffer from inadequacies of self-worth as a result of their learning disability. It is reported that these problems can best be alleviated intrinsically in the warm, accepting environment afforded by a therapeutic play group. The purpose of this study was to investigate the use of therapeutic self-directive play as a means of developing positive self-concepts and motivation in educationally handicapped children. Further consideration was also given to behavioral changes as viewed by the classroom teacher and aide.

RESEARCH METHODS AND DESIGN

The population of the study consisted of forty-seven educationally handicapped children ranging in age from six to thirteen years. The Self-Concept Motivational Inventory (SCAMIN) was administered to the entire population. The teacher and aide of each of the self-contained classes rated each child on the Burks' Behavior Rating Scales. Each of the four educationally handicapped classes participating in this study had an experimental group and a control group. The control group consisted of twenty-three subjects, representing a developmental first grade, an educationally handicapped primary class, and two intermediate educationally handicapped classes. The experimental group consisted of twenty-four subjects, representing a developmental first grade, an educationally handicapped primary class, and two intermediate educationally handicapped classes. The subjects were assigned at random to an experimental group or a nontreatment control group. Differences among pretest and post-test, experimental group and control group, teacher evaluations and aide evaluations were all done by appropriate grouping of raw data and the use of the t test.

INTERVENTION

Children in the experimental group received twenty-four therapeutic self-directive play sessions, meeting twice weekly for thirty minutes over a twelve-week period. Therapeutic self-directive play is based upon the premises that play is a child's natural means of expression, and the child has an intrinsic ability for and striving toward the development of mature behavior. The child was provided a playroom in which an accepting atmosphere allowed the expression and exploration of feelings about self and world. Although the responsibility for decisions and the direction of growth rested with the child, the facilitator assisted the child by recognizing and accepting the child as an individual capable of this responsibility. The control group received no intervention.

RESULTS

Significant positive changes in self-concept and motivational attributes, as measured by the mean of the group, were found among the experimental groups in some of the self-contained classes. Motivation was significantly higher for those students in the experimental group than for those in the control group. No significant positive change was found for any control group. Significant positive behavioral changes were found to be predominant in the experimental groups of most classes as viewed by both teachers and aides. When the entire group was considered, significant positive behavioral change was found in coordination, receptiveness, and academic skills, as viewed by the teacher. Teachers saw no significant positive changes within the entire control group.

COMMENTARY

Therapeutic self-directive play was particularly pertinent to the areas of difficulty experienced by most children with learning disabilities (i.e., poor physical strength, poor coordination, poor intellectuality, and poor academics), which contribute to the slow rate of learning. Gains in the improvement of coordination, receptiveness, and academic skills were highly significant. Children in the experimental group assumed responsibility for themselves and their behavior, which allowed them to experiment with choices, develop interpersonal relationships, and examine and accept self. It was concluded that educationally handicapped children profit from experiencing therapeutic self-directive play.

SOURCE

Wall, M. 1973. The effectiveness of therapeutic self-directed play on self-concept of educationally handicapped children in a Saratoga, CA, elementary school. Ph.D. diss., Oregon State University. *Dissertation Abstracts International* 34: 2315.

POSSIBLE DSM-IV-TR DIAGNOSES

315.xx   Learning Disorder
317/319 Mental Retardation

315.xx/307.x   Communication Disorders
299.xx   Pervasive Developmental Disorders

Play Therapy with Labeled Children in the Schools

Lynette Johnson, Elizabeth McLeod, and Marijane Fall

FOCUS

Six sessions of play therapy with labeled children in the schools are found to facilitate expression of feelings effectively and increase children's skills in coping with the issues of their lives.

INTRODUCTION

School-age children whose biological makeup makes learning more challenging often get labeled for their behavioral problems. Directive strategies such as behavior modification and retraining have proven effective in changing labeled behaviors, but these strategies do not address the additional problems resulting from being a labeled child. Labeled children often struggle with communicating their thoughts and feelings and building peer relationships. Furthermore, their sense of control and beliefs about their abilities to cope effectively with the world are threatened by the labels they receive. The purpose of this study was to determine if six sessions of child-centered play therapy effectively addressed the secondary problems of labeled children in the schools.

RESEARCH METHODS AND DESIGN

Participants in this study were six male children, ages five to nine, from two rural elementary schools, all of whom had been labeled due to results from standardized tests or physician's diagnosis. Their labels included attention deficit/hyperactivity disorder (ADHD), mental disability, developmental delay, autism, cerebral palsy, and obsessive compulsive disorder. Six weekly, thirty-minute sessions of nondirective, child-centered play therapy were conducted with each child. The therapists were nonjudgmentally accepting and focused on reflecting actions, feelings, and meanings expressed by the children's play, setting limits when appropriate to keep the children safe.

The thirty-six sessions were transcribed and analyzed by the three re-searchers, and categories were created and agreed upon to describe the play. The two major agreed-upon categories were expression of feelings and expression of control. The expression of feelings category included instances of children expressing their feelings through direct verbalization and through play. The expression of control category included instances of children controlling the toys, the therapists, and themselves.

RESULTS

With one exception, all the subjects displayed both feelings and control though language and actions in the play therapy sessions. Over the course of the study, the children's skills in coping with the issues of their lives were observed to increase. For instance, one child's initial violent play decreased greatly though the six sessions. He also shifted from ordering the therapist to including her in his play. Initially, the therapist was usually made to be the victim in his play. Toward the end of therapy, the child began taking a more benevolent role, helping the therapist or enlisting her as a partner. The progression moved from needing to dominate to being comfortable sharing control.

Other children made progress to degrees that were significant for them. An autistic child shifted from initially walking over the therapist as if she were not present in the room, to walking around her, looking her in the eye, holding her hand, and engaging her in verbalizations. A child with cerebral palsy shifted from initially expressing only helplessness and desire for the therapist to do everything for him. At the end of therapy, the child was exerting control and independence over toys and objects.

Results of this study showed that nondirective, child-centered play therapy provided the labeled children with opportunities to express feelings, experience control, and develop coping skills. The researchers surmised that these positive changes occurred because of the nonjudgmental acceptance of the therapists during their play and the sense of control and mastery the children experienced through their play.

COMMENTARY

The authors found support for the effectiveness of nondirective, child-centered play therapy sessions in helping address secondary problems of children who are labeled in the schools. Results of the play therapy experience generalized to the classroom, and teachers reported improvement in the behaviors that had precipitated referral. In play therapy, labeled children can receive acceptance unrelated to competencies of any kind, therefore balancing out the demand for better performance.

SOURCE

Johnson, L., McLeod, E., and Fall, M. 1997. Play therapy with labeled children in the schools. *Professional School Counseling* 1: 31–4.

POSSIBLE DSM-IV-TR DIAGNOSES

314.xx   Attention-Deficit/Hyperactivity Disorder
317/319 Mental Retardation
315.xx   Learning Disorders
299.00   Autistic Disorder
300.3   Obsessive Compulsive Disorder
312.9   Disruptive Behavior Disorder NOS

CHAPTER 15

Mentally Challenged (Handicapped)

Mentally challenged children are first and foremost people. They happen to have limitations and challenges, as do all people, to which specific labels have been attached. Like other people, they experience intense emotions and feelings. Until very recently, treatment for mentally challenged children typically involved medication and behavioral-control methodologies with little or no attention paid to their emotional or mental-health needs. Estimates of the incidence of emotional problems in mentally challenged individuals range up to 50 percent, with depression, low self-esteem, anxiety, and socialization problems being the most common. Play therapy is especially appropriate for these children because it provides a medium of communication and expression uniquely suited to the mental and developmental needs of the child, and the focus is on treatment for emotional problems rather than the exclusive goal of behavioral change. Although play therapy was slow to become part of the therapeutic procedures used with mentally challenged children, a 1985 survey in the Netherlands found that it was used in approximately 40 percent of the residential centers for mentally challenged people.

Group Play Therapy with Mentally Challenged Children

Benjamin Mehlman

FOCUS

Group play therapy is used to facilitate the psychological adjustment of mentally challenged children.

INTRODUCTION

A review of the literature found few references to the use of group play therapy with mentally challenged children. The consensus of the time was that "mental deficiency" was beyond limited psychotherapeutic assistance. This study recognized the importance of the emotional lives of children who are mentally challenged.

RESEARCH METHODS AND DESIGN

The subjects for this study were thirty-two children from the Syracuse State School for the Mentally Retarded. The children's ages ranged from 86 to 140 months, with a mean age of 120.8 months; the length of residence in the institution ranged from four months to forty-eight months, with a mean length of residence of eighteen months. The order of birth ranged from first to ninth.

Three groups took part in the study: (1) group play therapy, (2) group inactive, and (3) group movie. The group inactive had no contact with the treatment other than the pre- and post-testing. The group movie, in which children were shown short movies or were read stories for the duration of the experiment, was designed as a control for the disturbance of the institutional routine and the personality of the therapist. The play therapy group participated in biweekly, nondirective play therapy group sessions. Each session was fifty minutes long, and a total of twenty-nine sessions were held over a sixteen-week period.

Pretesting was conducted during the six-week period prior to commencement of the play therapy group; post-testing was completed in the six-week period following completion of the treatment group. The following instruments were used: the Revised Stanford Binet (Form L), the Grace Arthur Point Scale of Performance Tests (Revised Form II), the Rorschach, the Haggerty-Olson-Wickman Behavior Rating Scale, and the California Test of Personality.

INTERVENTION

Mehlman described the group play therapy as nondirective, "along the lines described by Axline."[1] An attempt was made to have an observer present during each play session. This was administratively feasible for only eighteen of the twenty-nine sessions. The therapist completed reports of each session, which were compared with the notes taken by the observer.

---

1. Virginia Axline, *Play Therapy* (New York: Ballantine Books, 1969).

RESULTS

The play therapy group evidenced positive behavioral and personality changes as compared to the other groups on the Haggerty-Olson-Wickman and on the Rorschach. There were no statistically significant changes in intelligence measures.

COMMENTARY

Although the statistical significance of the outcome measures was limited, there appeared to be considerable qualitative benefit for the children who participated in group play therapy. Mehlman noted that a basic assumption in the study was that the mentally challenged child, despite intellectual limitations, can grow in play therapy because therapeutic benefit does not depend on intellectual ability. The benefits of the play therapy relationship and the resultant therapeutic progress, while observable on a qualitative level, did not show quantitative significance. Clearly, quality of life for the mentally challenged child extends beyond intelligence measures.

SOURCE

Mehlman, B. 1953. Group play therapy with mentally retarded children. *The Journal of Abnormal and Social Psychology* 48 (1): 53–60.

POSSIBLE DSM-IV-TR DIAGNOSIS

319.0   Mental Retardation, Severity Unspecified

The Effect of Play Therapy on IQ and Emotional and Social Development of Mentally Challenged Children

Lydia Mundy

FOCUS

Individual play therapy is used to alleviate emotional disturbance and increase measured intelligence with mentally challenged children.

INTRODUCTION

Mundy conducted her research on psychotherapy with mentally challenged children at a time in the field of psychology when psychotherapy was deemed inadvisable with this population. Mentally challenged children who were experiencing neurosis and behavioral disturbance were placed in nondirective play therapy to assess the impact on IQ and social adjustment.

RESEARCH METHODS AND DESIGN

The subjects for this study were twenty-three children from the Fountain Hospital in London, England. These children represented the total treatment population, with a comparably matched control group pre- and post-tested as well. The average age was 8.5 years for children in the treatment group and 8.0 years for the control group, with a range of 5 to 12 years in both groups. The average age at the time of first hospitalization was 4.5 years for the treatment group and 4.9 for the control group. The initial average IQ of the treatment group was 45 and for the control group, 44; the difference is statistically nonsignificant.

The assessment instrument utilized for pre- and post-testing was the Revised Stanford Binet (Form L). Qualitative assessment was conducted to measure social adjustment change.

INTERVENTION

Because of the regressed developmental condition of the children, play therapy was selected as the most appropriate medium for communication. The treatment intervention was described as nondirective play therapy "modified by an analytically oriented therapist." The play therapy was carried out over a period of nine to thirteen months, with post-testing conducted within six months. The members of the control group were tested on a similar timetable.

Case details on one child (Janet) were provided in the study because of the pronounced change in her presentation. Although there was no significant change in her intellectual functioning, the "alteration of her behavioral adjustment was so striking that her case seems worth quoting." Janet, who had been virtually nonfunctioning (unintelligible speech, frequent tantrums, poor reality contact) made remarkable progress as evidenced by increased reality contact, decreased obsessional behaviors, increased comprehension and initiative, and markedly improved speech.

RESULTS

The quantitative results indicated relevant differences between the treatment and control group in terms of IQ measurement. The mean IQ of the treatment group increased nine points in the post-testing versus two points for the control group. Mundy asserted that it could be "assumed with fair certainty that the significant alteration . . . was due to the treatment." In a qualitative assessment of social adjustment, the majority of children in the treatment group were considered ready and suitable for special academic programs for which they were previously deemed inappropriate. There were decreases in temper tantrums and uncooperative behavior, as well as increased social cooperation and constructive behavior. One compelling observation was the noteworthy development of verbal ability in a group that initially appeared mentally incapable of verbalizing.

COMMENTARY

Mundy suggested that the most important finding in her study was that children who are mentally challenged exhibit minimal resistance to psychotherapy. The quantitative and qualitative measures support the provision of play therapy interventions with this challenging population. Mundy posited that the benefits of play therapy had far-reaching benefits for these children, noting that the improved social behavior that resulted from the therapy correlated with a greater desire for communication, which in turn produced increased speech and verbalization. The play therapy relationship effectively impacts children regardless of their limitations; mentally challenged children are no exception.

SOURCE

Mundy, L. 1957. Therapy with physically and mentally handicapped children in a mental deficiency hospital. *Journal of Clinical Psychology* 13-14, 3–9.

POSSIBLE DSM-IV-TR DIAGNOSIS

318.0   Moderate Mental Retardation

Play Therapy with Mentally Challenged Institutionalized Children

Barbara L. Newcomer and Thomas L. Morrison

FOCUS

Individual versus group play therapy and directive versus nondirective play therapy with institutionalized children who were mentally challenged are studied.

INTRODUCTION

Play therapy interventions were used with institutionalized children who were mentally challenged to assess the impact on social and intellectual functioning.

RESEARCH METHODS AND DESIGN

The subjects for this research were twelve children who were mildly and moderately mentally challenged and were institutionalized at a state facility. Their ages ranged from 5.1 to 11.75 years, with a mean age of 8 years. The children were randomly assigned to treatment groups, with four children receiving individual play therapy, four receiving group play therapy, and four forming a no-treatment control group.

The assessment instrument used was the Denver Developmental Screening Test, designed to measure subjects' developmental level. The test categories were (1) gross motor, (2) fine motor-adaptive, (3) language, and (4) personal-social.

INTERVENTION

The children assigned to group or individual play therapy received ten sessions of directive play therapy over a six-week period. Following this, they received ten sessions of nondirective play therapy over a six-week period. They then received ten more sessions of directive play therapy over the next six-week period. Control group members received no treatment. All children were evaluated with the Denver Developmental Screening Test before the commencement of treatment and after each six-week period.

During directive therapy the therapist assumed responsibility for the guidance of the play. In the nondirective therapy, the therapist left the responsibility and direction to the child. The same play materials were used in all treatment groups, and the same activities were introduced in the individual and group directive play experiences.

RESULTS

The mean scores of the children in the play therapy groups increased continuously over the thirty sessions (eighteen weeks) of therapy. The initial hypothesis that the play therapy intervention given to the children would have a beneficial effect on social and intellectual functioning was confirmed by analysis of variance of the data. The mean scores of the control group remained unchanged. Additional hypotheses regarding different results according to individual versus group play therapy and directive versus nondirective play therapy did not produce statistically significant results. Qualitative observations of the children involved also supported the quantitative results. The authors suggested in their qualitative analysis that directive play therapy seemed more beneficial than the nondirective approach.

COMMENTARY

Newcomer and Morrison suggested that a major benefit of the play therapy intervention was its unique response to the inherent social deprivation that occurs with institutionalization. The children involved in the treatment quickly became attached to the therapist and to the playroom. The authors additionally suggested that the play therapy intervention led to increased motivation on the part of the children involved in the treatment. These two elements may be significant factors in the measured increase in developmental level for the treatment subjects. The authors also posited that directive play therapy was perhaps more appropriate for this population because of the inherent disorganization of children who are mentally challenged. Although this was not shown to be significant in the quantitative results of the study, the more important issue appears to be the clear benefit of the play experience for an often disenfranchised population of children.

SOURCE

Newcomer, B. L., and Morrison, T. L. 1974. Play therapy with institutionalized mentally retarded children. *American Journal of Mental Deficiency* 78 (6): 727–33.

POSSIBLE DSM-IV-TR DIAGNOSIS

317/319   Mild Mental Retardation

Effects of Directive Versus Nondirective Play Therapy with Mentally Retarded Children

Thomas Morrison and Barbara Newcomer

FOCUS

The effects are studied of providing mentally retarded children with play therapy opportunities on increasing their language and motor skills, as well as their social skills.

INTRODUCTION

Play has been shown to increase the child's ability to learn, communicate, and experience. Children develop not only social skills but also language and motor skills through play. Mentally retarded children are typically deficit in these skills. Researchers hypothesized that play therapy would be beneficial for mentally retarded children in these skill areas. Researchers questioned whether directive play therapy or nondirective play therapy would produce greater gains in skills.

RESEARCH METHODS AND DESIGN

Fourteen children, residents of a large state training school for retarded people, were selected to participate in the study based on the following criteria: being less than eleven years of age, mildly or moderately retarded, and not involved in another treatment program. The children were randomly assigned to receive directive play therapy (5), nondirective play therapy (5), or no treatment (4). The Denver Developmental Screening Test was used to measure developmental level, including gross motor, fine motor-adaptive, language, and personal-social skills. The test was administered prior to treatment and within two days following treatment. Data was analyzed using repeated measures analyses of variance. Where interaction effects were found, the data was further analyzed by subsequent analyses of variance comparing two groups at a time.

INTERVENTION

Therapists were twelve student nurses trained briefly in play therapy and receiving supervision on working with mentally retarded children. Each therapist saw one child for eleven forty-five-minute treatment sessions spaced over three weeks. Six therapists each were randomly assigned to take a directive approach, and the other six were assigned to take a nondirective approach. In directive therapy, the therapist guided the play, initiating activities with predetermined materials. In nondirective therapy, the therapists left all choices about activities up to the child. The same materials in playrooms were provided for both approaches. The no-treatment group received no play sessions.

RESULTS

For the fine motor-adaptive and personal-social scales, there were significant interaction effects that could be attributed to greater gains by the treatment groups compared to the control group. The source of the interaction effect for the fine motor-adaptive scale was the relatively greater gain in the directive group, which also had the lower fine motor-adaptive score before treatment. Thus, the interaction effect represented the directive group catching up to the other two groups rather than surpassing them. The source of the interaction effect for the personal-social scale was the gain in both directive and nondirective groups compared to a decrease in the control group.

COMMENTARY

The results of this study give support to the hypothesis that play therapy is effective in increasing the developmental level of institutionalized mentally retarded children. There was no evidence that the directive therapy condition was more effective than the nondirective condition.

SOURCE

Morrison, T., and Newcomer, B. 1975. Effects of directive vs. nondirective play therapy with institutionalized mentally retarded children. *American Journal of Mental Deficiency* 79: 666–69.

POSSIBLE DSM-IV-TR DIAGNOSIS

317/319   Mental Retardation

CHAPTER 16

Reading Difficulties

Although the exact nature of the association between reading difficulties and emotional difficulties has not been established, the literature supports the hypothesis that a definite relationship exists. There is consensus that reading problems often stem from emotional maladjustment that has been contributed to by unmet needs. Historically, studies have shown that personality maladjustment frequently coexists with reading difficulties. Our society places such importance on reading achievement that failure in this area often has a negative impact on a child's self-concept. The feelings of frustration, failure, and discouragement that accompany reading difficulties may lead to emotional conflicts, and repeated failure in reading may contribute to making children regard themselves as failures. It is no wonder, therefore, that in such circumstances, children feel helpless, hopeless, worthless, impotent, powerless, and unable to change their situation and, thus, develop an external rather than internal locus of control. As demonstrated in the studies in this chapter, the unique nature of the play therapy relationship allows children to act out their feelings of frustration, anger, and powerlessness and returns control to children, thus building up their self-concept and empowering them, all of which are necessary in the development of an internal locus of control.

Teacher Use of Play Therapy Procedures for Poor Readers

Virginia Axline

FOCUS

A teacher uses play therapy procedures in the classroom to facilitate children's reading readiness.

INTRODUCTION

Children often have the capacity to learn but may not participate easily in the reading process. This lack of reading readiness is based on many factors, including the skill to translate printed symbols into meaningful words, social and emotional maturity, and life experiences that develop a verbal vocabulary. Teachers may be able to use play therapy procedures to alleviate such problems.

RESEARCH METHODS AND DESIGN

The thirty-seven children selected to participate in this study were initially identified by teachers, who were asked to refer seriously maladjusted readers in their classrooms. All those so identified were given the Gray Oral Reading Test and Gray Primary Reading Test. The thirty-seven who received the lowest scores were selected and placed in the same classroom. Their IQs ranged from 80 to 148. There were eight girls and twenty-nine boys. Four children had serious vision problems. Five were African American, and thirty-two were Anglo American.

The children's behavior was recorded in several ways. Trained observers recorded the behavior in the classroom weekly. The classroom teacher also kept notes on one-to-one interactions. On the basis of the teacher's interactions, it was discovered that most of the children had serious emotional problems: parental divorce, absence of a parent due to military service (war), verbal and/or physical abuse at home, abandonment by a parent, a seriously ill parent, a murdered parent, and so on. This personal information was not initially known and, therefore, not the basis for a child's being selected for this study. However, the researchers later identified emotional difficulties as key to the lack of reading readiness.

The classroom environment was set up to encourage personal expressiveness. The children were encouraged to interact with the teacher on a one-to-one basis. The teacher responded with child-centered therapeutic responses that included focusing on the child, validating feelings, and respecting the child and the child's world. A variety of media for self-expression was made available in the classroom, including toys, puppets, musical instruments, and art materials. Puppet shows and dramatic play were encouraged. The goal was to assist the children not only to express self but to problem-solve, think through a situation, and clarify their perceptions.

In reading groups, the children listened to stories, read stories, and told their own stories. None of them were required to come, but once they realized that reading groups were in fact an option, they came, ready and willing to participate.

Four children received thirty-minute individual play therapy sessions once a week for eight weeks. None of the children received any special remediation in the area of reading or any other intervention.

At the end of four months, all the children were given the same reading tests and IQ test.

RESULTS

One child dropped out of the study, leaving thirty-six children. The children's reading skills were subdivided into words, sentences, and paragraphs. In the area of words, twenty-one of the children improved beyond the typical growth expected. Their scores ranged from four months' to sixteen months' improvement. In the area of sentences, twenty students improved, ranging from four-and-a-half months to fifteen months. Twenty-two students improved over the expected level with reference to paragraphs; their scores ranged from four-and-a-half months to seventeen months. Only six children showed below-expected gains across all three reading skill areas.

In the area of IQ, four children increased their scores by eighteen, twenty-four, thirty-two, and thirty-six points. Three of the four had received the individual play therapy sessions.

The fourth child who had received individual play therapy sessions had an initial IQ score of 126 and did not show any dramatic increase; her reading scores, however, increased by twelve months in words and sentences and seventeen months in paragraphs.

COMMENTARY

It appears from this study that children can make advances in the areas of reading when provided with a classroom atmosphere in which the teacher is able to respond in a therapeutic manner, and the child's self-expression is honored and encouraged. The addition of only eight thirty-minute play therapy sessions resulted in even more dramatic changes for all four children who participated. As Axline commented in this study, there may be a significant emotional factor involved in the lives of children who experience difficulties in reading. However, the emotional factor may not be easily identified, thus not treated.

SOURCE

Axline, V. 1947. Nondirective therapy for poor readers. *Journal of Consulting Psychology* 11:61–9.

POSSIBLE DSM-IV-TR DIAGNOSES

315.00 Reading Disorder
Other diagnoses varied by child:
995.5   Physical Abuse of Child
V61.20 Parent-Child Relational Problem
300.02 Generalized Anxiety Disorder
309.00 Adjustment Disorder
309.21 Separation Anxiety Disorder

Brief Client-Centered Play Therapy to Increase Reading Skills

Robert E. Bills

FOCUS

Child-centered play therapy is used to improve reading skills in school-age children who are experiencing learning difficulties, especially in reading.

INTRODUCTION

Bills studied third graders who had been identified as slow learners and who had delayed reading development. Child-centered play therapy was used to remediate the problem based on the belief that poor reading resulted from an inconsistent attitude on the part of a child and a conflict between the child's viewing him- or herself as a good or poor reader.

RESEARCH METHODS AND DESIGN

A class of third graders, all identified as slow learners, was selected for this study. The slow learner designation was based on a child's inability to learn at an age-typical speed. None of the children had been placed in this special classroom because of emotional difficulties or limited intellectual factors. All twenty-two children in the selected class began the study; four dropped out for various reasons, leaving eighteen children from whom data were collected and analyzed. Eight children in the treatment group were selected based on intelligence quotient: four had very high intelligence (IQ 111–159), and four had average intelligence (IQ 99–111). The ten children who received no treatment formed a comparison group.

The study was designed to have three time periods: a control baseline phase, the treatment phase, and the posttreatment phase to assess any lasting effects of the treatment. Each phase consisted of thirty school days. The first phase allowed the children to serve as their own control group and established a baseline for their reading skills. At the beginning and end of this period all the children were given oral and silent reading tests. In the second phase, the eight selected children received one individual, client-centered play therapy session each week. A weekly client-centered group play therapy session was added during the last three weeks of this stage. At the end of the third stage, all the children received the oral and silent reading tests. No special intervention was given during this last stage.

RESULTS

The six individual and three group client-centered play therapy sessions resulted in statistically significant gains in reading by the children in the treatment group. All of the eight children in the treatment group increased their reading skills at the end of the second stage as compared to their scores at the end of the first phase. Taken as a group, the change was statistically significant at the .001 level of probability. The children's reading skills continued to grow during the third and final stage, although no further intervention was given. The group's gain during the third and final stage was statistically significant at the .01 level of probability.

The author indicated that the children were either learning at a more rapid pace because of the play therapy, or more likely, the play therapy allowed the children to maximize the information they already had but previously had been unable to use effectively.

COMMENTARY

One of the most exciting findings of this study was that statistically significant change occurred after only six individual play therapy sessions and three group play therapy sessions. Also, although these children were not selected on the basis of any emotional maladjustment, six of the eight also showed improvement in personal areas. These findings demonstrate the effectiveness of play therapy in facilitating change in the total child.

SOURCE

Bills, R. E. 1950. Nondirective play therapy with retarded readers. *Journal of Consulting Psychology* 14:140–49.

POSSIBLE DSM-IV-TR DIAGNOSIS

315.00   Reading Disorder

Play Therapy as an Intervention for a Reading Problem

Ray H. Bixler

FOCUS

Play therapy is used with a ten-year-old boy with poor reading performance and behavioral problems.

INTRODUCTION

William was initially referred for counseling because he was underachieving in school, specifically reading, and was at risk of failing the third grade. An IQ test indicated average intelligence, and an achievement test revealed he was working about one year behind his grade placement. His mother reported behavioral problems in the home, which included two brothers, one a year older and one aged three-and-a-half. His father was also in the home, and both parents were employed.

CASE STUDY

William began play therapy with a counselor with whom he developed a deep therapeutic relationship. After twenty sessions, his first counselor left, and a second counselor provided William's last eight play therapy sessions. Nondirective play therapy was used, with an emphasis on limit setting. William's mother was inconsistent in bringing him to his sessions, which often meant that several weeks elapsed between sessions, and she prematurely terminated treatment. During the play therapy intervention, it became apparent that William was having problems with sibling rivalry, which in turn led to scholastic problems.

During the first twenty sessions, William often talked about problems at school. He stated that his school was "one of the rottenest" and that he hated the school. William also expressed his wish to be able to read better. In the eighth session, he reported that his younger brother had broken his sailboat. In the ninth session, his interaction referred to both brothers. In his final two to three sessions with his first therapist, William struggled to work through the termination of that relationship. He threatened to lock up the therapist so he could not leave and to shoot pins at the new therapist.

In the first session with the new therapist, William expressed his disappointment with having to establish a new relationship. During this process, William tested the limits to see just what the new therapist would allow him to do and to identify the differences between the therapists. In the second session with the new therapist, a great deal of aggressive play occurred, during which William communicated that he did not like it when things did not go his way. William also expressed, through play, that even though he was taking the role of the "bad guy," he would rather be the "good guy." This conflict between good and bad continued for several sessions.

William continued to express aggression during work with the new therapist. The therapist continued to set firm, appropriate limits. The ongoing theme appeared to be focused around how much destructive behavior the therapist would tolerate and still accept William, particularly when the aggression was aimed at the baby dolls. When the therapist correctly reflected back William's feelings, William ceased being destructive and engaged in constructive play. When the therapist missed the feeling, however, or became too interpretive, William's aggressive and/or destructive play escalated.

William's mother terminated play therapy when his behavior problems cleared up at home and he began passing subjects at school. William, who had correctly spelled words in several of his sessions, brought his spelling list into his final session and misspelled all of them. This seemed to be a clear expression that he did not feel ready to terminate.

COMMENTARY

Bixler used this case example to identify the importance of treating the child and not the presenting problem or diagnosis. Bixler stated that nondirective play therapy results in a speedier resolution to children's problems in that children are allowed to deal with what is of importance to them. As in William's case, if intervention had focused on the reading problems through tutoring, the real cause of his problems would never have been addressed.

Bixler also detailed excerpts from the new therapist's sessions. Each session is followed by Bixler's assessment of the therapist's responses, identifying strong, appropriate responses, and contrasting those that were off target with examples of better responses. This format is of additional help to the play therapist as it facilitates understanding of where one might easily go astray in a session.

SOURCE

Bixler, R. H. 1945. Treatment of a reading problem through nondirective play therapy. *Journal of Consulting Psychology* 9:105–18.

POSSIBLE DSM-IV-TR DIAGNOSES

315.00   Reading Disorder
V61.8   Sibling Relational Problem

Nondirective Play Therapy with Low Achievers in Reading

Elizabeth Hoyser

FOCUS

The effectiveness is studied of nondirective play therapy with boys who are low achievers in reading.

INTRODUCTION

The purpose of this study was to investigate the effectiveness of therapeutic nondirective play treatment with third-grade boys who were low achievers in reading and to determine how treatment was associated with changes in reading achievement: vocabulary and comprehension; reading attitude and academic self-concept; role expectations and self-adequacy.

RESEARCH METHODS AND DESIGN

Subjects were chosen according to results from the Gates-MacGinitie Reading Test. Subjects whose reading comprehension age was one year and four months below mental age were designated as being underachievers in reading. Fifty-two boys who met the criteria were then administered pretests and post-tests on reading attitude (Primary Pupil Reading Attitude Inventory) and academic self-concept (Self-Concept and Motivation Inventory). The boys were then post-tested using the Gates-MacGinitie. The specific areas compared were reading achievement, reading attitude, and self-concept. Analysis of variance, one-way classification was applied to the pretest, post-test, and post-test/pretest group differences in order to determine if there were significant findings. Significance was determined at the .05 level.

INTERVENTION

The subjects were placed in four groups: therapeutic nondirective play and reading, therapeutic nondirective play only, reading only, or nonintervention control. The treatment groups met for twenty-seven sessions, and each session was thirty minutes long. The control group had only the pre- and post-testing.

RESULTS

The analysis of data revealed that the therapeutic nondirective play and reading group demonstrated greater significant gains (.05 and .01) in role expectations, an element of self-concept, and in total self-concept than the play-only, reading-only, or control groups. The play-only group produced more significant results (.01) in the measures of total self-concept than the reading-only or control groups. There were no significant differences among groups in reading achievement or reading attitude.

COMMENTARY

Play therapy appeared to positively impact the self-concept of low achievers in reading. This study supports other play therapy research that the intervention of play therapy is effective in increasing the self-concept of children. Although reading achievement was not improved, the increase in self-concept can be related to more positive academic experiences for those children experiencing difficulties in school.

SOURCE

Hoyser, E. 1971. Therapeutic non-directive play with low achievers in reading. Ph.D. diss., Oregon State University. *Dissertation Abstracts International* 71: 5426.

POSSIBLE DSM-IV-TR DIAGNOSIS

315.00   Reading Disorder

CHAPTER 17
Selective Mutism

Selective mutism, in which children remain silent in certain situations, is a relatively rare childhood disorder; some researchers estimate seven cases per thousand children. The 1994 DSM-IV changed the name of this disorder from elective mutism (DSM-III-R), which the committee felt was less descriptive and implied motivation, to selective mutism. The terms are used interchangeably in this chapter since the majority of articles in the literature refer to elective mutism. This condition is most frequently observed when the child talks at home but not at school, although there have been some cases in which the reverse is true. We are familiar with primary-grade children who will not talk in the classroom or read aloud in the reading circle but read at an advanced level at home. This can be an exasperating situation for the teacher who must give a grade for reading.

Children who are selectively mute tend to be oppositional, defiant, controlling, moody, aggressive, stubborn, sulky, strong willed, and distrustful and to have temper tantrums. They can also be submissive, sensitive, weepy, insecure, frightened, passive, anxious, fearful, and dependent. Play therapy is the recommended treatment of choice for children who are selectively mute because there is no pressure or expectation to verbalize. Play allows them to safely express feelings about the self they feel is unacceptable. The play therapist's acceptance of these feelings allows the children to experience themselves in a more positive way. As these children are able to accept themselves, they can relinquish the silence that has defended their sense of self.

Nondirective Play Therapy with an Elective Mute Child

Virginia M. Axline

FOCUS

Nondirective play therapy is used with a five-year-old boy with elective mutism and undersocialized behaviors.

INTRODUCTION

Billy was referred for play therapy because of the threat of expulsion from kindergarten. Billy would not interact with other children and would not speak to anyone. He crawled around the room close to the wall and, when approached by another child, rolled up into a ball and hid his face. He would not participate in any school activities and would not listen to stories. Billy had not been like this when he entered kindergarten six months earlier, however.

CASE STUDY

Billy's mother reported that his development appeared to be healthy until the age of three, when he suddenly stopped talking, stopped walking, and regressed to a completely infantile stage. This change in behavior followed the mother's (recent) hospitalization for emergency surgery. She took Billy to a physician, who diagnosed him as "feebleminded." She reported that Billy's brother was "feebleminded" (mentally retarded) and that she was fearful that Billy might also be. He was physically in good health but had received a psychometrist's report of an IQ score of 68.

INTERVENTION

Billy entered the playroom with a blank stare, drooping figure, and shuffling gait. He went to the middle of the room and stared and was told by the therapist that he could play with any of the toys if he wanted to. After standing for a long time, Billy played by sifting his hands in the sandbox for the entire session. He seemed more alert in the second session, playing again in the sand and occasionally looking silently at the therapist. During the third session, he played with cars in the sand and made a few comments to the therapist, who replied each time Billy spoke. When Billy came in for his fourth session, there was a significant change in his behavior. He did not drag his feet, he was more alert, and he talked with the therapist. Billy's mother reported a noticeable change at home, with Billy talking more, appearing less tense, and the regressive behavior disappearing. During the fifth week, the school called home to inquire about what was happening with Billy, as his behavior at school was also changing positively.

RESULTS

Billy continued to improve during the ensuing weeks of play therapy. He talked more with the therapist, and his play became more complex and imaginative and his demeanor more positive and free. The mother reported more assertive behavior at home and a greater willingness to venture out into the neighborhood. There were still some difficulties at school, however, where Billy had been labeled by the teachers and ostracized by the other students. The therapy was concluded with a series of group play therapy sessions that significantly reduced the social difficulties at school. One year after termination, the mother reported that Billy had adjusted excellently to a new school situation, was doing well academically (a new IQ score put him well within the average range), and was a "happy, relaxed child."

COMMENTARY

Axline postulated that a child behaves as he perceives himself in relation to others and that a child's behavior is dependent upon the current feeling of adequacy or inadequacy in coping with the particular circumstances. She believed that Billy's play therapy provided a freeing experience from the "chains of past experiences" and gave him a safe place in which to operate. It was in this environment that Billy was able to process his issues and express himself fully. The changes that occurred for Billy in the playroom naturally translated outside into his life at home and school. The safety and the relationship that Virginia Axline's approach offered Billy are conditions that the elective mute child seems to need in order to find the freedom so desired.

SOURCE

Axline, V. M. 1948. Some observations on play therapy. *Journal of Consulting Psychology* 12: 209–16.

POSSIBLE DSM-IV-TR DIAGNOSES

313.23   Selective Mutism
300.23   Social Phobia, Generalized
317.0   Mild Mental Retardation

Individual and Sibling Group Play Therapy with a Selective Mute Child

Karen Barlow, JoAnna Strother, and Garry Landreth

FOCUS

Individual and sibling group play therapy is used to treat selective mutism and enuresis in a five-year-old girl.

INTRODUCTION

Amy refused to talk at school or in any situation away from the home and exhibited excessive shyness, enuresis, and nighttime bedwetting. Amy's two brothers had also suffered from nighttime bedwetting. Previous research has shown high incidents of enuresis, excessive shyness, and immaturity among selective mute children.

CASE STUDY

Amy did not speak a single word during the first five months she was enrolled in the early childhood program at her school. She passed all the nonverbal items at the appropriate age level on an early childhood screening test and was put in a special education class. Amy's teachers observed her to be a passive little girl who sat and observed activity around her. Her social skills were virtually nonexistent. She did not play with groups of children but preferred to play alone or with an adult. An unusual behavior was that Amy did not show pain, even in extreme situations such as having her pierced earrings pulled through her ears while playing or when she fell in the gymnasium at school, which caused her mouth to bleed.

INTERVENTION

Amy was seen in a combination of individual and sibling group play therapy once a week for nine months. During the initial session in play therapy, she was totally nonverbal. She hid under the paint easel and gestured for forty-five minutes. In the second session, Amy refused to enter the playroom without a friend who had accompanied her to the center. In this session, Amy chatted and played contentedly with the friend. In later sessions, Amy's friend was not available, and it was decided to add Ben, her nine-year-old brother, and Ned, her two-year-old brother, to the sessions individually at different times. When Ben was in the playroom, he was the responsible one—for himself and for Amy. Ben talked and played for both of them. When Amy played in the playroom with Ned, she was the teacher and helper, although Ned was independent. When Amy played alone in the playroom, she remained shy, yet verbal. A combination of sibling play therapy, individual play therapy, and brief family consultation was found to be the most appropriate approach.

A theme that continued for most of the play sessions was Amy's need to be in total control, and she used silence to accomplish this by demanding that the play therapist be silent. As Amy became more independent, Ben dropped his role as protector and responsible member of the family. Amy's new confidence extended into the home and classroom as she began to express feelings more frequently and as talking, singing, and participating in class became fun for her. As Amy became more verbal and participated more actively in her world, the enuresis occurred less frequently.

COMMENTARY

Because elective mute children have a purpose for their behavior, verbal prodding by adults usually reaps few benefits. Play therapy provides the child with a safe place where there is no pressure to talk. The authors conclude that lack of verbal communication skills and underdeveloped social skills were paralyzing Amy's efforts to function in society beyond her immediate family. Individual play therapy in this case seemed to bring faster results because the issues could be defined immediately, and work in sessions and at home could begin on the shift in the communication pattern. The sibling group play therapy sessions provided an intimate environment in which Amy could interact safely.

SOURCE

Barlow, K., Strother, J., and Landreth, G. 1986. Sibling group play therapy: an effective alternative with an elective mute child. *The School Counselor* 34 (1): 44–50.

POSSIBLE DSM-IV-TR DIAGNOSES

317.23   Selective Mutism
307.6   Enuresis

Psychoanalytic Play Therapy with an Elective Mute Child

Morton Chetnik

FOCUS

Intensive treatment of a six-year-old girl with elective mutism, using play techniques, is studied.

INTRODUCTION

Amy was referred for treatment for elective mutism, together with noncompliance, multiple fears, and other parental concerns. The two years of Amy's psychoanalytic treatment included play therapy, doll play, and art and clay work.

CASE STUDY

Amy was reported to have had a "talking problem" all her life. In kindergarten, she had not spoken to her teachers or peers for the entire year. At home, she whispered occasionally with her parents or siblings and never to anyone else. Amy was generally described as stubborn, passive, and withdrawing and was considerably noncompliant at home. She also had a number of fears, including a strong fear of dogs, bedtime fears, and a fear of being alone. Amy experienced occasional enuresis and soiling at times of increased anxiety. Her parents expressed concern about Amy's vivid fantasy life, which would sometimes be intense and aggressive.

Amy was from a large family, the fifth of six children. She became hostile and aggressive toward her younger sibling at birth, and the infant had to be protected from her. At age three, Amy fell into a pool and had to be resuscitated after several minutes of unconsciousness. A resulting lung infection resulted in six weeks of hospitalization. She never spoke while hospitalized, and her eating and verbalization remained restrictive until the time of referral.

INTERVENTION

Treatment consisted of two years of intensive psychoanalytic play therapy. Amy was "totally silent" throughout the treatment process, although Chetnik reported many forms of "vivid communication" during the sessions. These included drawing, writing, intense play, body gestures, and, finally, sounds.

In the first few weeks of the therapy, Amy would play in a corner of the room in a "compulsive" manner, primarily focused on using the clay. During this early play, she was very distressed about messiness. Eventually, she moved to the doll family, where the play consisted of separations of family members and loving reunions. Amy also played out several pediatric visits. Another theme during these early months of treatment was role-playing animals and play with the scissors. Interpretive comments by the therapist during this play resulted in Amy's becoming increasingly anxious and regressive in her play.

Chetnik also worked with the parents during the course of treatment and reported that Amy's mother in particular had considerable negative emotions about her daughter's situation. A pattern of lateness and unpaid sessions became an issue during this process.

Chetnik reported markedly improved adjustment for Amy during the second year of treatment. He described Amy's "control" of the process, using examples of how Amy would sing on her way to the playroom but refuse to verbalize once in the room. She began to talk in most settings but not in the playroom. During this second year, her speech difficulties decreased and disappeared outside treatment. Amy began to participate in the classroom, made friends with several of her classmates, began to talk with neighbors, and greatly enjoyed talking on the phone. Chetnik also reported that Amy's relationship with her mother had shown remarkable improvement.

COMMENTARY

Play therapy provides a child with an opportunity to be in control, regardless of the specific therapeutic approach. Amy was able to process her need for power and control in the play sessions, which resulted in the amelioration of her presenting symptoms. She "communicated" in a variety of ways during the treatment process, which led to increased communication outside therapy. Chetnik concluded his report of the process with a discussion of psychoanalytic issues in the play, as well as diagnostic and prognostic concerns. Chetnik was able to keep in touch with the family and noted that Amy remained stable throughout her latency years. The psychoanalytic play experience was clearly beneficial for Amy, resulting not only in symptom reduction but also in the opportunity to gain mastery and control in the play and in her life.

SOURCE

Chetnik, M. 1973. The intensive treatment of an elective mute. *Journal of the American Academy of Child Psychiatry* 12 (3): 482–98.

POSSIBLE DSM-IV-TR DIAGNOSES

313.23   Selective Mutism
309.21   Separation Anxiety Disorder
313.81   Oppositional Defiant Disorder

CHAPTER 18

Self-Concept and Self-Esteem

The terms self-concept and self-esteem are often used synonymously and are therefore combined in this chapter. Self-concept is the internal measure of one's worth. The individual forms a sense of self based on external experiences and internal perceptions. Self-concept may be defined as the perceptions individuals hold about themselves or as a set of beliefs about the self—the evaluation a person usually maintains about self that suggests the degree to which an individual sees himself or herself to be capable, acceptable, successful, and important. Play is a key factor in a child's development, learning, and self-concept. Research studies have demonstrated a significantly positive correlation between self-concept and parental acceptance, academic achievement, classroom adjustment, perception of others, sociometric choice status, emotional adjustment, and overall personal adjustment. Children express their thoughts and feelings primarily through play. Play also allows a child to practice activities and to master skills. The play therapy relationship provides the necessary freedom for introspection and development of an inner life that are the prerequisites for a positive self-concept. In this relationship, in which responsibility is returned to the child, the child can begin to gain mastery over the environment and the self.

Play Therapy Increases the Self-Concept of Poor Readers

Judy Crow

FOCUS

Children who are poor readers often have low self-esteem. In this research study, play therapy is used to increase the self-esteem of poor readers.

INTRODUCTION

School-based play therapy sessions were provided for children identified as poor readers who had been held back in first grade. Because of the school schedule, slight modifications to the usual forty-five- to fifty-minute session were necessary.

RESEARCH METHODS AND DESIGN

The children for this study were initially identified as children who had been retained in the first grade and had the lowest scores on the Gates-MacGinitie Reading Test or the Stanford Reading Achievement Test. Children from two schools participated in the study; students in one school were the experimental group, and the students in the second school were the control group. All the children completed a battery of instruments before and after treatment. The instruments used to collect data were the Gates-MacGinitie Reading Test, the Piers-Harris Children's Self-Concept Scale (CSCS), and the Intellectual Achievement Responsibility Questionnaire.

INTERVENTION

For the ten weeks following the collection of the predata, the twelve children in the experimental group received one thirty-minute play therapy session each week. The author was the play therapist. She had been trained specifically in play therapy in the graduate program at the University of North Texas. She also had one year of supervised clinical experience in play therapy.

After the ten sessions of play therapy ended, the same instruments used to collect the predata were administered again. One child in each group, experimental and control, had moved, leaving eleven in each group. The resulting data were statistically analyzed using the analysis of covariance (ANCOVA) to take into account any initial differences between the two groups. (ANCOVA is also sensitive to any differences among group members.)

RESULTS

The children who received play therapy improved in their self-concept as measured by the Piers-Harris CSCS. The increase in self-concept was statistically significant at the .0435 level. The Intellectual Achievement Responsibility Questionnaire was used to measure the locus of control. The children involved in play therapy improved their internal locus of control; the children in the control group did not. All twenty-two children made gains in their reading ability as assessed by the Gates-MacGinitie Reading Test. There was no noticeable difference in the gains made between the children in the experimental or control groups.

The play therapist also identified changes in specific children over the course of the sessions. Several displayed play therapy behaviors that indicated an increase in attention span and the ability to focus. Another child, who never spoke during initial sessions, displayed greater self-confidence and frequently spoke in more complex sentences. A child who allowed her twin sister to initiate social and academic interactions developed her own sense of control and assertion skills during play therapy. A very aggressive boy, often identified as out of control, exhibited substantial aggression in the initial play therapy sessions. As his sessions continued, he developed self-control as evidenced in his development of more appropriately timed speech patterns.

COMMENTARY

School-based play therapy has been found very effective for children in need of improvement in self-concept and a wide variety of other problems and concerns. It is encouraging that thirty-minute sessions appear to be effective interventions. These shorter sessions fit more easily into the school schedule and allow the school counselor to serve more children. The shorter sessions also indicate to play therapists in a nonschool setting that significant therapeutic responses can occur.

SOURCE

Crow, J. 1990. Play therapy with low achievers in reading. Ph.D. diss., University of North Texas, 1989. *Dissertation Abstracts International* 50 (09): B2789.

POSSIBLE DSM-IV-TR DIAGNOSIS

315.00   Reading Disorder

Activity Play Therapy to Increase Elementary Students' Self-Concept

Myrna Frank Gould

FOCUS

Group play therapy is used to improve the self-concept of elementary school students.

INTRODUCTION

Research was conducted within a school system to discover the feasibility and effectiveness of providing group play therapy and discussion group experiences for children within that environment.

RESEARCH METHODS AND DESIGN

The Piers-Harris Children's Self-Concept Scale (CSCS) was administered to eighty-four elementary school children identified by teachers as having low self-image although not suffering from significant maladjustment. The children were then randomly assigned to experimental, placebo, and control groups, with twenty-one children in each group. Pretest and post-test scores from the Piers-Harris CSCS were compared for all groups using analysis of variance and *t* tests.

INTERVENTION

The children from the experimental group were divided into groups of three or four and participated in nondirective group play therapy once each week for twelve weeks. Children in the placebo group were divided into three groups of seven and participated in discussion groups under the same schedule. Half the children in the control group met only for administration of the pre- and post-tests; the remainder met only for administration of the post-test.

RESULTS

The mean difference for pre- and post-test scores on the Piers-Harris CSCS for both the play therapy group and the discussion group showed positive change. The strongest positive change was noted for the children who participated in group play therapy. No significant change was noted for the control group.

COMMENTARY

Gould suggested that the school is in a unique position to make a valuable contribution to the mental health of children. The opportunity to interact with each other in group play therapy and/or discussion groups provides children with the chance to learn and practice new social skills within a controlled environment, resulting in a measurable increase in self-concept. Gould suggests that both play therapy and discussion groups be conducted as part of the regular planned school program. It was the researcher's belief that all children could benefit from therapeutic interventions, which historically have been assigned to those defined as "at risk."

SOURCE

Gould, M. F. 1980. The effect of short-term intervention play therapy on the self-concept of selected elementary pupils. Ph.D. diss., Florida Institute of Technology. *Dissertation Abstracts International* 41 (03): B1090.

POSSIBLE DSM-IV-TR DIAGNOSIS

Insufficient information provided in the study.

Child-Centered Group Play Therapy as an Intervention to Increase Sociometric Status and Self-Concept

Reese Milton House

FOCUS

Child-centered group play therapy is used to bring about desired changes in self-concept in children identified as underchosen on a sociometric test.

INTRODUCTION

After conducting a review of the literature, House concluded that the effectiveness of child-centered group play therapy had not been validated. His study was designed to investigate the effects of child-centered group play on the self-concept and sociometric status of selected second-grade children in a public school setting.

RESEARCH METHODS AND DESIGN

Thirty-six children were selected for the sample. Twelve children—six boys and six girls—were randomly assigned to each of three groups: the experimental group, control group one, and control group two. The Self-Concept Motivational Inventory (SCAMIN) and a sociometric test were administered to the subjects before and at the conclusion of treatment. A two-factor mixed design with repeated measures on one-factor analysis of variance was used to compare experimental and control groups on each instrument.

INTERVENTION

Members selected for the experimental group participated in child-centered play therapy in groups of six for twenty thirty-minute sessions conducted by the researcher over a period of ten weeks. Members selected for control group one participated in a specialized reading program under the same regimen. Members assigned to control group two received no treatment other than pre- and post-tests.

RESULTS

The self-concept of members of the experimental group increased significantly over the ten week period, while the self-concept of members of both control groups decreased slightly, although not significantly. All three groups demonstrated a significant increase in sociometric status. House noted that since the stability of sociometric relationships is probably not firmly established by mid-October of the second grade, developing and changing relationships in the classroom may cause sociometric status to change at this age level. The experimental group did show a greater score gain in sociometric status than the control groups, although the difference was not significant. Since the teachers were aware of the underchosen members, perhaps they facilitated some changes in sociometric status through their attitudes toward these children. In the case of the two control groups, an increased status position apparently did not positively influence the children's view of self as measured by the SCAMIN self-concept scale. However, the self-concept of members of the control groups may increase eventually, especially if their higher sociometric status is maintained.

COMMENTARY

Participation in child-centered group play therapy provides a climate for change in which a child can learn to express feelings in appropriate ways, resulting in the development of positive regard for self and others. This change supports the premise that an individual has a strong capacity to grow toward mature behavior if given the freedom to do so. The value and importance of a healthy self-concept has been established in our society. Implications for the use of child-centered group play therapy in the public schools seem to be clear. Since two half-hour group play therapy sessions per week significantly enhanced the self-concept of children identified as underchosen, initiating an extensive program of child-centered group play therapy as part of any elementary counseling program would be highly recommended.

SOURCE

House, R. M. 1970. The effects of nondirective group play therapy upon the sociometric status and self-concept of selected second grade children. Ph.D. diss., Oregon State University. *Dissertation Abstracts International* 31 (06): A2684.

POSSIBLE DSM-IV-TR DIAGNOSIS

Insufficient information provided in the study.

Child-Centered Play Therapy to Increase Self-Efficacy in the Schools

Marijane Fall, Jane Balvanz, Lynette Johnson, and Linda Nelson

FOCUS

The effectiveness is studied of play therapy in the schools and its influence on self-efficacy.

INTRODUCTION

The authors have several purposes for this study. School counselors are expected to conduct counseling as part of their primary job function, but there is no empirical basis for supporting individual counseling interventions in schools. In addition, play therapy in the schools has not been supported by empirical research. The authors also believe that a child's sense of self-efficacy—an individual's belief about personal ability to transform knowledge and skills into necessary behaviors—is related to a child's learning performance. The authors hypothesize that play therapy may help to increase a child's self-efficacy, which will increase the child's success in the classroom.

RESEARCH METHODS AND DESIGN

Researchers asked teachers to submit a list of children whose coping mechanisms did not facilitate learning behaviors. Examples included children who were shy, withdrawn, using self-defeating coping mechanisms, easily frustrated, acting out, unwilling to take risks, seeking attention, and not excited about learning. Researchers ruled out children who were using medication for attentional concerns. The study included twenty children from one school, eighteen children from a second school, and twenty-four children from a third school for a total of sixty-two children. Thirty-one children were assigned to the experimental play therapy group, and thirty-one children were assigned to the control group. Thirty-one girls and thirty-one boys participated in the study. Children ranged from kindergarten to third grade. In a pretest/post-test design, the participants were administered three instruments, including a classroom observation, the Self-Efficacy Scale for Children (S-ES), and the Conners Teacher Rating Scale (CTRS). The instruments served as the dependent variables and were analyzed using a mixed analysis of variance (ANOVA) with one within-subjects variable, time (pre, post), and two between-subjects variables, group (control, experimental) and counselor (1, 2, 3).

INTERVENTION

The experimental group participated in weekly individual play therapy sessions for six weeks for thirty minutes each time. Play therapy sessions were facilitated by the school counselor for each school and according to child-centered theory. The control group children received no intervention.

RESULTS

The mean self-efficacy score decreased from pre- to post-test for the experimental group and slightly increased for the control group, with a decrease in score being favorable. The mean score of classroom behaviors reported on both the CTRS and the classroom observation decreased from pre- to post-test for both the experimental and control conditions, with a decrease in score being favorable.

COMMENTARY

This research study indicates that children's self-efficacy may be increased with a half-hour play therapy intervention once a week for six weeks. The authors note that children with a high sense of self-efficacy make more choices and take risks, persist at tasks, attribute failure to lack of personal effort, and increase necessary behaviors accordingly. In addition, this study demonstrates the effectiveness of play therapy conducted by school counselors as a counseling intervention in the schools.

SOURCE

Fall, M., Balvanz, J., Johnson, L., and Nelson, L. 1999. A play therapy intervention and its relationship to self-efficacy and learning behaviors. *Professional School Counseling* 2 (3): 194–204.

POSSIBLE DSM-IV-TR DIAGNOSES

312.9   Disruptive Behavior Disorder NOS
        Attention-Deficit/Hyperactivity Disorder, Combined Type
V62.3   Academic Problem

Effects of Intensive Group Play Media on Self-Concepts of Children

Alan Y. Strom

FOCUS

The effects are studied of intensive group play media on the self-concepts of second-grade children.

INTRODUCTION

The purpose of this study was to test the effects of Intensive Group Play Media on improving the self-concepts of selected second-grade children. Group Play Media is an approach that combines both nondirective and directive play therapy facilitated by a counselor.

RESEARCH METHODS AND DESIGN

The author used a sample of thirty-six second-grade children identified according to level of self-concept. The children were tested three times by the Piers-Harris Children's Self-Concept Scale and the Pictorial Self-Concept Scale for Children. A teacher rating form was also administered. Based on their scores, children were assigned to groups of high, middle, or low self-concept, then randomly assigned to experimental, placebo, or control groups. The analysis included a 3 × 3 analysis of covariance, with the pretest of each self-concept scale being the covariate for two hypotheses and the teacher rating form serving as the covariate for one hypothesis.

INTERVENTION

The experimental groups received a full Intensive Group Play Media approach, which included eleven sessions of nondirective group play media, two sessions of directed puppet role play, which dealt with peer and family situations, and two sessions for closure. The placebo groups received fifteen sessions of playtime only. There was no interaction from the counselor. The control groups remained in their classrooms throughout the study. There were four children in each group.

RESULTS

The results supported that the self-concepts of the experimental group were significantly higher after Intensive Group Play Media than those of the control and placebo groups, when initial differences in self-concepts are taken into account.

COMMENTARY

The Intensive Group Play Media approach was statistically supported in this study. Playtime for children as a means of improving self-concept was also statistically supported. The author concluded that research is still needed with other grade levels, larger initial sample sizes, and only low-self-concept children.

SOURCE

Strom, A. 1976. The effects of intensive group play media on the self-concepts of selected second grade children. Ph.D. diss., University of Denver. *Dissertation Abstracts International* 37: 4148.

POSSIBLE DSM-IV-TR DIAGNOSIS

Insufficient information provided in the study.

Impact of Play Therapy on At-Risk Students in the School

Phyllis Post

FOCUS

Child-centered play therapy is used as an intervention for self-esteem, locus-of-control, and anxiety problems in fourth-, fifth-, and sixth-grade students.

INTRODUCTION

While research has demonstrated that play therapy has had a positive impact on self-concept in students with academic problems, the literature focusing on using play therapy with at-risk children is sparse. Minority children and children of low socioeconomic status are particularly at risk for school dropout and subsequent problems. The purpose of this study was to address specifically the impact of child-centered play therapy on self-esteem, locus of control, and anxiety level among at-risk fourth-, fifth-, and sixth-grade children.

RESEARCH METHODS AND DESIGN

Participants were students in an inner-city school composed of 168 children in fourth, fifth, and sixth grade. Students were defined as at-risk based on characteristics such as economic disadvantage, being below age-grade-level achievement, referrals to special educational services, and family situations involving frequent house-member transitions, impoverishment, neglect, or violence. Ages ranged from nine to twelve, with a mean age of ten years; 82 percent were African American, 8% white, 7% Asian, and 3% identified as "other." Students were referred to the study by teachers, other school staff, and parents for issues including poor self-esteem, depression, anxiety, abuse, neglect, or incarceration of a parent or family member. Instruments, including the Coopersmith Self-Esteem Inventory, the Intellectual Achievement Responsibility Scale–Revised, and the State-Trait Anxiety Inventory, were administered in early November and during the last week of school. The experimental group consisted of seventy-seven students, and the control group consisted of ninety-one students. Students' pretest and post-test scores on the instruments were analyzed using analysis of variance to determine whether participating in play therapy, time, or an interaction between participation in play therapy and time affected students' post-test scores on each of these assessments.

INTERVENTION

Students in the experimental group were assigned to individual play therapy sessions with advanced graduate students in counselor education. The twelve graduate students had completed a play therapy course and received supervision in play therapy. Play therapy was conducted according to Garry Landreth's model to create a therapeutic environment through engaging in a child-centered way of being with the children. The number of play therapy sessions ranged from one to twenty-five, with a mean of four. Sessions were conducted weekly. The students in the control group received no intervention.

RESULTS

The results indicated that although participating in child-centered play therapy did not enhance at-risk students' overall self-esteem, the students not participating in play therapy demonstrated a decrease in self-esteem over the course of the school year. Over an academic year, at-risk elementary students who did not receive the intervention of play therapy appear to have ended the school year at greater risk in terms of these variables than when they began the school year. Additionally, findings indicated that members of the control group decreased in their locus of control over the course of the school year, while the experimental group remained the same. No differences were found regarding anxiety.

COMMENTARY

The researcher found strong support for the effectiveness of child-centered play therapy sessions in helping prevent at-risk fourth-, fifth-, and sixth-grade students from decreasing in self-esteem and locus of control over the course of a school year. Play therapy appeared to be beneficial in halting the downward spiral typical of at-risk students and, therefore, might be effective in helping to prevent school dropout.

SOURCE

Post, P. 1999. Impact of child-centered play therapy on the self-esteem, locus of control, and anxiety of at-risk fourth-, fifth-, and sixth-grade students. *International Journal of Play Therapy* 8 (2): 1–18.

POSSIBLE DSM-IV-TR DIAGNOSES

296.xx   Major Depressive Disorder
300.02   Generalized Anxiety Disorder
312.9   Disruptive Behavior Disorder NOS
995.5   Neglect of Child
995.54   Physical Abuse of Child
V62.3   Academic Problem

CHAPTER 19
Social Adjustment Problems

Perhaps more than any other single indicator, social interactions—or the lack thereof—provide essential clues to children's emotional growth and adjustment. When poor relationships exist with peers or siblings, underlying needs of children should be examined. Likewise, socially immature, shy, or withdrawn behavior should call attention to children's poor self-concepts, feelings of inadequacy, need for nurturing, lack of acceptance in their lives, or intense interpersonal conflicts. These children often exhibit poor impulse control or quietly withdraw into themselves. For children who perceive themselves as different from their peers or who have poor social interactions, group play therapy provides an especially effective modality for them to learn new social skills, to discover that they are capable, to receive the peer acceptance that is so crucial, and to develop self-control and self-acceptance. Group play therapy is especially indicated in day care centers, kindergartens, school settings, and residential treatment centers. Play therapists are cautioned to equip themselves with the necessary training and supervision in group play therapy before using this approach.

Group Play Therapy as an Intervention for Children with Peer and Sibling Relationship Problems

Claire M. Bloomberg

FOCUS

Group play therapy is used to improve peer relationships during group activities at school and relationships with siblings at home.

INTRODUCTION

The majority of children who have difficulty interacting with peer groups at school were also found to have problems with sibling rivalry. Group play therapy provided the setting for these children to deal with their interactional problems.

RESEARCH METHODS AND DESIGN

Two groups of five children were selected on the basis of Rorschach tests, teacher input, and therapist observations to participate in group play therapy sessions. The groups met once a week for an hour throughout the school year. The same play therapist worked with both play therapy groups using, as inferred from the description, a nondirective approach.

INTERVENTION

The children were free to choose the toys they wanted to play with; play activities were not suggested. Snacks, crackers, and juice were available whenever the children wanted them during the session. The play therapist allowed a wide range of behavior, including dumping water on the floor and smearing clay on the walls.

The play therapist indicated that the group members served as pseudosiblings and she as the pseudomother. Her approach was to reflect relationship interactions, such as, "I wonder if you know what you're fighting about? Are you fighting because you think I can't love more than one person at a time?"

Themes of the play included redefining the relationship between self and the sibling. Initially, the play was ambivalent—sometimes nurturing, sometimes aggressive. One child killed the baby doll and then brought it back to life just before the end of the session. As termination approached, the play was more nurturing and positive.

Another theme was the interaction between the children and the play therapist. At one stage, the children banded together against the play therapist. The play therapist saw this as the children, in reality, trying to work through their feelings regarding their mothers. Eventually, all the children were able to express positive feelings toward the play therapist.

The play therapist met twice with the parents during the year to assist them in identifying the purpose of their child's behavior. The therapist indicated that two meetings were not sufficient to establish a working relationship with the parents.

RESULTS

The author briefly discussed the positive benefit of the group play therapy in qualitative terms. The children were described as more collaborative and less negative in their family and social interactions. A primary benefit of the group play approach was that the children discovered they were not alone in having "bad feelings." Increased positive affect and self-esteem were also noted.

COMMENTARY

Children who had problems interacting with their siblings had similar problems interacting with peers at school. Nondirective group play therapy appears to have been an effective intervention for these children. The establishment of a pseudofamily to assist these children in learning to handle a wide variety of emotions in the presence of an accepting adult had positive and therapeutic results for these children. When children's needs are met in a supportive group, coping skills are released to develop more positive relationship skills.

SOURCE

Bloomberg, C. 1948. An experiment in play therapy. *Childhood Education* 25, 177–80.

POSSIBLE DSM-IV-TR DIAGNOSES

V61.20 Parent-Child Relational Problem
V61.8   Sibling Relational Problem
V61.81 Relational Problem NOS

Self-Directive Play Therapy as a Treatment for Socially Immature Kindergarten Children

Lee Edward Pelham

FOCUS

Group and individual play therapy is used as an intervention for socially immature kindergarten children.

INTRODUCTION

The purpose of this study was to determine whether self-directive play therapy
would be effective in increasing the social maturity of kindergarten students who
had been identified by their teachers as socially immature.

RESEARCH METHODS AND DESIGN

Nine kindergarten teachers referred fifty-two children characterized as "socially
immature." Eighteen were randomly selected for membership in a control
group that received no treatment. Of the thirty-four remaining students, seventeen received parental permission to participate in the study. Nine of the seventeen were assigned to receive group play therapy in three groups of three. The
remaining eight were assigned to receive individual play therapy. Instruments
used to test the hypothesis included the Missouri Children's Picture Series
(MCPS), the Children's Self-Social Constructs Test (CSSCT), and the Behavior
Problem Checklist (BPC). Comparisons were made regarding the relative effectiveness of group and individual play therapy. Statistical analysis of the data was
completed using analysis of covariance, with the pretest scores used as the control variable.

INTERVENTION

Each child received six to eight forty-five-minute self-directive play therapy sessions conducted by the author. Nine children received group play therapy, and the remaining eight participated in individual play therapy sessions.

RESULTS

Children who received either individual play therapy or group play therapy made positive gains in social maturity when compared to the control group. There was no significant difference in the amount of increase between the two groups. The children in these two groups scored more positively on the complexity scale of the CSSCT, which was used as a measure of self-concept and was also related to a person's ability to be flexible in response to new experiences. Teacher ratings of the BPC indicated that children receiving group and individual play therapy improved significantly in classroom behavior when compared to children in the control group. In retrospect, the author found that the MCPS did not measure maturity as identified by teachers and may not have been a valid measure of maturity for the younger children.

COMMENTARY

Play therapy, either individual or group, proved to be an effective intervention for immature kindergarten children. Improvements were seen in classroom behavior, self-concept, flexibility in new situations, and social maturity after only six to eight forty-five-minute sessions. Since more children can be served in a group play therapy format, this may be the most efficient use of time and resources in the school setting for this particular concern. Ineffective behaviors learned outside the play therapy group can be unlearned in the group.

SOURCE

Pelham, L. E. 1972. Self-directive play therapy with socially immature kindergarten students. Ph.D. diss., University of Northern Colorado, 1971. *Dissertation Abstracts International* 32 (07): A3798.

POSSIBLE DSM-IV-TR DIAGNOSIS

V62.81 Relational Problem NOS

Play Therapy for Children with School Adjustment Problems

Randall L. Quayle

FOCUS

Play therapy is used for young children having problems adjusting to school.

INTRODUCTION

Early elementary school children are frequently identified as being at risk for not making a satisfactory adjustment to the school setting. Without intervention, it is believed these children will become increasingly maladjusted, increasing the child's risk of dropping out of school and developing emotional and psychological problems.

RESEARCH METHODS AND DESIGN

Fifty-four children, five to nine years of age, were identified as being at risk for school adjustment through the use of the teacher-completed AML Behavior Rating Scale–Revised. The scale produced scores for acting out, moodiness, and learning problems.

The thirty-five boys and nineteen girls were divided into three groups. The treatment group received individual play therapy sessions; a second, comparison group received individual attention in the form of tutoring; the third group, the control group, received no special attention.

Pre- and postmeasures were accomplished through the use of three forms of the Child Rating Scale: Teachers, Associate, and Child. The teachers were not told which students were being taken for play therapy and which for individual tutoring. The child aides who provided both the play therapy and the individual tutoring attention completed the Associate Form. The resulting scores were analyzed using analysis of variance (ANOVA) and analysis of covariance (ANCOVA).

INTERVENTION

Eighteen children received twenty thirty-minute individual play therapy sessions, and eighteen received twenty thirty-minute individual tutoring sessions.

Children in the latter group went to a study room for assistance with homework or reading activities. The eighteen children in the control group received no special attention and remained in the classroom. All the children filled out, pre and post, the child version of the Child Rating Scale.

The two child aides who provided both the play therapy and the tutoring sessions had participated in the Primary Mental Health Project in this same school for at least three years and had attended six three-hour training sessions on reflective listening and child-centered play therapy. During this study, a play therapy session was periodically videotaped and reviewed during the aides' bimonthly supervision sessions.

RESULTS

Children in both the individual play therapy group and the individual attention group improved. Children participating in the former group showed more positive growth in a greater number of areas, six of fifteen areas. The children receiving special attention showed positive gains in four of fifteen. The control group experienced negative results in seven of eleven areas. The only area in which the control group children demonstrated positive growth was in assertive social skills, as identified by the teachers. This may have been learned as a result of interactions with the children in the other two groups as they improved in that same area.

The teachers rated children receiving play therapy as improving in learning skills, assertive social skills, task orientation, and peer social skills. The child aides' responses indicated that the children improved in interactive participation and self-confidence.

COMMENTARY

More significant results may have resulted if the individuals providing the play therapy had received more training. As indicated above, their training was less than the equivalent of one graduate class. Also, as the author indicated, having the same individuals provide both the play therapy and the individual attention tutoring may have confounded the results. The aides' same empathetic interaction may have resulted in greater improvement in the children receiving individual attention. Even with all these concerns, the children receiving individual play therapy experienced greater growth and improvement.

SOURCE

Quayle, R. L. 1991. The primary mental health project as a school-based approach for prevention of adjustment problems: an evaluation. Unpublished Ph.D. diss., Pennsylvania State University. *Dissertation Abstracts International* 52 (OHA): 1268.

POSSIBLE DSM-IV-TR DIAGNOSES

309.xx   Adjustment Disorder
300.02   Generalized Anxiety Disorder
V62.81   Relational Problem NOS
312.9   Disruptive Behavior Disorder NOS
313.81   Oppositional Defiant Disorder

Group Play Therapy as an Intervention Modality for Modifying the Social Adjustment of Primary-Grade Boys

Lauriane Tondow Smith

FOCUS

Which is more effective, directive or nondirective group play therapy, with socially withdrawn or aggressive children?

INTRODUCTION

This study compared the effectiveness of nondirective group play therapy and directive, problem-focused group play therapy in modifying the social adjustment, sociometric status, and self-concept of early-latency-aged boys.

RESEARCH METHODS AND DESIGN

The eighteen second and third graders in this study were seven-and-a-half to nine-and-a-half years old, from a white, upper-middle-class, public elementary school in the San Francisco Bay Area. Based on teacher reports, the sample represented students who were socially withdrawn or aggressive and appeared to have more difficulties in social adjustment in comparison to their peers. Three groups of six children were matched by age, grade, IQ, and type of behavior problem. Each group involved two socially aggressive and four socially withdrawn subjects. The subjects had experienced no form of psychotherapy. The intervention techniques were randomly assigned to two of the three groups: directive, problem-focused play therapy and nondirective play therapy. The third group served as the control group. A pre-/post-test control group design was used, and data were processed through analysis of variance and post hoc *t* tests. Scales were used to measure pre- and post- social status, social skills, and self-concept.

INTERVENTION

The children in the two play therapy groups received twelve forty-five-minute sessions over a ten-week period. The children in the control group received no special attention or intervention.

Directive group play therapy was defined as an organized, structured set of developmentally appropriate activities based on specific tasks and needs of latency-aged children using S. R. Slavson's[1] framework. The directive and developmentally phased activities were designed with personality development theory in mind. The therapist provided specific developmental goals for the group, encouraged communication on an emotional level, and subtly emphasized the group process rather than production of a group outcome. Each session had three basic segments. First, subjects were given directions regarding the activities for the session. Second, the subjects worked on a project. Third, the therapist directed discussion centered on feedback gathered during the activity. Activities for the sessions focused on getting acquainted, recognizing and understanding feelings, developing social skills and respect for others, and improving each child's ability to define problems, suggest alternatives, and understand the consequences of the alternatives for everyone involved.

The second group of children received traditional nondirective group play therapy based upon the principles and guidelines of Rogers[2] and the techniques of Virginia Axline.[3]

---

1. S. R. Slavson, *Child Psychotherapy* (New York: Columbia University Press, 1952).
2. Carl Rogers, *Client-Centered Therapy* (Boston: Houghton Mifflin, 1951).
3. Virginia Axline, *Play Therapy* (New York: Ballantine Books, 1969).

RESULTS

Subjects receiving directive group play therapy scored significantly higher on a measure of social status than subjects who received either nondirective group play therapy or no intervention. Both intervention groups scored significantly higher than the control group on the measures of social adjustment and self-concept. On each scale subjects receiving directive group play therapy scored significantly higher than those who received nondirective group play therapy.

COMMENTARY

The results of this study indicated that developmentally based, directive group play therapy was the most effective in changing the social adjustment of the subjects. In addition, the results indicated that in primary-grade boys, nondirective group play therapy was also an effective intervention in facilitating positive change in social skills and self-concept, although not as effective as the directive approach.

It is often the perception that early-latency-aged children exhibiting poor social behaviors are not in need of intervention as they will outgrow their social handicaps naturally. Children may or may not outgrow their problems, but an important implication of this investigation is that intervention moves faster than no intervention in effecting social adjustment and self-concept change. These results confirm the value of providing intervention for children with social adjustment and self-concept problems and suggest that the intervention should be directive in nature and developmentally rooted.

SOURCE

Smith, L. 1988. The relative effectiveness of two group play therapy approaches in modifying the social adjustment of primary-grade children. Ph.D. diss., Pacific Graduate School of Psychology, 1987. *Dissertation Abstracts International* 48 (07): B2112.

POSSIBLE DSM-IV-TR DIAGNOSES

312.9   Disruptive Behavior Disorder NOS
309.0   Adjustment Disorder with Depressed Mood
309.3   Adjustment Disorder with Disturbance of Conduct
V62.81   Relational Problem NOS

Development of Self-Control in Bilingual Children through Group Play Therapy

Susan L. Trostle

FOCUS

Group play therapy is used to develop greater social acceptance through increased self-control in young minority children.

INTRODUCTION

Bilingual, immigrant children frequently encounter social, language, and other adjustment problems when beginning school. Social acceptance of self and others is usually low, often resulting in aggressive behavior and lack of self-control. Group play therapy is explored as an effective intervention procedure.

RESEARCH METHODS AND DESIGN

Forty-eight Puerto Rican children aged three to six years were used in this study. Their teacher had identified them as having been in the United States for at least six months, and their primary language at home was Spanish. The children were randomly assigned to the play therapy or control groups, matching only the number of boys and girls in each group. Twenty-four children were assigned to six play therapy groups. The control group consisted of twenty-four children who received unstructured free play with their classmates, using a set of toys similar to those in the play therapy groups. Each group had a forty-minute session weekly for ten weeks. Group play therapy provided the children with an opportunity to develop their social, representational, and adaptive skills in the group settings.

RESULTS

Post-test results indicated that the children assigned to the play therapy groups showed significant improvements compared to those in the control group. The areas of improvement were self-control and higher-developmental-level fantasy and reality play behavior. Boys became more accepting of others than did either the girls in the play therapy groups or any of the children in the control group.

COMMENTARY

This study supports the findings of other studies that have indicated that play therapy affects how children display aggression and increases their ability for self-control. Additionally, gains were made in developmental levels of both fantasy and reality play for these minority children. This developmental gain may afford children a greater ability to work out strong emotions through the use of play. As a result, self-confidence and self-esteem increase. This, in turn, allows children to be more accepting of others. For minority children or other children who perceive themselves as different from their peers, group play therapy appears to be an effective option for increased self-control and self-acceptance.

SOURCE

Trostle, S. L. 1988. The effects of child-centered group play sessions on social-emotional growth of three-to-six-year-old bilingual Puerto Rican children. *Journal of Research in Childhood Education* 3 (2): 93–106.

POSSIBLE DSM-IV-TR DIAGNOSES

309.3   Adjustment Disorder with Disturbance of Conduct
309.4   Adjustment Disorder with Mixed Disturbance of Emotions and Conduct
V62.81 Relational Problem NOS

Child-Centered Play Therapy for Children with Personal-Social Problems in School

Katherine Hume

FOCUS

The effect is studied of play therapy and teacher guidance on children in first to fourth grade with personal-social maladjustment in school.

INTRODUCTION

The purpose of the study was to evaluate an experimental counseling and guidance project for grades one through four. The focus was to investigate the possible preventive value of early identification and intervention to help emotionally maladjusted children in the school setting. The procedures included child-centered play therapy and an in-service course in guidance for teachers, designed to help the children achieve better mental health.

RESEARCH METHODS AND DESIGN

In each of eight grades, including two grades on each level from one through four, the children who manifested symptoms of personal-social maladjustment were identified during the first six weeks of school. They were identified according to criteria listed in Kough and DeHaan's *Identifying Children with Special Needs* and several sociometric measures. Twenty children were chosen to participate in the study. The researcher determined effectiveness according to the Descriptive Behavior Observation Guide used by teachers to make systematic observations of the subjects. The same instrument was used for a six-month follow-up and a two-year follow-up. The researcher also gathered data from parent interviews, sociometric measures, and academic reports. The researcher reported on each child individually and on group results.

INTERVENTION

The twenty children were placed in four experimental groups. The first group of eight children received play therapy, and their four teachers received in-service guidance training. In the second group, four teachers of four children received in-service guidance training only. In the third group, four children received play therapy, and teachers received no guidance. The fourth group served as a control group, and the four teachers and four children received no intervention. Subjects in play therapy met once a week for forty-five minutes in a variation of group and individual sessions over six months. The sessions were led according to the philosophy of child-centered play therapy. In-service course in guidance for teachers met one hour each week for six months and provided information to help teachers learn ways of creating growth conditions in their classroom and gain understanding of children in classes.

RESULTS

Child-centered play therapy seemed to provide a secondary preventive measure; all but one subject receiving play therapy showed considerable improvement in their behavior in school, at home, and in play therapy by end of school year and at follow-up evaluations. Play therapy appeared to be most effective when combined with teacher in-service. In-service appeared to be only partially helpful in making any impact in changing the behavior of subjects in the group not receiving play therapy. In follow-up, the control group continued to show poor mental health.

COMMENTARY

The study supported the value of two counselor functions on the elementary school level for facilitating prevention of emotional maladjustment of children. With one exception, play therapy provided for twelve emotionally maladjusted children on a once-a-week basis for seven months appeared to have a lasting effect over a two year period in helping to improve mental health. The eight subjects receiving play therapy whose teachers also participated in the in-service course in guidance made the greatest improvement in their mental health. The in-service course for teachers provided some limited short-term help. Without any counselor intervention, the follow-up data indicated that children do not outgrow their difficulties or improve in their mental health.

SOURCE

Hume, K. 1967. A counseling service project for grades one through four. Ph.D. diss., Boston University School of Education, 1966. *Dissertation Abstracts* 27: 4130.

POSSIBLE DSM-IV-TR DIAGNOSES

312.9   Disruptive Behavior Disorder NOS
V62.3   Academic Problem
V62.81 Relational Problem NOS

Group Play Therapy with Children Who Are Socially Isolated

Marshall Thombs and James Muro

FOCUS

The effect is studied of group play therapy and group verbal counseling on the sociometric status of second-grade children.

INTRODUCTION

The use of play media as a counseling tool has been documented in testimonial publications. Up to the publication of this study, no studies had attempted to employ play media in a group counseling investigation. The purpose of this study was to determine the effects of play media group counseling and verbal group counseling on the sociometric status of second-grade children.

RESEARCH METHODS AND DESIGN

Among four second-grade classrooms, the authors administered a sociometric instrument. Each child was asked to select five of his peers with whom he would like to work on a class project. Selected students were then assigned weighted scores with a first choice receiving a score of five and a fifth choice a score of one. The sum of the weighted scores for each child was then converted into social scores. Thirty-six students were identified as social isolates and were selected to participate in the study. Each was randomly assigned to one of five groups. Two groups of six children were placed in verbal counseling groups, while twelve other children were assigned to two play media groups. Twelve children were designated as controls and received no group counseling. Significant differences among the groups in social position did not exist before the initiation of group counseling. Three weeks after the termination of counseling, all subjects were readministered the sociometric scale.

INTERVENTION

All experimental groups met for thirty minutes each day for fifteen consecutive school days with a school counselor. The counselor facilitated the groups according to relationship theory or the conditions that provide a unique growth experience for the child. The counselor's primary focus was the individual's present level of functioning and the expressions of the child, not the child's problems, symptoms, or cures. The play media groups were facilitated according to a nondirective approach.

RESULTS

Children who received group counseling made significant gains in sociometric status when they were compared to the control groups. When verbal counseling groups were compared with the control groups, there was no significant difference.

Likewise, no significant differences were found when the play media groups were compared to the verbal groups. Thus, groups of children who were engaged in play media counseling showed a greater positive change in social position than did those who were in verbal group counseling sessions.

COMMENTARY

The authors note that the children who were counseled through use of play media were enthusiastic about the sessions and voiced a reluctance to terminate the process, unlike those involved in the verbal group, who frequently requested to bring toys. This study provided empirical support for using play media in counseling with young children.

SOURCE

Thombs, M., and Muro, J. 1973. Group counseling and the sociometric status of second grade children. *Elementary School Guidance and Counseling* 7: 194–97.

POSSIBLE DSM-IV-TR DIAGNOSIS

V62.81 Relational Problem NOS

CHAPTER 20

Speech Difficulties

In this chapter, we are not concerned with children who experience simple articulation problems but rather with children who exhibit a matrix of unsatisfactory communication that usually interferes with social interaction, academic achievement, and/or feelings about self. Speech therapy for these children is generally designed to make interpersonal exchange more satisfying and more successful but may not provide for the emotional development necessary for general language development. Delayed speech development and/or speech difficulties should call attention to the need to consider emotional factors as contributing to the difficulty. Children's problems do not exist in isolation but rather reverberate throughout the child's organism. For example, difficulties in speech may be accompanied by aggressive or withdrawn behavior. Play therapy provides children with an opportunity to release negative, restricting feelings that may have been inhibiting normal adjustment and to develop a positive self-image necessary for emotional development and growth. The permissive attitude of the play therapist, the opportunity to interact with peers without adult interference, consistent limit setting in a constructive and positive manner, and acceptance of the child provide the setting essential for children's growth and development, including speech.

Nondirective Group Play Therapy to Facilitate Speech and Language Development in Preschool Children

Kenneth Bouillion

FOCUS

The comparative effectiveness, appropriateness, and efficiency of nondirective group play therapy is studied as an intervention modality for preschool children with speech or language delay.

INTRODUCTION

Speech and language delay in preschool children is a commonly found problem. This study compared four intervention/treatment modalities, including group play therapy.

RESEARCH METHODS AND DESIGN

Forty-three children were involved in this study. The children, who ranged in age from three years, six months to six years, two months, were functioning at least at the average intelligence level and showed no evidence of hearing difficulties. All were capable of following directions to perform simple physical-motor tasks. Each child was diagnosed as speech or language delayed based on a one-year lag between the child's measured articulation or receptive skills and the child's chronological age.

The forty-three children were randomly assigned to one of four treatment programs. Ten children were assigned to group play therapy, eight to individual direct speech therapy, nine to group speech lessons, seven to physical-motor training, and nine to a control group. Each treatment group met five days a week, thirty minutes each day, for fourteen weeks.

Pre- and post-testing were accomplished through the use of standardized articulation and language instruments. The resulting scores were analyzed by analysis of variance and correlational statistics.

RESULTS

The children who participated in group play therapy achieved significantly higher scores than the other treatment groups in the areas of fluency and articulation. These same children showed the least improvement, however, in remediating receptive language deficits. Bouillion speculated that nondirective group play therapy may be most effective for the early stages of intervention when the emphasis is on developing a therapeutic relationship at the child's own pace. He hypothesized that the supportive play therapy environment resulted in decreased anxiety and more comfort in the intervention situation, increased self-esteem, and development of both linguistic and affective expressive abilities. The general conclusion of this study was that a more holistic approach to therapeutic speech remediations, in which several intervention modalities could be combined, would be the most beneficial to the child.

COMMENTARY

The findings of this study indicate that group play therapy proved most effective in the remediation of expressive language skills in preschool children. Other interventions were more effective in the remediation of receptive language skills in preschool children. Understanding this, developmental speech programs can more effectively intervene appropriately, matching the intervention to the needs of the individual child.

SOURCE

Bouillion, K. 1974. The comparative efficacy of nondirective group play therapy with preschool, speech- or language delayed children. Ph.D. diss., Texas Tech University, 1973. *Dissertation Abstracts International* 35 (01): B495.

POSSIBLE DSM-IV-TR DIAGNOSES

315.31 Expressive Language Disorder
315.31 Mixed Receptive-Expressive Language Disorder
315.39 Phonological Disorder

Play Therapy Intervention for Regression of Speech in a Young Child

Lydia Jackson

FOCUS

Play therapy intervention is used with a child with severely regressed speech.

INTRODUCTION

This child reacted to the birth of two younger siblings and a negative change in discipline from his mother in such a severe manner that he was initially misdiagnosed as mentally retarded. His speech regression was so severe that he gave no evidence of hearing or understanding what was requested of him.

CASE STUDY

Terry was described as a happy, pleasant baby until the birth of his first sister when he was twenty months old. He had begun to say a few words and was feeding himself. A maternal aunt who came to take care of him used "smacking" as a form of discipline and convinced his mother to continue this. Terry stopped talking and tried to take the new baby away from his mother. During the same period, Terry was hospitalized for two days for a circumcision, and for the following six months, he had nightly "screaming fits." When Terry was almost three-and-a-half, his youngest sister was born. Regression was again noted, as well as aggressive behavior toward younger children. Terry became very attached to his mother and followed her everywhere. He was enuretic and encopretic and made no attempt to self-regulate toileting. Although he often did not respond to being talked to, at night he could be heard humming or singing softly in his bedroom. As Terry did not respond to an attempt to assess his intelligence, he was labeled mentally retarded. At this point his mother sought a second opinion.

INTERVENTION

Terry was seen weekly for forty-five minutes of play therapy for eighteen months. In the initial sessions, he explored the playroom and became so absorbed in his activity that it was as though the play therapist was not even present. His manipulation of toys and materials was excellent, inconsistent with the ability level of a mentally retarded child. In an early session, after receiving the play therapist's permission to put a toy in the water tray, Terry often filled the tray with numerous toys. He responded positively to limits set on what he could put into the water. In the sixth session, Terry began his first real constructive play: building a bridge in the water tray.

Terry continued to play at the water table, and in the eighth session, the play therapist introduced a doll family, naming three of them after Terry and his two sisters. The play therapist then enacted a scene with the dolls arguing and the parent dolls taking the boy doll's side. Terry responded by throwing water on the dolls until they fell over. Each time the play therapist stood them up again, Terry's water play would "sink them."

In subsequent sessions, the play therapist continued to introduce various scenarios with the dolls. In one scene, she had a male doll pretend to urinate in the water tray. Terry took the doll and threw it to the other end of the room every time this scene was played out. After a few sessions of this play, however, Terry began to speak in bursts of "jargon talk."

After his fourteenth session, Terry was enrolled in a nursery school specially selected for its tolerant headmistress. He quickly began to respond to toilet training and other self-help skills. After an initial aggressive phase, Terry became protective of younger children at the school.

In the seventeenth session, Terry began to alternate between messy and constructive play. His behavior at home became very aggressive. He broke favorite items of his mother, threw his sisters' dolls in water, and frequently attacked the dolls, urinating on them and their beds. Supportive parent consultation was essential during this time. Following the aggressive phase, Terry's behavior was marked by mischievousness.

A two-month break in play therapy was necessary at this time because of minor illnesses and summer vacation. Upon returning to the clinic, Terry was very affectionate, to the point of needing to kiss everyone goodbye before leaving. His play became conflicted: building and destroying, dirtying and cleaning. In session twenty-four, for the first time, Terry whispered a direct answer to a question by the play therapist. The interpretation was that Terry no longer needed to hide behind his impenetrable defense of "not hearing." Indeed, his variety of play continued to expand, and although he was still very focused in his play, he no longer shut out the play therapist. In the twenty-ninth session, Terry spontaneously looked up at the play therapist and smiled. His play continued to increase in healthy and positive content, while ambivalent and destructive play decreased. In the forty-first session, free verbal give and take between Terry and the therapist occurred and continued in subsequent sessions. Meanwhile, at home, all the previous problem behavior had ceased. In a joint session, Terry and his sisters were very friendly and happily played together.

RESULTS

Play therapy was discontinued after sixty-four sessions. Terry continued to have brief contact with his play therapist when he was in the clinic for speech therapy and assistance in development of reading skills. At seven years of age, Terry was found to have an IQ of 149 and a mental age of ten years, eight months. Even though he still had language problems, such as telescoping sentences and cutting out conjunctions and prepositions, he presented himself as an attractive boy with lots of energy and good social skills.

COMMENTARY

This case reminds us of how powerfully a child can react to changes within the family. A child's view of his or her self and world can necessitate lengthy intervention. It is important that the play therapist continue to trust the process, while advocating for the child with the parents and school. The safety of the play therapy relationship allowed this child to venture forth into a world he had decided to shut out.

SOURCE

Jackson, L. 1950. Non-speaking children. *British Journal of Medical Psychology* 23:87–100.

POSSIBLE DSM-IV-TR DIAGNOSES

299.00   Autistic Disorder
299.10   Childhood Disintegrative Disorder (if behavior had begun after 24 months, rather than 20 months, as in Terry's case)
299.80   Pervasive Developmental Disorder NOS
313.81   Oppositional Defiant Disorder
313.23   Selective Mutism

Theraplay with Articulation Disorders

Phyllis Kupperman, Sally Bligh, and Marjorie Goodban

FOCUS

A special form of Theraplay used to remediate the articulation disorders of young children is studied.

INTRODUCTION

Speech Theraplay was studied to determine its effectiveness in working with young children who have not activated their articulation acquisition. This form of intrusive interaction intensifies and mirrors normal parent-child interaction that promotes communication development. The goal of the sessions was not to teach the phonemes but to activate the interaction that develops the desire and ability to increase communication.

RESEARCH METHODS AND DESIGN

Six children enrolled in a university speech clinic were selected for participation in this study. Four of the children were preschoolers, aged three years, two months to four years, six months. The other two were six-year-olds who had made little or no progress during six months of traditional remediation.

The clinicians were six undergraduate student clinicians who had participated in a twenty-hour training course and/or a supervised clinical practicum. The Theraplay training included role-playing, lectures, videotapes, group discussions, and supervision.

Pre- and post-testing were accomplished by using the Fisher-Logemann Test of Articulation Competence. Specific phonemes were identified for each child either through the use of distinctive features or developmental rationale. These phonemes became the focus of the intervention sessions.

INTERVENTION

Each child had two half-hour speech Theraplay sessions a week for six weeks. During the sessions, the child's attention was drawn to the targeted phonemes embedded within a meaningful interchange or as part of a play sequence. In

Theraplay, the repertoire of prespeech interactions includes smiling, cooing and gurgling responsively, singing, counting fingers and toes, playing peek-a-boo, and other such activities. These activities activate normal articulation acquisition and, therefore, are used with children of all ages. No props or toys are used. The child and the clinician sit facing each other on a mat on the floor. Physical contact, in the form of stroking, touching, and cuddling, occurs often. The clinicians often give high affect responses to encourage the child and help the child feel good about self.

RESULTS

The number of misarticulated items was reduced by each of the six children. The average reduction of errors in articulation was 10.8 items. The pattern of articulation acquisition varied for each child. The two six-year-olds gained proficiency in sounds. The preschoolers varied in their gains: one gained word endings; another, nearly all consonant blends; another, voiceless phonemes. In several cases, parents reported the child's making articulation changes at home before they became evident in the sessions.

Given the short duration of the study, six weeks, the authors did not believe that maturation was the cause of the growth. They hypothesized that the intensity of the positive affect associated with the stimulation resulted in higher self-esteem. The unconditional clinician approval may have also motivated the children to communicate more precisely.

COMMENTARY

Theraplay appears to be effective in activating or reactivating a child's normal speech development. The significance of a nurturing relationship to a child's healthy development is evident. This is not to imply the parents were not nurturing. However, the Theraplay sessions provided intensive and somewhat exaggerated positive interactions. The fact that the children began demonstrating improvement at home, rather than in the sessions, indicates the children's positive response to their parents.

SOURCE

Kupperman, P., Bligh, S., and Goodban, M. 1980. Activating articulation skills through Theraplay. *Journal of Speech & Hearing Disorders* 45 (4): 540–48.

POSSIBLE DSM-IV-TR DIAGNOSES

315.39   Phonological Disorder
315.31   Expressive Language Disorder

Group Play Therapy to Improve Speech, Social Skills, Personality Attributes, and Intelligence

Martin Sokoloff

FOCUS

Group play therapy is used with children who have cerebral palsy and associated speech difficulties.

INTRODUCTION

Children with cerebral palsy often have problematic articulation due to paralysis, weakness, or incoordination of muscles (dysarthria). This research sought to discover which therapy, individual speech therapy or group play therapy, was more effective in alleviating these speech problems. Possible changes in social adjustment, personality, and intelligence were also investigated.

RESEARCH METHODS AND DESIGN

Twenty-four children with cerebral palsy, identified as nonseverely dysarthric speech-handicapped, participated in this research. Pre- and postdata were collected using the Ammons Full Range Picture Vocabulary Test (to identify an intelligence quotient), the Vineland Social Maturity Scale (to assess social adjustment), and a personality rating scale. The children were also audiotaped as they responded to Blackie Pictures, which were rated for communicative abilities by a panel of experts.

Random assignment was made to either group play therapy or individual speech therapy. The two groups were balanced for IQ (an average of 81.4), age (average of 5.55 years), and gender (eight boys and four girls).

INTERVENTION

Four children were assigned to each of three play therapy groups. The groups met for one hour twice a week for thirty sessions. Two play therapy groups were led by a clinical psychologist, and the third was facilitated by a doctoral student.

The twelve children in individual speech therapy were seen twice a week for thirty minutes for a total of thirty sessions.

RESULTS

The children who received group play therapy showed statistically significant improvement ($p < .01$) in the areas of attention, concentration, responsiveness to therapeutic techniques, social confidence, self-confidence, and appropriate expression of nonverbal and verbal hostility.

Social maturity scores indicated that the children receiving group play therapy improved at a statistically significant level ($p < .05$). The personality rating of the children in group play therapy also improved at a statistically significant level ($p =< .01$).

There was no statistically significant difference between the two groups as to IQ. However, the children who received group play therapy did have an increase in the group's average IQ, from 82.5 (pre) to 86.4 (post). The range of IQ scores for children in group play therapy changed from 47 to 110 to 47 to 130. The children who received speech therapy actually lost IQ points, from an average of 80.3 (pre) to 78.2 (post).

The panel indicated that the children who received group play therapy improved significantly in communicative abilities. These included, specifically, articulation, intelligibility, voice, vocabulary, and language level. There were also interesting differences in improvement according to the child's age group. Children aged five to seven years improved most in articulation, general intelligibility, and language and vocabulary level. Children aged seven to ten years were fairly equal in areas of improvement. Children aged ten to thirteen years improved most in intelligibility, vocabulary level, and general communicative ability.

According to the author, significant factors in the group play therapy were the permissive attitude of the play therapist, the opportunity to interact with peers without adult interference, consistent limit setting in a constructive and positive manner, and the acceptance of the child.

COMMENTARY

Group play therapy was found to be an effective means by which certain children with cerebral palsy could improve speech skills, social adjustment, and their view of self. These results, many at a statistically significant level, were found after fifteen weeks of intervention. It would be interesting to see the possibilities of change for these children if group play therapy could be a standard part of the scholastic routine. One might postulate there would be an eventual plateau of gains, but to date it appears no one has discovered what these limitations might be.

SOURCE

Sokoloff, M. A. 1959. A comparison of gains in communicative skills, resulting from group play therapy and individual speech therapy, among a group of non-severely dysarthric, speech handicapped cerebral palsied children. Ph.D. diss., New York University. *Dissertation Abstracts International* 20 (02): B803.

POSSIBLE DSM-IV-TR DIAGNOSES

315.31 Expressive Language Disorder
315.39 Phonological Disorder

Group Play Therapy for Japanese Children Who Stutter

Yoko Yamaguchi Wakaba

FOCUS

Group play therapy with children who stutter is conducted to reduce their stuttering and improve social adaptation.

INTRODUCTION

Children who stutter are characterized by emotionally immature and meager expression, an introverted type of character, severe anxiety, and delayed interpersonal relations. Play therapy seems to be effective for such children. Group play therapy seems to be particularly effective in improving interpersonal relations.

RESEARCH METHODS AND DESIGN

Three boys, ages four to five years old, participated in the study. The author revealed the background history for each boy. All three boys began to stutter between the ages of two and three years old. One hour of group play therapy was provided once a week for five months (a total of 21 sessions). Group play therapy was facilitated according to the eight principles of Virginia Axline. In addition to the therapy, another therapist counseled the boys' mothers in order to improve the family environment and relations between mother and son. A verbal test and a test of social maturity (TAKEN Social Maturity Scale) were performed at the start and end of therapy. During testing, three observers recorded the demonstration of stuttering symptoms through a one-way mirror. These symptoms were rated on the Scale for Rating Severity of Stuttering. Follow-up surveys were taken six months and five years after therapy.

RESULTS

As therapy progressed, a definite process of change was observed in each child, from a period of anxiety, to the appearance of aggressive behavior, to increasing frequency of aggressive behavior, to a decrease in aggressive behavior. After the appearance of aggressive behavior, a fluctuation in stuttering occurred as cooperative play with other children was established. This was followed by a decrease in stuttering. The follow-up survey showed that stuttering had declined and social adjustment had improved.

COMMENTARY

The author found that therapy is more effective if it is continued until the period of disappearance in stuttering symptoms is observed in the therapy situation. In addition, the appearance of aggressive behavior during therapy is thought to be of major significance for the disappearance of stuttering and for interpersonal relationships. The author concluded that group play therapy was an effective treatment for stuttering symptoms.

SOURCE

Wakaba, Y. 1983. Group play therapy for Japanese children who stutter. *Journal of Fluency Disorders* 8:93–118.

POSSIBLE DSM-IV-TR DIAGNOSIS

307.0   Stuttering

CHAPTER 21

Traumatization

In this chapter, we use the term "trauma" to refer to the broader, more inclusive context of children's experiences that may be stressful and traumatic as defined by David Levy. Psychological trauma is an extremely stressful event or happening that is usually atypical in the life experiences of the child and is distressing to the point of being overwhelming, causing an inability to cope. Young children should not be expected to describe such experiences verbally because they do not have the facility required to do so; such experiences are usually too threatening for the child to consciously describe. The natural reaction of children is to reenact or play out the traumatic experience in an unconscious effort to comprehend, overcome, develop a sense of control of, or assimilate the experience. Repetitive playing out of the experience is the child's natural self-healing process. Some of the aspects of posttraumatic play as identified by Lenore Terr are appropriate here to help play therapists recognize such behaviors: "compulsive repetition; unconscious link between the play and the traumatic event; literalness of play with simple defenses only; failure to relieve anxiety; danger; use of doodling, talking, typing, and audio duplication as modes of repeated play; and possibility of therapeutically retracing posttraumatic play to an earlier trauma."[1]

---

1. Lenore Terr, Play Therapy and Psychic Trauma: A Preliminary Report, in *Handbook of Play Therapy*, ed. C. E. Schaefer and K. J. O'Connor, 308–19 (New York: Wiley, 1983), 308.

Child-Centered Play Therapy with a Neglected Child Traumatized by Hospitalization

Eliana Gil

FOCUS

Toy hospital equipment used in nondirective play provided the opportunity for a neglected child to work through feelings about a sudden hospitalization due to appendicitis.

INTRODUCTION

Physical traumas are often misinterpreted by young children as rejection and punishment for misbehavior. In the following case, fears of abandonment were confirmed when the child's parents were not located until four days after her hospitalization. Child-centered play therapy was selected to give the child a sense of control over her environment. The issue of the hospitalization was not introduced until the child made reference to her surgery. At that point, the therapist provided the toy hospital equipment and followed the child's lead as she used the toys to reenact her own hospitalization.

CASE STUDY

Laurie, aged seven, was referred for "reunification" treatment. She had been in foster care for eighteen months while her parents completed a drug rehabilitation program. Her parents had been successfully drug-free for eighteen months and were continuing in therapy. Laurie had been made a dependent of the court at the time of her hospitalization since her parents could not be located. She was described as a classic victim of neglect, suffering from malnourishment, minor infections, impetigo, and an untreated visual problem. During foster placement, Laurie developed a strong positive attachment to her foster family. Her foster parents described her as compliant, helpful, and at times almost invisible.

INTERVENTION

Laurie had been reunited with her biological parents before play therapy began and was seen for a period of nine months. The treatment plan described by the therapist included using nondirective play sessions to establish a strong therapeutic alliance; the sessions became directive at points with talk about Laurie's life with her biological parents and about her surgery. Conjoint family sessions were also scheduled to discuss parenting issues and problems surrounding the reunification. A plan for making contact with the foster parents was formed to help reduce animosity and help Laurie with her separation issues.

During initial sessions, Laurie chose to color or read quietly. The therapist engaged in parallel play, which seemed to help Laurie relax. Because of Laurie's expressed interest in reading, the therapist made available a book written for children in foster care. Eventually, Laurie moved to the dollhouse and doll family, recreating scenes with her former foster family and describing the fun she remembered having with them. Laurie's parents had continued to show animosity toward the foster parents, even refusing to let her talk about them. A meeting arranged between the parents and foster parents successfully alleviated the antagonism and displaced anger, resulting in a positive alliance between both sets of parents.

Laurie's first self-portrait, done at the request of the therapist, showed a very small child with no hands or feet and a hole in the middle. As Laurie became more comfortable with the play therapy room and with her parents, her play changed. She frequently played with the dollhouse, showing her "ideal family." She also played ball with the therapist, displaying confidence and pride as her catching skills improved. Her self-portrait also looked different. The hole in the middle was gone, and Laurie said it was getting better. This was the first time she had referred to her surgery, and the therapist took this opportunity to bring out the toy hospital equipment, which became Laurie's primary source of play. For the next eight weeks, Laurie depicted scenes of a little girl being taken to a hospital in an ambulance and undergoing an operation. Her posttraumatic play was constricted and robotlike. The play was repetitive, and anxiety remained constant. The parents reported regressive behavior at home, thumb sucking, and nightmares. At the ninth session, the therapist intervened by providing a commentary on the events throughout the play. At first Laurie seemed surprised, but then paced herself to the therapist's commentary and added her own, eventually responding to the therapist's occasional questions about the child's feelings. This commentary seemed to enable her to observe, while experiencing and processing, the difficult and frightening negative feelings associated with the traumatic event. After many weeks, the therapist began to refer to the girl doll as "Laurie." In the final elaboration of her play, the therapist asked Laurie to put the little girl's feelings into words and tell the ambulance people, the doctors, the counselor, the social worker, and her parents how she felt. The most difficult was for Laurie to tell her parents; she did not know how they would respond. Rather than answer her questions during play, the therapist helped Laurie ask her parents in a joint session directly why they had left her. After being prepared for the meeting by their therapist, the parents were able to reassure Laurie that her feelings of abandonment, fear, sadness, and anger were valid. The final phase of treatment involved Laurie's working through the painful process of understanding her feelings of anger toward her parents.

COMMENTARY

Laurie had successfully developed coping strategies to deal with her parents' severe neglect, but the trauma of hospitalization, surgery, and resulting foster placement completely disrupted her life. The successful multidimensional treatment provided for this family underscores the importance of creating a safe place for a child not only in the playroom but in the home, too. This child's need to take care of her parents interfered with her working on her own issues of fear around the hospitalization, sadness at losing her foster family, and anger toward her parents for abandoning her. The nonintrusive style of play therapy allowed the child to deal with her issues in the order that worked best for her. Separation from her foster family and development of some confidence in herself arose first, even though the trauma of the hospitalization most deeply affected Laurie's relationship with her parents.

SOURCE

Gil, E. 1991. *The Healing Power of Play: Working with Abused Children*. New York: Guilford.

POSSIBLE DSM-IV-TR DIAGNOSES

309.81   Posttraumatic Stress Disorder
309.28   Adjustment Disorder with Mixed Anxiety and Depressed Mood
V61.20   Parent-Child Relational Problem
995.5   Neglect of Child

Intensive Play Therapy with Child Witnesses of Domestic Violence

Sarina Kot

FOCUS

This study looks at the effectiveness of intensive child-centered play therapy on improving the self-concepts, internalizing and externalizing behaviors, problem behaviors, and playroom behaviors of child witnesses of domestic violence.

INTRODUCTION

Child witnesses of domestic violence exhibit a broad range of emotional and behavioral difficulties. The effectiveness of intensive child-centered play therapy for such children was investigated in (1) improving self-concept; (2) reducing internalizing behavior problems such as withdrawal, somatic complaints, anxiety, and depression; (3) reducing externalizing behavior problems, such as aggression and delinquency; (4) reducing overall behavior problems including internalizing and externalizing behavior problems and social problems, thought problems, and attention problems; and (5) improving play behaviors in the areas of affection, contact, physical proximity, self-direction, aggression, mood, play themes, and food nurturing themes.

RESEARCH METHODS AND DESIGN

A pretest/post-test control group design was used. Twenty-two children aged three to ten were recruited from three domestic violence shelters. The children were placed in two groups: an experimental group that received play therapy and a control group that did not. Children in both groups received basic shelter services that included three educational and/or recreational groups per week. Both experimental and control group children participated in pre- and postplay therapy sessions that were videotaped. The videotapes were rated using the Children's Play Session Behavior Rating Scale. All the children completed the Joseph Pre-School and Primary Self-Concept Screening Test. The mothers completed the Child Behavior Checklist.

INTERVENTION

The experimental group—eleven child witnesses of domestic violence—received twelve play therapy sessions within a two-week period. Each session lasted forty-five minutes. Trained play therapists, two at the master's level and one at the doctoral level, provided the play therapy.

RESULTS

Analyses of covariance revealed that the child witnesses in the experimental group demonstrated (1) significant improvement in their self-concept, (2) significant reduction in their externalizing behavior problems, (3) significant reduction in their total behavior problems, and (4) significant improvement in the play behaviors of physical proximity and play themes. Insignificant results were found in internalizing behavior problems and the play behaviors of affection, contact, self-direction, aggression, mood, and food nurturing themes.

COMMENTARY

This study supports intensive child-centered play therapy as a viable intervention for treating certain problem areas exhibited by child witnesses of domestic violence. Intensive play therapy can be used to deal with the traumatic aspects of witnessing interparental violence. The short time duration required for completing the intensive play therapy fits particularly well with the unstable and transient life situations of families suffering from domestic violence.

SOURCE

Kot, S. 1995. Intensive play therapy with child witnesses of domestic violence. Unpublished dissertation, University of North Texas, Denton.

POSSIBLE DSM-IV-TR DIAGNOSES

309.4   Adjustment Disorder with Mixed Disturbance of Emotions and Conduct
309.81   Posttraumatic Stress Disorder

Psychoanalytic Play Therapy with a Child Suffering from Traumatic Neurosis

G. Maclean

FOCUS

Psychoanalytic play therapy is used with a three-and-a-half-year-old boy suffering from traumatic shock.

INTRODUCTION

Freud was concerned with the characteristics of psychic trauma throughout his professional career. He posited a sequential set of components to describe the process and outcome of psychic trauma. The precipitating stimulus is followed by an intrapsychic process that consists of a breakthrough of the protective stimulus barrier between the conscious and the unconscious, resulting in a state of psychic helplessness and, consequently, painful and unpleasurable affect. The outcome of any given case is dependent upon the context and intensity of the original trauma, the strength of the traumatized person's ego, and that person's subsequent life experiences.

CASE STUDY

The child was referred by his father five months after they both had been attacked by a leopard in a pet store. He was the only child of an upper-middle-class family. The parents were described as industrious, successful people with a good relationship and an interest in parenting, as well as the ability to parent. Jason (a name the reviewer chose) was suffering from frequent nightmares about "animals and monsters." He exhibited extreme anxiety about and reluctance toward being apart from his mother and excessive concern regarding the whereabouts of both parents. These symptoms appeared as a marked regression from Jason's formerly normal development.

INTERVENTION

Jason was diagnosed with traumatic neurosis and received individual play therapy once each week for a period of eight months, with at least one conjoint interview each month that included the parents. Throughout the sessions the reenactment in play of the traumatic event was a major theme. Jason would review every detail of the leopard attack verbally or symbolically, often over and over.

During the first few sessions Jason focused primarily on reenacting the attack. Several times he adopted the appearance of the leopard and attacked the therapist. Following these attacks, Jason asked to leave the playroom, therefore cutting the sessions short. The therapist interpreted this as Jason's fear of retaliation for the attacks. Another major issue of transference became Jason's anger at his parents, especially his father, for allowing the attack to occur. After setting up a situation in which the toys were attacked by the vicious toy leopard, Jason would angrily accuse the therapist of not protecting them. The therapist interpreted these accusations in the context of the original leopard attack and took on the role of the father, who did not protect Jason in the pet shop. At times Jason's initial response to this interpretation was an escalation in anger. When the interpretation was repeated, he would begin to play quietly, possibly needing to make recompense for his angry outburst.

Jason expressed a wide range of emotions during the therapy; each would surface, then rapidly disappear. He had a variety of defenses for dealing with these feelings and the conflict that often ensued. He dealt with his fear and anger by identifying with the aggressive leopard and attacking the therapist. He also exhibited the defense of identification by acting like a mother, father, or therapist, often assuming the role of his father during the reenactment. As Jason began to project his anger onto the environment, his fear of retaliation often surfaced. For example, if Jason identified with the leopard and swatted the therapist across the neck, this would immediately be followed by his entertaining the therapist. Over the eight months of therapy, the child's symptoms decreased and at the time of termination they had disappeared.

COMMENTARY

This case illustrates the use of psychoanalytic play therapy to treat the phenomena of trauma. Maclean described how a definable traumatic event interrupted the process of an otherwise normally developing child. The shock of the leopard's attack overwhelmed the ego, as it produced feelings of abandonment, separation anxiety, anger, and expected punishment. These emotions were congruent with identical, preexisting emotions of fear, anger, and guilt derived from the age-appropriate oedipal conflict. Working through these conflicts and reestablishing the boy's normal development was accomplished in play therapy with the internal meaning of the traumatic event moving from unconscious to conscious awareness.

SOURCE

Maclean, G. 1977. Psychic trauma and traumatic neurosis: play therapy with a four-year old boy. *Canadian Psychiatric Association Journal* 22 (2): 71–6.

POSSIBLE DSM-IV-TR DIAGNOSES

309.81 Posttraumatic Stress Disorder
309.21 Separation Anxiety Disorder
307.47 Nightmare Disorder
309.24 Adjustment Disorder with Anxiety

Racial Differences Cause Extreme Rejection in Play Therapy: An Issue for Therapist and Child

May Tung

FOCUS

Acknowledging personal fears of what is different and unknown begins a boy's process from acute paranoia to healthy curiosity.

INTRODUCTION

A Caucasian child reacted with extreme rejection of a Chinese therapist. The therapist struggled with countertransference issues related to racial difference, resulting in self-awareness that greatly enhanced the relationship.

CASE STUDY

When John first came to the clinic, he was almost ten years old. He was short, overweight, behaved much younger than his chronological age, and walked pigeon-toed. The presenting problems included temper tantrums, talking and laughing to himself, and peer difficulties. John lived with his mother and younger sister. John's mother was short and obese, and her conversation was interrupted by explosive and inappropriate laughter. John's father had suffered years of emotional disturbance and been frequently hospitalized until his suicide when John was eight. John's mother related that John's father had not wanted children and was physically and verbally abusive to John until shortly before the suicide. Since that time, the family's life had been somewhat unstable, with frequent moves. Psychological testing revealed an extremely constricted and barren world in which John protected himself from the things that frightened him by not moving, not thinking, and not feeling.

INTERVENTION

Individual play therapy sessions were held approximately once a week for a period of eleven months. John's therapy progressed through a pattern of six stages: (1)

distrust and distancing, (2) ambivalence, (3) reality testing of the nature and meaning of the apparent racial differences, (4) finding out if Tung could help him, (5) showing positive feelings toward Tung, and (6) accepting Tung as a helping figure.

In the initial sessions, John's distrust of the therapist was observed in the absence of significant content in his play. John would rarely accept anything from the therapist, including cookies. Tung honored John's need for physical and emotional distance by sitting in a corner of the room while John played on the floor, making his presence known by asking occasional questions or handing John a toy.

John had acknowledged that Tung was Chinese by making specific comments about Chinese people in the first two sessions. The topic did not come up again for four months. In the fifth month of therapy and for the following six months, the topic was raised in every session. John seemed to use Tung's ethnicity as his vehicle for developing trust. At first Tung's being Chinese appeared to frighten John and be too unusual for him to accept. Could such a person be trusted? Would such a person get as angry and hurtful as John's father? Would this person go back to his own people, abandoning John? John's solution before the development of trust was to kill all the "Chinks" so that Tung would have no one to go home to. Tung interpreted John's fears as being that people who look and speak differently can be frightening and that not knowing whether or not someone will hurt you when he or she is angry is frightening. He allowed sufficient time for John to work through his fears. He also reassured John that he did not intend to leave him.

It was during this trust-building period that countertransference issues were most evident for Tung. Repeatedly hearing the term "Chinks" as John killed all the Chinese in his imaginary play caused Tung to be both uncomfortable and resentful. At the point that John's feelings of ambivalence toward Tung were most acute, Tung recognized John's pain and confusion. During this time, the possibility of Tung's leaving the clinic came up, and Tung began to feel personally responsible for causing or at least exacerbating John's pain. At this point, Tung sought consultation. The greatest insight Tung developed through these consultations included acknowledging his own feelings of guilt for possibly damaging a child and also accepting that sadness is a part of life and belongs in the realm of the therapeutic relationship. This crisis period for Tung lasted about a month. Resolution coincided with Tung's not leaving the clinic and the beginning of the last stage of John's play therapy experience.

COMMENTARY

In this case study, a young boy reacted negatively and with fear to the most obvious feature of the therapist, his ethnicity. The therapist was a nonintruding and interested adult who accepted John's initial fears and gave John the time and support to go through his own healing process. This case demonstrates the very personal nature of the play therapy relationship and the importance of therapist self-awareness. Patience and understanding by the therapist in the face of personal rejection facilitated this child's understanding and acceptance of himself, thus enabling him to be accepting of others.

SOURCE

Tung, M. 1981. On being seen as a "Chinese therapist" by a Caucasian child. *American Journal of Orthopsychiatry* 5 (4): 654–61.

POSSIBLE DSM-IV-TR DIAGNOSES

300.4   Dysthymic Disorder
V62.81   Relational Problem NOS
995.5   Physical Abuse of Child
300.00   Anxiety Disorder NOS

Group Play Therapy for Preschoolers Exposed to Domestic Violence

Alissa Huth-Bocks, Allison Schettini, and Valerie Shebroe

FOCUS

Group play therapy is used with preschoolers exposed to domestic violence and other traumas.

INTRODUCTION

Many child witnesses of domestic violence also experience the loss of a caregiver, and only a small number of preschoolers receive treatment for such problems. Less attention has been given to preschool witnesses than their older counterparts, despite the fact that preschoolers may be more vulnerable to negative effects due to developmental limitations. Preschoolers who witness domestic

violence have been shown to demonstrate more behavior problems, social difficulties, posttraumatic stress symptoms, and anxiety and poorer self-esteem than
nonwitnesses.

Many preschool witnesses of domestic abuse also lose a caregiver through
a breakup of the relationship, imprisonment, child removal from the home,
abandonment, or death. Preschool children who experience significant loss are
at risk for problems such as regressive behaviors, temper tantrums, aggression
and defiance, fear, excessive guilt, eating and sleeping difficulties, social impairment, and school failure. Although the need for intervention is clear, only
a small percentage of preschool witnesses of domestic violence receive treatment. There has been some debate about the ability of young children to benefit from group interventions. Preschoolers are in the preoperational period of
development, characterized by egocentricity and concrete thought. Therefore,
a group designed for preschoolers must take into consideration their developmental needs. This researcher found that a group designed for young children
exposed to domestic violence and related traumas had a positive impact on
participants.

INTERVENTION

Group sessions were conducted in a Head Start preschool for no more than six
children. The children were age four to five. Treatment consisted of fourteen
weekly sessions lasting for sixty minutes each. Because of the characteristic un-
predictability and chaos of the lives of the children participating, care was taken
to ensure that each session took place at the same time each week in the same
room, with the same therapists playing the same roles each session. Goals of the
group included helping children learn to identify and express their feelings, helping them learn problem-solving and conflict-resolution skills, providing children
with a safe place for self-expression, correcting misconceptions that were thought
to lead to children's guilt feelings, and providing children with corrective emotional experiences through interactions with the therapists.

Each session began with a warm-up activity and a time for each child to receive a brown paper sack to be his or her own puppet. Children picked out faces
depicting various feelings to assign to their puppets. The leader introduced the
topic of the day in a brief concrete explanation, followed by a concrete activity.
Children were then given twenty-five minutes of unstructured free play during
which the therapists reflected and interpreted the children's play. It was expected
that having free play after the structured activities in which themes were introduced would provide the children with an opportunity to work through conflicts
and emotions arising from those themes.

The leaders offered warm, nurturing snacks to the children as they opened discussion around a table. After snack, the children were led into that day's play activity. For the last ten to fifteen minutes of each session, the group leaders followed the children's cues as to how to end the session and transitioned the children back into their regular day.

RESULTS

Because of the preschooler's developmental level, bibliotherapy and storytelling worked well with this age group. Likewise, puppets and dolls were found to be useful for role-play situations. It is believed that the children were helped by projecting their own feelings and concerns onto other characters. Furthermore, the unstructured play was found to be helpful by providing the traumatized children with an opportunity for them to repeatedly recreate traumatic experiences in order to gain mastery over them. Conducting the group in a Head Start preschool rather than a domestic violence agency eliminated many attendance and time issues that other researchers encountered. It also made treatment available to children who otherwise would not have been recognized.

COMMENTARY

These researchers found the group designed for preschool witnesses of domestic violence had a positive impact on participants, as concluded from observations by teachers and parents of the preschoolers. They emphasized the importance of parental involvement and suggested enhancing the group's benefits by concurrently conducting a parenting group as well. Because many children who participate in groups such as these will have been repeatedly traumatized, problems should not be expected to completely abate during or after one group treatment experience. However, in conjunction with parental involvement, such a group can result in behavioral improvement for preschool witnesses of domestic violence.

SOURCE

Huth-Bocks, A., Schettini, A., and Shebroe, V. 2001. Group play therapy for preschoolers exposed to domestic violence. *Journal of Child and Adolescent Group Therapy* 11 (1): 19–34.

POSSIBLE DSM-IV-TR DIAGNOSES

309.81   Posttraumatic Stress Disorder
313.89   Reactive Attachment Disorder of Infancy or Early Childhood
995.5   Neglect of Child

Intensive Group Play Therapy with Child Witnesses of Domestic Violence

Sarina Kot, Garry Landreth, and Maria Giordano

FOCUS

Group play therapy for sets of siblings who have witnessed domestic violence is found to be equally effective as individual play therapy in improving self-concept and reducing behavioral problems.

INTRODUCTION

It has long been known that child witnesses of domestic violence become part of an at-risk population for developing adjustment difficulties. They often exhibit increased aggressiveness, hyperactivity, anxiety, social withdrawal, suicidal ideation, school problems, clinging behaviors, somatic complaints, and developmental delays. Sibling relationships often have a protective effect on child witnesses of domestic violence, and children with high levels of sibling support also demonstrate higher levels of self-esteem and social competence.

Individual play therapy has been found to have positive results in working with child witnesses of domestic violence, particularly in improving self-concept and reducing behavioral problems. At the same time, group play therapy gives children of varied ages the opportunity to use both play and verbalization as needed as a means of catharsis, social experimentation, collaboration, and motivation and support of change. Therefore, the authors hypothesize that the intensive play therapy model has potential to achieve even greater results by incorporating the benefits of group play therapy and sibling support.

RESEARCH METHODS AND DESIGN

Participants were ten children volunteers, six girls and four boys, ages four to nine, recruited from battered women's shelters in a large metropolitan area. A control group of eleven children on a waiting list for treatment was also sampled. The Joseph Pre-School and Primary Self-Concept Screening Test was administered to measure the children's self-concepts. The Child Behavior Checklist was administered to record behavioral symptoms and competencies as perceived by parents or caregivers. Instruments were administered pre- and posttreatment. The children who participated received twelve forty-five minutes sessions, spanning twelve days. Sessions were facilitated by a therapist trained in child-centered play therapy. There were two siblings in each play therapy group. Children on the waiting list control group were assessed using the same instruments within three days of arriving at the shelter and two weeks later.

RESULTS

The assessment results for both the children in the experimental group and the children in the control group were compared against results in Kot, Landreth, and Giordano's 1998 study, *Intensive Play Therapy with Child Witnesses of Domestic Violence*. The Kot et al. study demonstrated positive results using intensive individual play therapy with child witnesses residing in battered women's shelters. The authors of this study found that children in the intensive group play experimental group scored significantly higher on the Joseph Self-Concept Screening Test and on several subscales of the Child Behavior Checklist, including the Externalizing Behavior Problems, Aggressive Behavior, and Anxious/Depressed subscales, than the children in the control group. The experimental group also scored significantly higher on the Total Behavior Problems Scale of the Child Behavior Checklist. The experimental group in Kot et al. and the experimental group in this study scored comparably with no significant differences.

COMMENTARY

The authors found strong support for the effectiveness of intensive sibling group play therapy in a variety of areas with child witnesses of domestic violence. For example, the siblings who received group play therapy showed significant increases in self-concept, while children in the control group showed a decline in self-concept. In addition, group play therapy was found to be equally as effective as the individual play therapy intervention. The intensive group play therapy model appears to be an effective and efficient means of treating child witnesses of domestic violence during their limited stay at a battered women's shelter.

SOURCE

Kot, S., Landreth, G., and Giordano, M. 1998. Intensive child-centered play therapy with child witnesses of domestic violence. *International Journal of Play Therapy* 7 (2): 17–36.

POSSIBLE DSM-IV-TR DIAGNOSES

296.xx   Major Depressive Disorder
300.02   Generalized Anxiety Disorder
309.xx   Adjustment Disorder
309.81   Posttraumatic Stress Disorder
312.9   Disruptive Behavior Disorder NOS
995.5   Neglect of Child

CHAPTER 22

Withdrawn Children

Shy, quiet, withdrawn children can be a real challenge for play therapists who want to achieve results quickly. Efforts to entice, coax, encourage, or maneuver withdrawn children into some kind of response or activity with the play materials are usually met with resistance and result in immediate defeat. Withdrawn children are especially sensitive to such efforts and seem determined to remain on their chosen course of noninvolvement. They may interpret the play therapist's struggle as rejection since the play therapist seems to be working hard to have them change. As is demonstrated in Virginia Axline's work in this chapter, persistent patience frees the child from the restrictions of past experiences, including perception of self in relation to those experiences, and provides the child a safety zone in which to experiment with new perceptions of self and, thus, new behaviors in a relationship of acceptance.

For some withdrawn children, group play therapy is especially effective because it is less threatening for them to enter new experiences in the company of two or three children. The presence of several children seems to speed up the development of a relationship between the play therapist and each child. It may be that the group accelerates the child's awareness of the permissiveness of the setting and also provides an opportunity for vicarious experiences.

Child-Centered Play Therapy with an Extremely Withdrawn Boy

Virginia Axline

FOCUS

A young, withdrawn child is helped to release anxiety through child-centered play therapy.

INTRODUCTION

Virginia Axline, founder of child-centered play therapy, describes her relationship with a withdrawn child and discusses her profound belief in allowing the child to express here-and-now feelings, attitudes, and issues. As this is allowed to occur, the child comes to know self better and to experience self-acceptance and the freedom to develop self-confidence and self-adequacy. The playroom and therapeutic relationship provide the space within which the child can safely explore a personal world.

CASE STUDY

Five-year-old Billy was facing possible expulsion from kindergarten because of his extremely withdrawn behavior at school. He would not talk or interact with other children, and if another child attempted to initiate contact, Billy would cover his face with his hands and arms and roll up into a ball. He would not respond to instructions from the teacher. The school-administered Stanford-Binet indicated an IQ of 68.

Billy's mother reported normal childhood development until age three, when he stopped walking and talking and began to exhibit infantile behavior. Just before this sudden change, she had been extremely ill and required emergency surgery. When she sought help for Billy, she was told he was retarded; unwilling to accept this diagnosis, she spent a great deal of time with him, teaching him to name colors, count, cut and paste, write his name, and so on.

INTERVENTION

Billy participated in weekly, forty-five-minute, individual, child-centered play therapy sessions. He entered the initial session with a shuffling gait and stood in the middle of the room with drooping posture and a blank stare. Eventually, he went to the sandbox, where he spent the remainder of the session and ran sand through his fingers. During the next four sessions, he added small elaborations to his play, such as moving cars in the sand and adding a few comments. He appeared increasingly more alert, and his walk had more energy. After the fourth session, his mother indicated having observed significant improvement. Billy's regressive behavior had decreased, and he was talking more and appeared less tense. After the fifth session, Billy's teacher noted that although he still did not fully participate in classroom activities, his social interaction had increased.

Continued improvement was shown in the sixth through tenth sessions. Billy's play became more imaginative and complex, and he was more spontaneous and increased his verbal interaction. In the waiting room, he talked easily with others, moved with a quick, firm step, and displayed bright facial expressions. In preparation for termination, several sessions of group play therapy assisted Billy in continuing his growth in social skills.

A one-year follow-up revealed that Billy continued to be happy and relaxed, with vivid and spontaneous expressive skills. He had several friends in his new school and testing had revealed an IQ of 105.

COMMENTARY

As demonstrated in this case, withdrawal may be severe enough not only to affect social relationships but also to place the child in jeopardy of a possible, but incorrect, diagnosis of mild mental retardation. Without a therapist-driven agenda, this child was able to meet his own needs in play therapy and, in the process, to free natural developmental coping skills.

SOURCE

Axline, V. 1948. Some observations on play therapy. *Journal of Consulting Psychology* 12:209–16.

POSSIBLE DSM-IV-TR DIAGNOSES

300.23 Social Phobia, Generalized
313.23 Selective Mutism

The Use of Operant Conditioning in Nondirective Group Play Therapy with Withdrawn Third-Grade Boys

Paul W. Clement and D. Courtney Milne

FOCUS

Behavioral techniques in group play therapy bring about changes in withdrawn, introverted, and friendless eight- and nine-year-old boys.

INTRODUCTION

Children, if quiet and subdued, rarely receive intervention, especially if the social withdrawal does not affect scholastic performance. However, helping such children learn skills to interact socially is always an important consideration. Group play therapy affords that opportunity.

RESEARCH METHODS AND DESIGN

Eleven boys were selected from 2,761 third-grade children. Teachers identified boys in their classrooms who were socially withdrawn, introverted, very quiet, friendless, and lacked spontaneity. The eleven were selected from a pool of boys whose parents consented to participate in the study. The boys had psychological evaluations that included the Bender-Gestalt, the Children's Manifest Anxiety Scale, the California Test of Mental Maturity, and selected Rorschach cards. The subjects had an IQ range of 80 to 123. The boys were then randomly assigned to a token group, a verbal group, and a control group.

INTERVENTION

Each group met for one fifty-minute session per week for fourteen weeks. The token group's treatment was based on the group play therapy methods of Haim Ginott.[1] Brass tokens were given in the sessions for socially acceptable behavior.

---

1. Haim Ginott, *Group Psychotherapy with Children: The Theory and Practice of Play Therapy* (New York: McGraw-Hill, 1961).

At the end of each session, the tokens could be traded for small toys and candy. The verbal group was run the same way as the token group, except that verbal reinforcement rather than the token was given. The senior investigator was the therapist for both groups. The control group met in the same play therapy room but without a therapist. This group was observed behind a one-way mirror to ensure the safety of the children. The mothers participated in concurrent guidance groups led by the junior investigator. These sessions were also based on the work of Ginott.

Pre-, mid-, and postdata were collected on the boys' productivity, anxiety, general psychological adjustment, and problem behaviors. The data included grades on report cards and standardized assessment instruments. Social adjustment was measured by observing the behavior of each boy during the group play therapy sessions.

RESULTS

The two treatment groups achieved statistically significant change in the area of social adjustment during the fourteen sessions. The boys in the token group improved in three areas; the boys in the verbal group improved in two areas, but got worse in one area. The boys in the control group showed no change. During the group play therapy sessions, the token group boys showed increases in verbal communication with each other ($p < .05$); in time spent in social play ($p < .01$); and in proximity, or getting closer to each other, during the group play therapy sessions ($p < .01$).

The boys in the verbal group displayed less dependence on the therapist by decreasing therapist-directed verbalization and increasing verbalization with their peers ($p < .01$); they also showed an increase in proximity ($p < .01$). The amount of time spent in social play, however, decreased for this group ($p < .01$).

The only change in problem behaviors occurred in the token group. The Behavior Problem Checklist completed by the mothers indicated statistically significant improvement during the fourteen sessions ($p < .05$).

As measured by report card grades, performance showed no significant change. According to the authors, the preintervention data, which indicated that all of the boys were average students with no reported scholastic problems, accounted for this. The authors also indicated that anxiety, often reduced during play therapy, also showed no significant change during this study. In this case as well, the boys scored in the typical range of anxiety for their age range before this study began.

COMMENTARY

Group play therapy provides withdrawn children with the opportunity to develop social skills and process self-concept issues. Using a nondirective approach with the addition of operant conditioning through positive reinforcers resulted in significant improvement for the children participating in this study. The play therapy experience by itself provides positive reinforcement as children learn to accept themselves through the acceptance of the play therapist. The often-overlooked withdrawn child needs this experience.

SOURCE

Clement, P., and Milne, D. C. 1967. Group play therapy and tangible reinforcers used to modify the behavior of eight-year-old boys. *Behavior Research & Theory* 5:301–12.

POSSIBLE DSM-IV-TR DIAGNOSES

309.9   Adjustment Disorder, Unspecified
V62.81 Relational Problem NOS

Behavioral Learning Theory Applied to Play Therapy as an Intervention with a Withdrawn, Noneating Child

John Graham White

FOCUS

Behavioral play therapy is used to facilitate the return of normal eating patterns in a child who had withdrawn from eating.

INTRODUCTION

Children withdraw from normal patterns of living for various reasons. The child described in this study initially withdrew from other family members because of pampering by her father. After his death, she increasingly withdrew in her eating behavior until she took in only liquids. The author described the application of learning theory to play therapy to resolve this child's withdrawal.

CASE STUDY

The child in this case was born five years after her older sister. Her father was away, serving in a war, during the first four years of the sister's life; the sister was identified as the mother's baby. After the father returned, the client child was born; she became identified as the father's baby. He fed her almost from the time she was born, played with her, and lavished care on her. When her father fed her, she would play with his shirt collar and, subsequently, would not fall asleep unless she could hold onto a shirt collar.

By age three, the child began demanding that her main meal of the day be fed to her by her father upon his return home from work. He would hold her on his knee during the meal, during which both of them ignored the mother and older sister. At bedtime, she would not allow her mother to put her to bed and screamed until her father came in and read several books. Finally, she would fall asleep.

Just before she was five years old, her father became very ill and spent seven weeks in the hospital. During this time the child could not see him but still slept at night holding onto the collar of one of his shirts. When the father returned home, and until he died two months later, she spent the majority of her time in his room. After his death, she still expected his return as her mother told her he had gone "to God's hospital." When her mother began working, the child's appetite deteriorated despite the wide variety of games and entertainment various family members used to attempt to get her to eat. Once she commented to her mother, "Dr. B. says if I don't eat I'll never be a big girl. If I grow into a big girl my daddy won't recognize me, will he?" After six weeks of being bedridden, with a diagnosis of acute rheumatism, she stopped eating any solid food and was hospitalized.

INTERVENTION

This child's case was conceptualized from a behavioral learning theory perspective, identifying the father as the conditioned stimulus upon which the conditioned response of eating was based. The treatment plan was to provide a male psychologist as a stimulus-substitution of her father, later providing a generalization continuum to include members of the child's family.

The child was initially seen one hour a day during the first week of hospitalization. The sessions took place in a playroom set up like a large playhouse with child-size furniture, utensils for cooking, and a child's tea set. In the first session the therapist and child took care of the dolls, which included feeding them. In the next four sessions, the child ate miniature cookies and drank milk from the small teacups but refused to eat solid food on the ward. At the end of the first week, she was discharged from the hospital.

Upon return to the hospital for outpatient treatment the following Monday, her mother reported that she had eaten a small amount of solid food during a visit to her paternal aunt and uncle. During the second week of daily play therapy sessions, full-size cups and cookies were substituted for the doll-size ones. At midweek, the mother reported having been embarrassed on one occasion when a neighbor chastised her for saying that this child would not eat because the child had eaten two plates of food at the neighbor's home. Another neighbor, who had stopped by the child's house for a visit, reported to the mother that the child said, "I don't eat at this house. I don't eat for my mummy." Although there were no play therapy sessions over the next six days because of the Christmas holiday, the child sat down to meals with her mother and older sister, even though she would not consistently eat with them.

During the next three weeks, she had at least four play therapy sessions a week. The child began to prepare meals for herself and her therapist during these sessions. She also began taking the lead in other play activities. The therapist continued to play the role of her permissive, doting father. Six weeks after the play therapy sessions began, the child had the therapist drinking to the beat of her hammer pounding a pegboard. At this time, the therapist decided to shift the pseudo father-daughter relationship from child focused to more reality focused. He began to retrain her from exploiting the relationship to being rewarded by responses to other stimuli. One example was having her assist the therapist in small, useful jobs around the clinic, in addition to participation in the playtime. At home, she continued to eat better, including eating breakfast regularly and telling her mother when she was hungry. She continued to improve and suffered a brief relapse of only three to four days' duration when her mother returned to work.

Six months after her initial hospitalization, even with a six-week break because of measles and chicken pox, she continued to express an interest in food and developed some special favorites. Because she was now able to eat both at home and in the home of relatives, her eating was no longer the cause of concern.

At a three-year follow-up she continued to be eating normally. Nocturnal enuresis, which had been present at the time of hospitalization, cleared up twelve months after her eating problem was resolved. This child had suffered no relapse during the three-year period, even though her grandmother and a favorite uncle, who had become a father substitute, died. She was described as healthy and fairly well adjusted with her peers at home and at school.

COMMENTARY

This child's failure to transfer her stimulus response of eating from her father to others was resolved through the use of behavioral play therapy. The play therapy also provided the development of more assertive skills as seen in her being allowed to become responsible for the direction of her play.

SOURCE

White, J. G. 1957. The use of learning theory in the psychological treatment of children. *Journal of Clinical Psychology* 15:227–30.

POSSIBLE DSM-IV-TR DIAGNOSES

307.59   Feeding Disorder of Infancy or Early Childhood
309.9   Adjustment Disorder, Unspecified
V62.82   Bereavement
V61.20   Parent-Child Relational Problem

Child-Centered Play Therapy with a Withdrawn Child

Virginia Axline

FOCUS

Child-centered play therapy is used with a socially withdrawn, selectively mute, emotionally disturbed child.

INTRODUCTION

Axline's description of the case of five-year-old Dibs has become a classic in the field of play therapy. Dibs's challenging behaviors ranged from mute and almost catatonic behavior in the classroom and at home to having violent temper tantrums. Although he did not attend a school for the mentally challenged or emotionally disturbed, Dibs was considered possibly both, or as having suffered some type of neurological damage. Nondirective or child-centered play therapy was employed.

CASE STUDY

Dibs was a puzzle to the adults in his life. His parents, teachers, the school psychologist, and the school pediatrician were unsure about the etiology or treatment for his bizarre behavior. Dibs had been in an exclusive private school for two years and exhibited severe withdrawn and mute behaviors. In general, he did not talk and sometimes would not move. At times, he crawled around the classroom on the floor, oblivious to teachers or other students. At other times, he had violent temper tantrums. Appearing to be mentally challenged, on occasion Dibs responded quickly and displayed flashes of superior intelligence.

His mother had used her influence with the private school to get him accepted into the program with the constant request that the teachers give him more time to change. His father was reportedly a gifted scientist, and his younger sister was described as the "perfect child." Before entering treatment with Axline, the parents had concluded that Dibs was mentally challenged and requested referrals for programs to handle such children.

INTERVENTION

Axline observed Dibs in the classroom and had the initial play therapy session at his school. She described Dibs as seeming lonely and depressed: "There seemed to be no laughter or happiness in this child. Life, for him, was a grim business." Although there was limited interaction in the first session, Axline noted that she saw great potential and courage in Dibs. The following play therapy sessions were held at a local child guidance clinic.

A playroom with a wide variety of play materials was made available. Axline employed a nondirective, or child-centered, approach and left the direction of the therapy to Dibs, interacting with him at his request. As Dibs became more comfortable and explored the playroom, he began to be more emotionally expressive. Positive changes in his home and school behavior became evident as well. Although his parents initially asked not to be involved in the treatment process, Dibs's mother made an appointment with Axline to discuss the changes that were having an effect on the mother and the family, such as Dibs's coming out of his room more often but also appearing very controlled and depressed. He began to enter and leave the therapy clinic in a much quieter and cooperative manner.

The positive changes in Dibs were reportedly having a positive effect on his family. The systemic effect included indications that Dibs was being treated with "more consideration, understanding, and respect at home." His playroom play became happier and included positive artwork and songs he composed to sing. He began to express positive and negative emotions verbally in the playroom and at home. Dibs's school behavior also improved. His teachers reported that he responded in the classroom, occasionally initiated conversations, and was "happy, calm, and showing an interest in other children." The temper tantrums ceased.

At the conclusion of the play therapy sessions, a standardized intelligence test was administered and Dibs achieved an overall IQ score of 168. The brilliant and gifted child that had been buried underneath such emotional turmoil had emerged in play therapy.

COMMENTARY

Dibs was offered a child-centered play therapy experience during a time when corrective and intrusive measures were often prescribed, including institutionalization. It is unlikely that this child, however, would have emerged had such severe measures been taken. Dibs was offered a safe place in which to explore and find himself, and having been given the opportunity, he reclaimed his childhood. A child who had been written off as neurologically and emotionally damaged was able to establish positive relationships as a result of the healing power of the child-centered play therapy relationship.

SOURCE

Axline, V. 1964. *Dibs: In Search of Self.* New York: Ballantine Books.

POSSIBLE DSM-IV-TR DIAGNOSES

300.23   Social Phobia, Generalized
312.8   Conduct Disorder
309.9   Adjustment Disorder, Unspecified (Social Withdrawal), Chronic
313.89   Reactive Attachment Disorder of Infancy or Early Childhood

Index

abreactive play therapy, 114–16
abuse and neglect, 1–13; child-centered
play, pseudomother role, and self-
healing, 11–13; overview, 1;
processing through puppet play, 1–4;
reunification treatment for child
traumatized by, 228–30; safety and
concrete play's role in disclosure of,
6–8; self-psychology and reflection in
treatment of deprivation, 4–6. *See also*
sexual abuse; witnesses of domestic
violence
acceptance, need for: by selective mute
children, 175; by withdrawn children,
243
acting out. *See* aggression and acting out;
drama therapy for enuresis and acting-
out problems
adjustment problems, 41–43. *See also*
acute illness, psychosocial adjustment,
and play; mentally challenged
children; psychosocial adjustment
adolescent girls, psychotic, 83–85
adopted children: cognitive, reflective,
and psychodynamic therapies
promoting attachment, 48–50; role of
mother in therapy, 49–50
aggression and acting out, 15–43; brief or
release play therapy for temper

tantrums, 28–30; child-centered sand
and water play, 32–34; developmental
play group counseling and classroom-
disturbance behavior, 26–28; Jungian
play therapy and interpretive language,
15–17; nondirective therapist's
relationship with institutionalized
child, 30–32; operant techniques and
social responsibility in playgroups,
23–26; oppositional disorder, video
feedback, and parent-child relations,
18–20; overview, 15; psychoanalytic
therapy using expressive art, 35–37;
and self-control in bilingual children,
207–9; in treatment for stuttering and
social adjustment problems, 224. *See
also* individual play therapy; touch and
developmental play therapy
Alexander, Eugene D., 105
Allan, John, 15, 76
anxiety. *See* fear and anxiety
Armstrong, Hubert E., 23
art, expressive, 35–37
articulation difficulties, 219–21
associations, loose, 79
asthma, 63–66
at-risk children, 193–95
attachment difficulties, 45–50; in adopted
child, 48–50; child-centered play

255

emotionally disturbed children, 87–96;
mentally challenged, 155; overview,
87; with trichotillomania and
microcephaly, play and family therapy
for, 89–91; use of developmental
playgroups to treat, 87–89. *See also*
school
emotional maladjustment: and drama
therapy for enuresis and acting-out,
99; play therapy and teacher guidance
for, 208–10; and reading difficulties,
165
Enberg, S., 138
encopresis, 97–104; and cognitive-
behavioral play therapy for language
deficit, 100–102; mother-child
relationship in psychodynamic therapy
for, 102–4; overview, 97
enuresis, 97–104; individual and sibling
group therapy to treat selective
mutism and, 178–80; overview, 97.
See also drama therapy for enuresis and
acting-out problems; encopresis
epileptic children, 70–71
exploration of self. *See* self-exploration
expressive art, 35–37
expressive language, 214–15

Fall, Marijane, 152, 189
family therapy, 89–91. *See also*
pseudofamily, therapeutic
fear and anxiety, 105–18; assessment of
using Missouri Children's Picture
Series, 135–36; in at-risk children, and
school-based therapy, 193–95; child-
centered play therapy to treat hair
pulling, 107–9; hospitalization related,
study of reduction of through play,
134–36; overview, 105; pain related,
and maternal home therapy for toilet
training, 112–14; projection of on
puppets, 132–34; related to surgery,
and situational doll play, 129–32;
release or abreactive therapy for
stammering due to, 114–16;

separation, focused play to resolve,
116–18; use of structured play to
uncover root causes of, 109–12. *See
also* Palmar Sweat Index (PSI); school,
phobia of
Fear Thermometer, 144
fecal incontinence. *See* encopresis
feelings, expression of by labeled children,
152–54
filial therapy. *See* mothers
focused play to resolve separation anxiety,
116–18
freedom, 176–78
Freud, Sigmund, 232–33
Friedman, David, 4
Fuchs, Natalie Rogers, 112

Gaulden, Gary Lloyd, 26
Gil, Eliana, 228
Giordano, Maria, 240, 241
Goodban, Marjorie, 219
Gorman, Jane, 78
Gould, Myrna Frank, 186
grief, 119–27; nondirective puppet play
and treatment of traumatic, 122–23;
normalization and peer support in
playgroups to treat, 124–25; overview,
119; and sand play therapy, 119–21;
use of child-centered therapy to treat,
126–27
group play therapy. *See* playgroups
guidance programs for teachers, 208–10
Gumaer, Jim, 87

hair pulling, 107–9
handicaps, educational, 149–52. *See also*
mentally challenged children
healing, 65. *See also* self-healing
Healy, Mark, 57
hide-and-seek games, 98–99
high-functioning autism: importance of
child's communication during
treatment, 53–54; psychodynamic play
therapy for, 51–54; use of puppets in
treatment of, 51–54

home play therapy for toilet training, 112–14

hospitalization, 129–45; mastery of intrusive procedures in chronically ill children, 136–38; nondirective, child-centered play therapy and psychosocial adjustment, 143–45; outpatient department and waiting room play programs, 139–40; overview, 129; reunification treatment for child traumatized by, 228–30; situational doll play and surgery-related trust and fear issues, 129. *See also* acute illness, psychosocial adjustment, and play; burn victims; fear and anxiety; puppet play

hostility. *See* aggression and acting out

House, Reese Milton, 187

Hoyser, Elizabeth, 172

Hume, Katherine, 208

Huth-Bocks, Alissa, 237

hyperkinetic disorders, 70–71

illness. *See* acute illness, psychosocial adjustment, and play; chronic illness

immaturity, social, 200–201

incontinence, fecal. *See* encopresis

individual attention tutoring, 202–4

individual play therapy: child-centered, for children with adjustment problems, 41–43; for emotionally disturbed children in schools, 94–96; for institutionalized mentally challenged children, 160–62; intensive, for children with IDDM, 66–68; and parent counseling for conduct disorder children, 37–39; and school adjustment problems, 202–4; to treat enuresis and selective mutism, 178–80; for withdrawn and aggressive behaviors, 39–41

institutionalized children: mentally challenged, 160–62; nondirective therapist's relationship with, 30–32

insulin-dependent diabetes mellitus (IDDM), 66–68

intelligence quotient (IQ): of children with cerebral palsy, 221–23; of mentally challenged children, 157–59

intensive child-centered therapy, 230–32

Intensive Group Play Media approach, 191–93

Intensive Play Therapy with Child Witnesses of Domestic Violence, 241

intensive psychoanalytic play therapy, 180–82

intensive sibling group therapy, 240–42

interpretive language, 15–17, 54–55

intrapsychic issues and chronic illness, 64–65

intrusive procedures, mastery of, 136–38

Irwin, Bernadine, 81

Jackson, Lydia, 216

Johnson, Lynette, 152, 189

Johnson, Patricia, 141, 143

Jones, Elizabeth M., 66

Jungian play therapy: and interpretive language, 15–17; in treatment of sexually abused schizophrenic, 76–78

Kawai, Hayao, 70

Kawai, Itsuo, 70

Klem, Patricia R., 6

Knell, Susan, 100

Kot, Sarina, 230, 240, 241

Kupperman, Phyllis, 219

labeled children, 152–54

Landreth, Garry, 107, 178, 240, 241

language: deficit, cognitive-behavioral play therapy for, 100–102; interpretive, 15–17; skills, expressive and receptive, 214–15. *See also* reading difficulties; selective mutism; speech difficulties

Lanyado, Monica, 54

Lawton-Speert, Sarah, 76

About the Editors

Garry L. Landreth, Ed.D., LPC, RPT-S, is regents professor in the Department of Counseling, Development, and Higher Education and founder of the Center for Play Therapy at the University of North Texas. Dr. Landreth is director emeritus of the Association for Play Therapy. He is internationally recognized for his writing and work in promoting play therapy. He received the Virginia Axline Distinguished Professional Award for his work in conceptualizing and advancing the child-centered approach to play therapy.

Daniel S. Sweeney, Ph.D., LPC, LMFT, RPT-S, is associate professor and director of the Northwest Center for Play Therapy Studies in the Graduate Department of Counseling at George Fox University. He is a member of the board of directors of the Association for Play Therapy. Dr. Sweeney has presented at numerous national and international conferences and has multiple publications on the topics of play therapy, filial therapy, and sandtray therapy.

Dee C. Ray, Ph.D., LPC-S, NCC, RPT-S, is assistant professor in the Department of Counseling, Development, and Higher Education and director of the Child and Family Resource Clinic at the University of North Texas. Dr. Ray is editor of the *International Journal of Play Therapy* and president of the Texas Association for Counselor Education and Supervision. She is a frequent presenter at Association for Play Therapy International Conferences and other national and state conferences. She has published and presented extensively on the effectiveness of play therapy and play therapy in schools.

Linda E. Homeyer, Ph.D., LPC, RPT-S, is associate professor in the professional counseling program at Texas State University–San Marcos. She has served as president on both state and national boards of the Association for Play Therapy. Dr.

Homeyer has traveled extensively in the United States, South Africa, India and Malaysia training therapists in play therapy and sandtray therapy. She has published several books and numerous journal articles.

Geraldine J. Glover, Ph.D., LPC, RPT-S, is Child and Adolescent Behavioral Health Services Coordinator for the Alamo Navajo Health Clinic in Magdalena, New Mexico. She is a contributing author to several books primarily in the area of multicultural issues in play therapy and working with Native American clients. Dr. Glover is a member of the board of directors of the Association for Play Therapy and has been president of the New Mexico Association for Play Therapy.

Breinigsville, PA USA
09 August 2010
243212BV00002B/2/P

2575